From Liberation to Remediation

Writing Research, Pedagogy, and Policy

Elizabeth Wardle, Director of the Howe Center for Writing Excellence at Miami University, Series Editor

Distant Readings of Disciplinarity: Knowing and Doing in Composition/Rhetoric Dissertations
Benjamin Miller

From Liberation to Remediation: The Rhetoric of General Education
Kelly Ritter

Policy Regimes: College Writing and Public Education Policy in the United States
Tyler S. Branson

A Shared History: Writing in the High School, College, and University, 1856–1886
Amy J. Lueck

From Liberation to Remediation

The Rhetoric of General Education

KELLY RITTER

UTAH STATE UNIVERSITY PRESS
Logan

© 2026 by University Press of Colorado

Published by Utah State University Press
An imprint of University Press of Colorado
1580 North Logan Street, Suite 660
PMB 39883
Denver, Colorado 80203–1942

All rights reserved

 The University Press of Colorado is a proud member of
Association of University Presses.

The University Press of Colorado is a cooperative publishing enterprise supported, in part, by Adams State University, Colorado School of Mines, Colorado State University, Fort Lewis College, Metropolitan State University of Denver, University of Alaska Fairbanks, University of Colorado, University of Denver, University of Northern Colorado, University of Wyoming, Utah State University, and Western Colorado University.

ISBN: 978-1-64642-795-6 (hardcover)
ISBN: 978-1-64642-796-3 (paperback)
ISBN: 978-1-64642-797-0 (ebook)
https://doi.org/10.7330/9781646427970

Library of Congress Cataloging-in-Publication Data

Names: Ritter, Kelly, author.
Title: From liberation to remediation : the rhetoric of general education / Kelly Ritter.
Other titles: Writing research, pedagogy, and policy.
Description: Logan : Utah State University Press, [2026] | Series: Writing research, pedagogy, and policy | Includes bibliographical references and index.
Identifiers: LCCN 2025032533 (print) | LCCN 2025032534 (ebook) | ISBN 9781646427956 (hardcover) | ISBN 9781646427963 (paperback) | ISBN 9781646427970 (ebook)
Subjects: LCSH: General education—United States. | General education—United States—History. | Universities and colleges—Curricula—United States. | English language—Rhetoric—Study and teaching (Higher)—United States. | Education, Higher—United States. | Education, Higher—United States—History.
Classification: LCC LC985 .R58 2026 (print) | LCC LC985 (ebook)
LC record available at https://lccn.loc.gov/2025032533
LC ebook record available at https://lccn.loc.gov/2025032534

Publication of books in the Writing Research, Pedagogy, and Policy series is supported by the Roger and Joyce Howe Center for Writing Excellence at Miami University.

Cover photograph of Suzzallo Library, University of Washington, by Cameron Stewart/Unsplash

Contents

Acknowledgments vii

Introduction: The Story of General Education 3

1. Educating the Great Community: Postwar Gen Ed Philosophies and the Variable of Student Choice 30

2. "The Interests of the State": Curricular Sameness and Public University Systems 61

3. To AP or Not to AP: Advanced Placement and the Rhetorics of Exemption 107

4. Liberatory Mythologies: Dual Enrollment / Dual Credit and the Rhetoric of Writing Studies 152

Conclusion: Will the Circle Be Unbroken? The Challenges of the Paper Ceiling 188

Notes 207

Works Cited 231

Index 249

About the Author 261

Acknowledgments

This book would not have been possible without help and moral support from a number of people across my life and work. First, I thank Elizabeth Wardle and Michael Spooner for believing in this project (including Liz's entirely correct insistence that I should "get to the point!" in my revisions), and the two anonymous reviewers for making this book much stronger than it was in its original draft form. Second, I thank my fellow school chairs here at Georgia Tech—John Lyon, Victoria Thompson, and Cassidy Sugimoto—for cheering me on through the completion of this book, and through the work of chairing in general.

Further, I thank the archivists at the University of Georgia, Georgia Institute of Technology, and the State of Georgia—the latter of whom endured many requests for files, and photocopying, across my multiple visits to their spaces in Morrow, Georgia. Along for those trips, and serving as my intrepid research assistant for archival work, was Jessica Rose. I am grateful for her help in uncovering the historical intersections of race and education that this book aims to highlight regarding General Education. I am also grateful to Jessie for introducing me to aspects of culture and life in Georgia across our archival travels, including the bizarre but endearing Dwarf House restaurants.

I thank my colleagues in English Studies and Writing Studies, who, each in their own ways, helped to shape the content of this book. Those are Zachary

Beare, Courtney Adams Wooten, Jacob Babb, Doug Hesse, Melissa Ianetta, Alison Johnson, and Annie Mendenhall. This book would literally not be what it is today without your conversation, insight, and guidance.

I thank my former colleagues at University of Illinois Urbana-Champaign who also had a part in this book. These include Alaina Pincus, my colleague for almost two years on the Grand Challenge Learning Initiative in the Office of the Provost. My thanks to Alaina for spending countless hours talking with me about how Gen Ed works—and doesn't; how our UIUC students might benefit from new conceptions of Gen Ed on the ground; and how we will "never know what students don't choose" in relation to their Gen Ed coursework. Alaina's thinking helped me to shape some foundational arguments here about student choices, or lack thereof, in Gen Ed. Equally important to the foundations of this book is Chuck Tucker, former Vice Provost for Undergraduate Education at UIUC, who hired me to be a Provost's Fellow for Undergraduate Education and lead of the Grand Challenges Initiative. Chuck, I will always value your belief in my work, and also your ability to fix almost anything, mechanically speaking, with just a handful of pennies. And last but not least, I thank my other colleagues in the Provost's Office, Kathy Martensen, Kristi Kuntz, and Staci Provezis, each of whom knows more about the way universities work than anyone I will ever work with again. Ladies, you are the reason why West Side is the Best Side.

I thank my former colleagues in the Office of the Dean of Liberal Arts and Sciences at UIUC, who endured many conversations with me about General Education, and who might remember the years I carried around a print copy of the first volume of *The Journal of General Education*, promising that someday I would write about it. Those are Amy Elli, a generous and fantastic colleague who spent four years helping me lead our college Gen Ed committee and navigate also the infamous Senate Educational Policy Committee, or EPC; Matthew Ando, the best associate dean of mathematics and science around and the most genuinely curious, empathetic, and kind person I have ever met; and Clare Crowston, the best associate dean of humanities and French historian in the business and a lifesaver to me so many times over. I also thank Barbara Hancin, who for many years led the UIUC Student Office in LAS with care, dignity, and wisdom. I miss you all, friends.

And last but never least, I thank my husband, Josh Rosenberg, and my daughter, Sarah Catherine Rosenberg, for their unwavering love and support. I dedicate this book to Sarah Catherine, with the belief that she, and millions of other students nationwide, deserve a more equitable, affordable, and meaningful K–16 system than the United States currently is able, or willing, to provide.

FROM LIBERATION TO REMEDIATION

INTRODUCTION

The Story of General Education

In the process of doing research for this book, I chatted with colleagues and friends about its subject matter. When I said I was writing about General Education, I received a variety of responses. These ranged from "Gen Ed—you mean like those classes I had to take when I started college?" to "General Education . . . yeah, I don't know very much about that," to "What's Gen Ed?" One of my former deans, an economist by training, insisted that she had never heard the term "general education" used at either of her previous institutions, where Gen Ed had been labeled as "liberal education" and "distribution requirements," respectively. She further objected to the term itself, proclaiming "'general' sounds like *nothing*."

None of these reactions were surprising to me. Unless a faculty member has worked in admissions, undergraduate studies, or with staff who regularly interact with students and the public, they are unlikely to know much about Gen Ed's content, and certainly not its nomenclature, or history. This is especially true for faculty in disciplines not included in the Gen Ed curriculum (for example, engineering, nursing, business) or who teach only upper-division undergraduate or graduate students and who thus may have never really thought about Gen Ed at all. Such sedimented ignorance of Gen Ed's principles over generations can also be true for faculty in the liberal arts since, as a rule, academics are most knowledgeable about what they themselves teach and study, and less so about what others do, by comparison.

As for the public, Gen Ed is just one of many obstacles in higher education as a whole that slows progress to the valuable college degree. Many in the public who value a college degree but are unhappy about its costs, or the time it takes to complete, hope Gen Ed will just move out of the way to make way for truly important things—like specialized major coursework and other professional training that directly relates to preparation for a specific career. Other members of the general public eschew college and higher education altogether. Each of these people, who are hardworking members of American society—our neighbors, family members, and coworkers—have no good reasons at present to care about whether Gen Ed persists, is revived, or is reinvigorated, especially given its framing over the last thirty-odd years as a sum-total negative. To much of the public, Gen Ed was created to get more of their tuition dollars and to make their children repeat work that they already did in high school. Gen Ed is a box of jacks spread out on the floor that players hope to gather up in one bounce of the ball—at most two—so that they can win the game of higher education. Gen Ed is, with apologies to Shakespeare, sound and fury, signifying nothing.

With all the above viewpoints in mind, the goal of this book is to get you, the reader, to change your mind about General Education. Whether you are a student, faculty member, administrator, parent, or policymaker, or none of the above, I want to persuade you that General Education—or the set of core, introductory courses across academic subjects that are required for a four-year college degree—is more valuable than you think. By exploring the rhetorical histories and futures of Gen Ed—that is, the way it is spoken and written about, promoted, and also, minimized—I am asking you to see the story of Gen Ed as intrinsic to and indivisible from the story of modern higher education in the United States. In telling this multilayered story, I make key stops along the way to examine discourse on Gen Ed within academic communities, local histories of schooling, national testing movements, and higher education policy implications on the students Gen Ed was meant to serve, in order to illustrate how Gen Ed has devolved in both its purpose and execution since its origins some eighty years ago.

No system, educational or otherwise, is perfect. General Education, in its many forms and permutations, is only as strong as the faculty, administrators, and policymakers who articulate and implement its teachings on their campuses, and the students who take Gen Ed courses and choose (or not) to use the lessons learned in their educational and professional lives. In telling

Gen Ed's story, I provide both historical and contemporary evidence to support my claims about Gen Ed's value and its precarity, some of which may be painful to read, especially if what you learn about the enterprise of schooling in the United States is either new or long since forgotten. As much as we tout education as a fundamental tenet of our democracy, this book will teach you that there are still clear educational winners and losers when it comes to getting a college degree, depending upon how (or whether) that degree was completed, and under what circumstances.

I start this story in 1945, with Gen Ed's initial articulations as both a program and a social movement, which represented deeply held, principled views of how to live and work in a participatory democracy, including the belief in the edification that college can bring. This story ends just about eighty years later, with the widespread rhetorical reconstruction of Gen Ed that sharply contrasts with its postwar origins, backed by many citizens' beliefs that a four-year degree is a financial burden, an elitist pursuit, and worst of all, a waste of time (and money). This tale of Gen Ed—which I tell from my perspective as a first-generation humanities faculty member who is deeply invested in undergraduate education and the benefits college can provide especially to the marginalized and disadvantaged among us—will show you how many Americans have gone from valuing higher education to shunning it, out of fear, confusion, and a blind (and often uninformed) worship of both school and workplace efficiencies.

If you are still willing to hear my good reasons for how our wrongheaded thinking about higher education is 100 percent dependent on the vilification of General Education, please read on. I'll focus the remainder of this introduction on some fundamental facts about Gen Ed; a brief history of its origins at Harvard; what I mean by the "rhetoric" of Gen Ed, in practice; the realities of Gen Ed courses and credits on the ground, including in my own field of rhetoric and writing studies; and finally, a brief overview of what the rest of the chapters of this book will discuss and how they might be useful to you and to making Gen Ed better in the future.

So, please settle in to hear this important tale. We have a lot of ground to cover together.

The Fundamentals of General Education in Perilous Educational Times

Let's begin with some contextual definitions and foundations and other key information for readers less well-versed in General Education as a curriculum or a concept. Such readers have good reasons not to know much, as Gen Ed's recent (i.e., twenty- to thirty-year) history has been one of marginalization and obfuscation both on and off college campuses. Gen Ed in the twenty-first century operates thusly: You, the student, take a menu of Gen Ed courses in usually your first and second years of college, courses designed for those with no prior knowledge in the subject at hand and aimed at a cross-sectional audience hoping to gain a broad background and shared understanding of the parameters and importance of a particular field or discipline(s). These courses may be small or large in size, in person or virtual, taught by faculty or graduate students, and in total, equal anywhere from thirty to sixty credits of your four-year bachelor's degree (or the majority of your two-year associate's degree). This is the case, however, *only if* you didn't place out of some or all of these Gen Ed courses in high school, via Advanced Placement (AP), College-Level Examination Program (CLEP), International Baccalaureate (IB), or ACT or SAT requisite subscores (for the English and math sections), *or* dual enrollment / dual credit programs, where you gained credit for *both* high school and college courses *at the same time*.

If you did end up taking a full menu of General Education courses, you are in the distinct minority in the United States. That's because many students—especially white students from privileged backgrounds—come to college with double-digit credits of Gen Ed already (most frequently in English and in other humanities, such as history, followed by mathematics and the social sciences), while others were able to earn an entire associate's degree (or 60 credits of a 120-credit bachelor's degree) while still *in* high school, by taking advantage of one or more of the various credit options noted above.

This galvanizing construction of Gen Ed as a curriculum that happens off a college campus (or in the cases of distance or virtual learning, outside a college classroom) is reliant upon the key belief that college can be a waste of time and money, akin to remedial education as a whole, and that Gen Ed is simply a menu of check-box courses that only exist as an expensive, repetitive hurdle to earning that degree. For example, a May 2024 report from the Pew Research Center found that "about half of Americans say that a college degree is less important today than it was 20 years ago." Such views are skewed along political party lines, with 57 percent of Republicans and 43 percent of Democrats holding these beliefs, and those without a college education also agreeing with this assertion more than those without a college education (30% and 22%, respectively). And 38 percent of those with a bachelor's degree—less than half, but certainly a nontrivial number—assert that their four-year degree was "not too or not at all useful" in their ability to obtain a "well-paying job" (Fry et al.).

Similarly, a survey reported on by the Gates Foundation in March 2024 revealed that both high schoolers and "non-enrollees" (those not in a degree program and also not currently in high school) felt that the most important reason to get a college degree was "to be able to make more money" (71% of non-enrollees, 81% of high schoolers). They also believed that on-the-job training was more valuable than a four-year college degree, with 77 percent of non-enrollees reporting job training as an "excellent/good value" versus only 57 percent reporting the same for a college degree. And finally, 38 percent of high schoolers and 33 percent of non-enrollees agreed that having more dual enrollment courses in high school was "extremely helpful" in completing a college degree.[1] And a 2022 report of an online survey of 1,006 students and 605 parents by the College Board—which also administers both the AP and CLEP programs—notes that "80% of all US high school students and parents believe there is value in a college education" but also indicates that only 32 percent see college as primarily a "valuable investment," versus 66 percent believing college is primarily important to "get the job I want after high school." Importantly, only 27 percent of students surveyed believe that the primary reason to attend college is because it will "expose me to many different types of people and perspectives." Notably, Black adults are more likely than Latinx or White adults to see college as much or somewhat *more* valuable than before the COVID-19 pandemic (37% versus 26% and 22%, respectively).[2]

Such views about the relative value of college, particularly those cast in economic terms, are the reality across large segments of American culture, which now has a US president at the helm also determined to devalue education even further by rolling back payment forgiveness on student loans, eliminating the US Department of Education, and targeting his own presidential rhetorics toward working-class citizens, some of whom he had led to believe would benefit socioeconomically from his anti-intellectual, anti-education platform.[3] More important than any one leader's current views, however, is how the growing disregard for higher education is also antithetical to General Education's original design: as an equalizing measure for *all* students, and a site for discovering intellectual ideas and opportunities that a student may not have otherwise known even existed, which in turn helps them to not just secure a "good" job but also better function in a democracy—which, at least for the moment, is still what the United States wants to be.

In this book, I historicize these original benefits of General Education and contrast them with the prevailing rhetorics that now control it—namely those of efficiency, economy, and remediation. From my particular viewpoint as a scholar of rhetoric and writing studies, this book also takes as its central premise that introductory college writing courses are *the* foundational experiences within General Education programs. Such a premise leans on the fundamental, even dogged, belief among the public that literacy is the key to advancement and success in our economy—even as many within that public repeatedly diminish and marginalize literacy pedagogies. The histories of General Education and literacy education are thus forever intertwined, as both rhetorically complex and as prone to the political whims and fleeting trends that characterize our equally complex views of literacy and democracy in the United States.

It is my further contention that first-year writing courses, as part of General Education, have suffered the most among all core Gen Ed subjects, as the result of shifting institutional, public, and even corporate rhetorics of the latter half of the twentieth century regarding what Gen Ed is, or could be. On occasion, this suffering has been at the hands of those who design and operate writing programs and who lack a full understanding of their role in enacting the principles of General Education. In making this assertion, I do not discount that a mathematician could write their own book, parallel to this one, about the fate of mathematics as a core requirement in the history of Gen Ed—nor do I think such a book is unwarranted, given the contemporary frenzied (over)emphasis on STEM education and concomitant calls for better and more extended K–12 preparation in math (and the physical and natural sciences, and computer science), especially for minority and also first-generation students.[4]

Yet literacy instruction, in contrast to other subjects, continues to be framed as corrective rather than additive or knowledge-gaining. Despite constant industry calls for college graduates to be "good communicators," the instruction designed to make these postgraduate identities possible is still seen by the general public as a fix-up, clean-up shop. In contrast, instruction in mathematics is understood to be the *building* of technical knowledge of increasing, scaffolded complexity (i.e., from college algebra to calculus III) in the service of STEM careers requiring mastery of such concepts as a baseline for hire. This identity admittedly elides the more complex, theoretical side of mathematics as much as the public conception of literacy and writing instruction ignores the broader pursuits of the field of Rhetoric and Writing Studies itself. And certainly, the debate over the place of basic (i.e., "pre-college" level) math in college curricula rages on. Yet as a public, we do not talk about writing instruction in the same ways that we do instruction in other subjects, partially because writing itself is seen as subjectless, and because "poor" writing skills are often associated with lower social class.[5]

This book therefore also focuses on the postwar history of General Education as it affects the position of first-year writing instruction, and argues that each has been victim to misconceptions of what a socioeconomically minded liberal education can and cannot provide for a democracy, especially one now in the throes of late-stage capitalism. But you, the reader, need not be an expert in either rhetoric and writing studies or any other field to follow this story, because you likely have already heard some of the public declarations about higher education that I amplify in this book. For example, in 2003, Harvard University President Derek Bok declared that "a university must have a clear sense of the values needed to pursue its goals with a high degree of quality and integrity. When the values become blurred and begin to lose their hold, the urge to make money quickly spreads throughout the institution" (*Universities* 6). Yet such a declaration was undercut some twenty years later by the Thiel Foundation, backed by PayPal founder and venture-capitalist billionaire Peter Thiel, in its promises of "$100,000 to young people who want to build new things instead of sitting in a classroom."[6] How do stakeholders in higher education decide which of these rhetorics is the "right" one to follow when they both sound equally compelling in our fraught financial times?

Value alliances that form between corporate giants and the US government, and against academic leaders with investment in college as a greater good, certainly can portend a dangerous future for higher education as a whole. But as I show, such alliances become near-perfect rhetorical frameworks for devaluing General Education as nonspecific to a major, introductory in its typical approaches, and offering instruction in areas that students may never study again (for example, biology for an English major, literature for a computer science major), never mind the cross-applicability of such experiences to actual life and career practices. General Education's history is laden with the damages incurred from the uptake of these circulated values (though our current political arena evinces an anti-intellectualism not seen in any other postwar US presidential administrations to date). Its history is also jeopardized by our collective public conceptions about writing, literacy, and social uplift, which become reflected in the critical courses that make up the Gen Ed curriculum, as well as whom these courses do and do not ultimately serve.

In order to understand how we got to this place, let me first summarize the rhetorical and pragmatic origins of General Education as born at Harvard University. With an acknowledgment that programming in General Education existed before and during the time of Harvard's initiative (including at Columbia University, the University of Chicago, the University of Iowa, and the

University of Minnesota, among others), I submit that it is the Harvard model that is most evident in our current conceptions of Gen Ed, and that Harvard's is the most high-profile origin story as well, in terms of its architects and ensuing publications lauding and promoting its work.

General Education at Harvard: Postwar Education as Liberation

In his February 25, 1938, speech "The Mission of American Universities," then president of Harvard University James Bryant Conant declared that "At least half of higher education is a matter of selecting, sorting, and classifying students."[7] This mantra stands as one of the earliest declarations of higher education's potential to provide, on the one hand, social uplift and class ascension and on the other, to preemptively disenfranchise students, especially those from nondominant populations. Conant's subsequent leadership of Harvard's 1945 vaunted publication *General Education in a Free Society* (Harvard Committee), colloquially known as the "Redbook," provided a very public preamble to his later executive roles with the Educational Testing Service (ETS) and the College Board, including the now-ubiquitous Advanced Placement program. Each of these roles allowed Conant a wide platform for shaping how the "regular" student—who is neither a family legacy nor of gifted or talented status—could succeed in higher education and, subsequently, in American life.

By Conant's design, Harvard's General Education initiative was originally crafted to help ameliorate the effects of inherent sorting mechanisms in academe, at least to a degree, by presenting Gen Ed as a baseline set of core subjects that all students should study in their college years, regardless of their preparation or future professional aspirations. Informed by enrollment shifts at Harvard and other elite institutions following World War II, as well as their economic impact on institutional operations and the demographics of graduating classes, Conant's plan served as a widely accepted blueprint for other institutions nationwide for the Gen Ed menu of core required, usually introductory courses in the arts, humanities, mathematics, physical and natural sciences, and social sciences.[8] The Harvard plan also influenced how secondary schools would organize their curricula, notably including the expansion of programs designed to address students' overall health and hygiene, such as physical education. Though the University of Chicago memorialized its own in *The Idea and Practice of General Education* (1950), it is Harvard's plan that remains the most commonly referenced template for how modern General Education curricula have been imagined and implemented as core areas of study for the first two years of a student's college education.[9]

General Education in a Free Society was the result of work by the University Committee on the Objectives of General Education in a Free Society, which began work in 1943 and ended with the Redbook's publication in 1945. The committee was made up of twelve Harvard faculty from Arts and Sciences and also Education and drew upon reams of research and consultation both inside and outside Harvard's gates. This publication and its aims have been the subject of scores of studies in higher education since then, alongside copious scholarship on Conant himself; indeed, in Wilson Smith and Thomas Bender's substantial compendium *American Higher Education Transformed 1940–2005*, an excerpt and summary of the Redbook is the lead artifact.[10]

The committee members were Paul H. Buck (chairman), John H. Finley Jr. (vice-chair), Raphael Demos, Leigh Hoadley, Byron S. Hollingshead, Wilbur K. Jordan, Ivor A. Richards (more commonly known to rhetoricians as I. A. Richards), Phillip J. Rulon, Arthur M. Schlesinger, Robert Ulich, George Wald, and Benjamin F. Wright. These faculty—all white men, and all tenured—represented the disciplines of history, classics, philosophy, biology, education, English and rhetoric, biology and chemistry, and political science. Complementing these was Conant's own training as a chemist. These men largely attended elite high schools or boarding schools as children, and elite universities for their undergraduate and graduate education. Hence the three pages of acknowledgments that lists seventy-five external men and women consultants—from companies such as International Harvester and Pratt and Whitney, numerous public and private high schools, many private and public colleges and universities, labor unions, and state boards of education, as well as thirty-five other Harvard faculty (including Theodore Morrison, Director of English "A," aka first-year writing), and, finally, the three secretaries who "prepared the manuscript for publication." A description of the committee's collective process is in the book's introduction, in the form of a letter of transmittal to Conant:

> We maintained a central office in which memoranda poured and where daily groups smaller than the whole committee met informally to discuss our problems. We sought advice from both our colleagues in the university and from persons of various walks of life and sections of the country. We brought consultants to Cambridge as individuals and in groups. We operated through subcommittees and by conferences. All in all, we tapped so far as was in our power the rich and varied thinking and experiences of American education. (Harvard Committee xiv)

Such a process may sound familiar to readers who themselves have been on councils or boards of undergraduate education at their college or university, or on committees to revise their own institution's General Education requirements. But where Harvard's work differs from the typical curricular revisions we undertake today is its massive scope and national aim to change the conversation about and processes for educating American citizens. This work was intensive and complex, undertaken by faculty who were both invested in the task and also inexperienced in much of what the final report would ask colleges and their faculty to do in the classroom and in the community with the new population of postwar students. The labors of the committee may be found across several linear feet of documents in the Harvard University Archives.[11]

In this same letter of transmittal that opens the Redbook, the committee repeats the value statement that would characterize the overall committee charge, sent forth to them by Conant on January 11, 1943: "The primary concern of American education today is not the development of the appreciation of the 'good life' in young gentlemen born to the purple. It is the infusion of the liberal and humane tradition into our entire educational system. Our purpose is to cultivate in the largest possible number of our future citizens an appreciation of both the responsibilities and the benefits which come to them because they are Americans and are free" (Harvard Committee xv). Taking this directive, the group constructed a philosophically and civically minded 267-page plan divided into the following sections: "Education in the United States"; "Theory of General Education" (including chapters titled "General and Special Education" and "The Good Man and the Citizen"); "Problems of Diversity";[12] "Areas of General Education: The Secondary Schools"; "General Education in Harvard College"; and "General Education in the Community."

As noted in the first section of the Redbook, a core consideration of the committee was to search for "some overall logic, some strong, not easily broken frame within which both college and school may fulfill their at once diversifying and uniting tasks. This logic must be wide enough to embrace the actual richness and variegation of modern life—a richness partly, if not wholly, reflected in the complexity of our present educational system. It also must be strong enough to give direction to this system—something much less clear at present" (40). Indeed, the Redbook was designed to be a broad proclamation against the primacy of "special education," or that which was meant for professional or advanced study. The committee envisioned General Education as a tool for strengthening our democracy and collective civic responsibilities and addressing, if not eliminating, the decidedly diverse social and educational needs of postwar American youth.[13]

Despite its aim to provide equalizing educational programming, the committee did *not* see General Education as a nominal vessel housing generic course requirements, as it so often functions today. In particular, the committee did not intend for General Education to mean

> some airy education in knowledge in general (if there be such knowledge), nor does it mean education for all in the sense of universal education. It is used to indicate that part of a student's whole education which looks first of all to his life as a responsible human being and citizen; while the term, special education, indicates that part which looks to the student's competence in some occupation.... Clearly, general education has somewhat the meaning of liberal education, except that, by applying to high school as well as to college, it envisages immensely greater numbers of students and thus escapes the invidium which, rightly or wrongly, attaches to liberal education in the minds of some people. But if one clings to the root meaning of liberal as that which befits or helps to make free men, then general and liberal education have identical goals. (Harvard Committee 51–52)

This imperative was both intellectual and pragmatic in its design, for Harvard (like many other elite colleges postwar) now found itself educating a new group of citizens, significantly as a result of the GI Bill (which directed government funds to institutions as well as students) and the slow stream of women entering Harvard from Radcliffe College during wartime to occupy seats vacated by enlisted men. To stay financially solvent, and socially current with the times, General Education was a necessary instructional plan that would soon become adapted across the country, for similar reasons.

With this brief overview above, I want to emphasize to readers unfamiliar with Harvard's work just how much the Redbook influenced higher education to see General Education as a requisite set of courses providing intellectual gain for all who take them, in a college setting. This belief stands in sharp contrast to the rhetoric of General Education today, which divides academics and the public regarding its true educational value, rapidly devolving in perceived purpose to something only for students who *lack* proper K–12 educational training and coursework. Further still, the Redbook had no mention of, or even thoughts toward, the current characterization of General Education as a curricular enterprise that is nonspecific and thus interchangeable across all institutional types and educational levels. Instead, it made explicit connections between high school and college but avoided declaring that a student might *only* engage in Gen Ed within the secondary school setting. Instead, it upheld the evolutionary view of college as the start of a lifelong pursuit of engaged citizenry—to use today's terms, a "K–16" endeavor—but not the kind based on efficiency principles that now elide levels of personal and intellectual development toward avoiding so-called instructional redundancies. Nothing about General Education, to its Harvard founders, was aligned with redundancy; rather, it was based on recursive *reinforcement* across levels, and adoption of principles key to democracy.

Conant's later (1953) book *Education and Liberty* narrated such a process, arguing that by the mid-twentieth century, college

> came to be more and more justified as preparation for citizenship. It was more and more divorced from any connection with professional training which was the province of a university: law, medicine, theology, and gradually the sciences with the exception of engineering came to be regarded as postgraduate subjects. The logical outcome of this development was a continuous demand for a wide variety of new subjects to be taught in school as well as college. The drive for general education—"education for citizenship"—affected the high schools even more than the colleges.... In less than fifty years the pattern of full-time schooling ... was completely altered. (47)

As Conant further argues, "If you combine a belief in equality with a belief in the desirability of a full-time education leading to the collegiate degree for all who can afford it, the American pattern of education is the logical outcome" (46).

For Conant, the "average" student could only succeed through possession of core knowledge of all the means of intellectual inquiry present in the university's curriculum; such was his protest reaction against postsecondary emphases on specialization and narrow training that presumed a different kind of student than was entering US colleges mid-century. Indeed, Conant observed that "experimenting with various types of college courses" across the General Education framework was a way to address the shift from an entirely elite, "highly literate" student body to the postwar college population that also included returning soldiers and lower- and middle-class students lacking the benefit of college-educated parents helping them with their studies. As Conant asserted, "the cultural background of the students is too diverse, the impact of modern science and scholarship has been far too great. These two factors have made necessary a re-examination of the older idea of a liberal education" (*Education and Liberty* 52).

Today, the competing forces that drive Gen Ed in and out of view—as an educational *movement* born of a postwar ideal regarding social class rarely realized on a wide scale—have wreaked havoc on its original equalizing and liberating purposes and its wide use value and applicability to all students. And Conant's point about all students who can "afford" college has been massively complicated by the rising price of a college degree, secondary to severe cuts in funding to state universities and the high price of student loans in relation to the salaries for college graduates in many fields. The continuing value and position of General Education in its current incarnation in the twenty-first century, when set against Harvard's original plans and Conant's core ideals, is thus put to the test by asking two key questions: Is it a movement designed to provide tools for enculturation, assimilation, and uplift, or for civic engagement, liberation, and social action? And is it delivering on one or both of these promises, or neither?

General Education Today: Rhetorics Bought and Sold on the Educational Marketplace

In the chapters to follow, I tell the story of the rhetoric and, to borrow from James Berlin, the *reality*, of General Education from the mid-1940s to the present day, so as to interrogate how the "selling" of Gen Ed has waxed, waned, and been colonized by various actors who are associated with, or who can benefit from, the enterprise of higher education. But what do I mean by the "rhetorics" of General Education, exactly?

I use *rhetoric* in its simplest term throughout this book: that which uses the available means of persuasion, performed by any number of actors (rhetors) in order to influence one or more audiences. In presenting these rhetorics, some readers might see me performing what John Schilb would call my own "rhetoric of refusal," since, as a faculty member and also a school administrator with many years of experience in General Education instruction, I am expressing and enacting a "particular disassociation: that between a procedure their audience expects them to follow and a presumably better course" (*Rhetorical Refusals* 35). Further still, my fellow academic readers will likely see my work here as seeking "the audience's assent to another principle, cast as a higher priority" in relation to General Education (3). In other words, this book does not do what is "rhetorically normal" in discussing Gen Ed—that is, propose particular reconstructions of curricula that better fit societal and institutional priorities, as valuable as those efforts are. Nor do I, as this book's author, tow what many in the Gen Ed industry would consider the party line. In this book, I am focused on how we *speak, write, and argue about* General Education. Because no amount of Gen Ed reform in the world will work unless we first change these modes of discourse.

That Gen Ed industry, as I construct it throughout this book, is made up of testing companies, state legislatures, other local politicians, and even some university administrators themselves, who form a collective *anti*-literacy sponsorship, to borrow from scholar Deborah Brandt's well-known concept. I say this because these stakeholders have become invested in using rhetorics that diminish and sideline General Education away from college campuses, to the extent that these actors benefit far more from its absence than its presence in completion metrics, selectivity, and curricular configurations that also may allow streamlined entry into graduate programs for highly qualified students. Indeed, Gen Ed is a curriculum that almost *everyone*, not just students, seeks to get out of the way, by any means necessary.

But this did not happen overnight; it took many decades of chipping away at the original promises of the Redbook for us to get to where we are now. Some questions I'll ask about the rhetorics surrounding Gen Ed are as follows: How have public responses to Gen Ed curricular content and requirements (both positive and negative) affected writing's place in American universities? What role have local and state politics played in these decisions, including those related to race and educational attainment? What impact have credit-by-exemption programs and concepts such as seamless transfer had on the quality and import of Gen Ed programming, including the universality of the first-year writing course? And finally, what populations have benefited from Gen Ed as a movement, including within first-year writing, and which have been left behind?

Indeed, General Education is a hot topic in higher education, even as faculty in individual disciplines tend to look inward at adjustments and amendments to their own curricula, rarely discussing or understanding how those curricula fit into larger educational systems that all college students experience. The literature on General Education as a concept thus circulates most widely amongst scholars and researchers who study and assess teaching and learning per se, including those who undertake theoretical examinations of the evolving structures of colleges and universities. Part of the problem with promoting General Education is understanding what is meant by the term "general"—a term prone to rhetorical miscasting as well, as it hails an identity that is nonspecific, generic, or devoid of meaning altogether, as noted at the start of this introduction. The frequently substituted term of "liberal education" can be equally problematic—in that some citizens believe a liberal education (or the liberal arts, even) is equal to left-wing politics, when in fact its roots are quite fundamentally democratic (even conservative by some measures). On my campus, the term for Gen Ed is "core curriculum," which emphasizes its centrality. Other institutions use terms such as "foundations," "first- and second-year studies," or other similarly broad labels. To borrow from a common saying, Gen Ed, like the Devil, goes by many names.

National organizations have attempted to create a common understanding of Gen Ed across these local nomenclatures and permutations, some emphasizing liberal education as the most ideal, and capacious, framework within which to house Gen Ed. The American Association of Colleges and Universities, for example—more commonly referred to as the AAC&U and a leader in "advancing the democratic purposes of education," per its website—has published various treatises on liberal education as part of its core organizational mission. On an extensive page within its site, entitled "What Is Liberal Education?," the AAC&U defines it as "an approach to undergraduate education that promotes integration of learning across the curriculum and co-curriculum, and between academic and experiential learning, in order to develop specific learning outcomes that are essential for work, citizenship, and life." This AAC&U definition is in harmony with the Harvard group's defining goals, minus the "outcomes" language not yet part of the professional lexicon in 1945.

The AAC&U further notes that the key components of liberal education come in four parts. These are (1) "Essential Learning Outcomes"; (2) "High-Impact Practices" (e.g., capstone courses, portfolios, first-year experience courses); (3) "Signature Work" (a student immersing themselves in an original project); and (4) "Authentic Assessment" (rubrics that align with the AAC&U's VALUE initiative).[14] The essential learning outcomes are framed by four specific areas: knowledge of human cultures and the physical and material world; intellectual and practical skills; personal and social responsibility, including civic knowledge and engagement; and integrative and applied learning (AAC&U, "Trending Topic").

The first of these four aspects—framed in this paradigm using the heading of "Essential Learning Outcomes"—are what we would consider the foundational components of the original General Education movement still offered at most postsecondary institutions, and areas also often invoked in institutional General Education program outcomes.[15] In the immediate postwar era, of course, assessment was still a nascent concept, and terms of art such as "high-impact practices" were not in academia's vocabulary. But the interconnectedness of foundational coursework across the areas outlined above, with further, deeper investigations of problems across the curriculum was very much a principle that early Gen Ed proponents encouraged.

What clouds the mission of Gen Ed in the twenty-first century is the splintering of the first of the four areas of knowledge away from the other higher-order, specialized work that comes chronologically after it (in most cases, with the exception of first-year experience); this splintering is anathema to scholars such as Chris Gallagher, who has argued for a more integrated four-year curriculum. Many colleges and universities value—even vociferously promote—these "signature" aspects of a college degree to prospective students. The idea of "hands-on learning" within a college curriculum is a big selling point in recruitment, as it promises to provide an experience that adds value—implicitly *practical* value—to a college degree. Yet these same colleges may simultaneously enable, if not encourage, students to bring in AP or other test-based credits in order to bypass the fundamental Gen Ed subject areas noted above—which are seen by the public as divisible and interchangeable by design.

Given these conditions, though "liberal" and "general" become synonymous in discussions of General Education both past and present, the execution of educational experiences labeled by these two terms may be very different in practice. As Terrel L. Rhodes (2010) has also observed, General Education committees working on reform and reinvention of the curriculum today face "more restrictive definitions" that omit "much of the earlier intent to form character and judgment in students through an intentional intellectual and social development process grounded in experiences requiring practical application of knowledge" (244).

As a result, outside the genre of scholarship discussed above that directly addresses core values within General Education and how to reform curricular structures so as to make these values visible to all, research in higher education that encompasses General Education more broadly pivots toward the changing requirements of college and their relationship to student mobility, particularly in terms of initial college requirements (often but not always framed as barriers) that may be exempted or waived. It also engages sometimes with doomsday rhetorics about the end of the liberal arts, though not as tied to Gen Ed histories in any consistent way. This approach is reflected in books such as Moner et al.'s *Redesigning Liberal Education* and Davidson's *The New Education* (2017). Here, the focus is not on General Education per se as a movement, nor on its rhetorical impact in terms of social class and marginalized students, though of course there are numerous titles over the last decade, significantly from sociologists studying higher education, that do address social inequities in higher education.[16]

Despite this fairly vast array of scholarship that exists on how and why General Education curricula should be revised, revamped, or rebooted, little specific attention has been paid to the rhetorical currency of Gen Ed as a movement with equalizing aims, including how writing curricula have been reduced and streamlined as a central part of Gen Ed, and how the Gen Ed movement's overall value has been depleted or negated entirely in the decades since the Harvard plan. The story I tell of Gen Ed in this book recovers that rhetorical history, toward my contention that its import—indeed, its rhetorical label—has shifted completely from *liberation* to *remediation*.

This shift has particularly dire consequences for the student groups who most frequently come to college campuses without test or other course credits, who are statistically speaking often first-generation students, students of color, and students from underserved areas (rural as well as urban). This aggregated population is a primary focus of concern in my story of Gen Ed, since its devaluation via pre-college mechanisms is even more potentially stratifying when we consider how such mechanisms often work in tandem with private tutoring and coaching usually afforded to upper-income students. Positionalities of lower-income, first-generation, and Black and Hispanic students toward college are also important in this conversation, as they inform how such students approach the curriculum itself. In addition to prevailing rhetoric regarding Gen Ed's use value, these students, as sociologist Ann L. Mullen has argued, "may embrace some elements of the instrumental order (e.g., the idea of earning a degree in order to obtain better employment) yet reject other aspects (e.g., the valorization of theoretical knowledge, and the assumption that holding theoretical knowledge enhances one's value)" ("You Don't" 143). This makes the higher purposes of General Education, as well as other subject matter, less translatable to students who are already influenced heavily by financial and social pressures related to college, even as such students are more likely to be required to take Gen Ed courses as part of a college degree than are their more affluent, suburban, white peers.

I thus argue that the problem, long since framed rhetorically as one of *access* to pre-college curricula and credits for these students at the margins, is much larger than this—and that therefore, such access arguments are a red herring. The real problem lies with the accepted equivalency that has emerged between General Education and underpreparedness, secondary to accelerated timelines for college completion and streamlined degree programs by agencies such as Complete College America (CCA). CCA contends that programs like dual credit and early college are equalizing, in that they increase college graduation rates for students of color—hence providing important "momentum." CCA argues, "Data tells us the best way to create that momentum is to remove unnecessary barriers and ensure students hit essential milestones like completing gateway courses and accumulating credits as soon as possible" (https://completecollege.org/momentum/).

CCA's particular rhetorical stance—which uses "gateway" as a stand-in term for Gen Ed, and values credit "accumulation" over earned, scaffolded college coursework—creates a false equivalency between pre-college-level "milestones" to be dispatched in high school, and General Education curricula as a whole. This is the mantra that students internalize as further voiced by parents, mentors, pundits, and most importantly, universities themselves, encouraging students to test out of Gen Ed courses as much as possible. It is a race to *completion*, framed not so differently than one might describe a quest to win in one of those now ubiquitous "escape room" competitions, where one needs to find all the missing artifacts in order to unlock the door before the timer goes off. In the paradigm of a college education, the timer ticks ever loudly, and so everyone wants to find a way to shut it off and escape—with a college degree.

In this time-based framework, creating more access to AP curricula or other pre-college credit mechanisms simply feeds the beast of remediation arguments surrounding Gen Ed. To wit: If *every* entering college student took a full menu of Gen Ed courses, *on* college campuses, and if the United States' commitment to higher education would be reinvigorated such that college was truly affordable for all, then we would not need testing and pre-college credit programs, and we would not therefore need to expand access to them.[17] As a result, the very initiative that was meant to *better* prepare students in a variety of subjects as part of a holistic liberal education has been relegated to the margins of our curriculum, and reframed as coursework for the unlucky or the (deemed) unworthy among us.

Gen Ed, Rhetoric and Writing Studies, and Credits and Courses on the Ground

Ideally, the diverse group of readers of this book includes some from my own field of rhetoric and writing studies. These readers know that a crisis regarding the position of college writing in the curriculum has been present for decades, as defined by its labor and associated funding models, and its rapid decline as a standard experience for all first-year students—three issues that are not mutually exclusive. Yet a surprisingly scant amount of the field's literature takes on the overarching mechanisms that hold our college writing program operations in place. And the *biggest* mechanism—General Education—has been mostly talked *around* in our field, rather than talked about, with a few notable exceptions, for example Branson's *Policy Regimes: College Writing and Public Education Policy in the United States*, Hansen and Farris's *College Credit for Writing in High School*, and Tinberg and Sullivan's *What Is College-Level Writing?* (volumes 1 and 2), as well as Adler-Kassner's *The Activist WPA*. Each of these are key policy-minded books to which my story of Gen Ed, and its framings, owes considerable debt.[18]

Just as I am not the first scholar to highlight the problems with shortcutting General Education curricula through pre-college programs, testing, or other similar means, neither have I been an innocent bystander to the industry that demeans Gen Ed, as a former writing program administrator, associate dean for curricula, department head, and now, a humanities school chair. From each of these vantage points, I have seen how Gen Ed as an ecosystem, and first-year writing as a biotic part of it, has been relegated to the margins of the curriculum and consequently earmarked for those who come to campus *lacking* the intellectual work in core subjects that heretofore was the provenance of college instruction alone.

As an associate dean of liberal arts, I managed Gen Ed from a global position, seeking to keep our college's Gen Ed enrollments appropriately high, because 99 percent of all the students at my university came through our college's doors by virtue of Gen Ed courses. My job entailed wrangling competing departmental requests to create new Gen Ed courses simply to boost unit-level enrollments, for revenue, while receiving regular pressure from outside forces—including the College Board itself—for quicker, easier, *seamless* ways for students to bring in pre-college credits in order to make way for either a shorter time to degree or a space for students to use the hours otherwise devoted to Gen Ed to complete a second major.[19]

Thus, I faced internally competing discourse: On the one hand, Gen Ed makes us (the college) money, as these are required courses offered on a massive scale almost exclusively in the liberal arts, and are intrinsic to our mission. On the other hand, students (and parents) want to spend their tuition dollars elsewhere in the college, on curricula they have been taught *matters more* than Gen Ed (including other colleges' majors and minors), so we should marginalize and minimize its place in our requirements in favor of investing in other new degree programs and associated enrollments. To borrow from Elizabeth Bishop, the art of such losses and gains are, sadly, not hard for administrators to eventually master.

This balancing act was informed by the seventeen prior years I served as a writing program administrator (WPA) across three different universities. As a WPA, I oversaw the various means for exemption from first-year writing courses. On a local level correspondent to my own field identity, I faced similar internal contradictions to the later work I would do as an associate dean. I promoted the value of college writing courses, but I also learned that enrollment management is a complicated math problem, whereby there are never enough instructors to serve all the students, and that *this*—more than ability testing, curricular scaffolding, or course outcomes—drove how students entered and moved through our program.

Each university where I was a faculty member, true to all writing instruction being a local endeavor, had its own way of handling placement and enrollments, each of which I inherited as a WPA and was able to do little to change during my tenure. At my first university, placement was determined via a timed essay test, which decided whether students should go into basic writing, Comp I, or Comp II (the ubiquitous "research writing" course).[20] This was familiar to me, as it also had been our placement mechanism at my doctoral institution, where I oversaw placement as an assistant (graduate) director of composition. These were large-scale mechanisms designed to quickly and in rote fashion assess students' abilities upon intake and roughly place them into something resembling an acceptable starting point for their postsecondary literacy education.

At my second university, there was no placement test, but students could be exempted from one or both writing courses via AP Literature or Language exam or SAT English exam subscores. Since non-credit-bearing basic writing and basic math courses were not allowed at the college level, per that state's legislature, the intake placement mechanisms only determined whether students would be able to bypass one or two of the standard comp courses, not whether they needed an additional preparatory course as well. My third university, where I later undertook the associate dean responsibilities described above, had a program with a similar placement structure, with 50 percent of all students being exempted from the standard composition course by means of SAT English subscores, or AP Literature or Language scores.

These three universities took as a guiding principle that some reliable percentage would "place out" of the first-year writing sequence, in whole or in part. This was key to the labor model for teaching; as I used to remind our staff, we *could not teach* all our first-year students each year if a significant percentage of them were not exempted. Our tenure-stream faculty did not teach these courses (at two of these three universities), and we did not have the non-tenure-track faculty to teach the whole first-year class. We also shared the belief that we should not grow our English graduate program to irresponsibly large levels *just* to bring on graduate TAs to staff sections of first-year writing, without a clear promise of academic jobs awaiting them upon completion.

Indeed, it's impossible to tell any story about General Education without first recognizing that it has become a system that students are literally *taught to bypass* in various explicit ways. It is also important to recognize that universities are economically shaped to rely on such bypassing of requirements, particularly first-year writing. Much like invitations to a wedding, wherein the bride assumes 20 percent of her guests will be unable to attend, or seating on an airplane, where maybe 5 percent of passengers will not show up before the boarding doors close, writing programs are built around a presence of absence—namely, the students who "test out" and bypass the requirement. Placement is thus but one of those ways that students can avoid first-year writing, through institutionally sanctioned means. The assumptions we make about students and their abilities through systems such as placement in 2026 are also the assumptions that James Bryant Conant in 1945 was hoping General Education might respond to and even negate. Placement is a means by which students can be segregated into the haves and the have-nots of our educational system, starting before the first day of college.

I have also been a parent participating in the unequal system of Gen Ed. Our daughter accumulated seventeen college credits from AP in high school, which gave her an exemption from first-year writing, history, and other social sciences. Even though her AP Language and Composition course was admittedly one of the best that she took in high school, others—notably the infamous APUSH (AP US History)—were no more than hectic and stress-inducing races to the finish line, with little time for deeper knowledge or applied learning. AP courses were the only advanced option available in many subjects at her high school, which did not do multilevel tracking as some other schools do. But throughout, our daughter's school counselor and the administration as a whole nonetheless pushed AP courses *hard* on many higher-income students and their parents, often regardless of their ability levels.

This is because high schools are rated by *US News and World Report* and other national aggregators on the basis of the number of AP courses they offer, the number of students who enroll in them, and the percentage of those students who receive a "passing" score of 3 or higher on the exams themselves. So it behooves high schools to fill these courses with students whom they feel are the most likely to score well on the exam. According to *USNWR*, our daughter's high school at the time of this writing has a 39 percent participation rate in AP and a 30 percent pass rate. Our daughter, who is white, regularly questioned how a diverse school such as hers, with just over 50 percent Black and Hispanic students and 56 percent low-income enrollment students (of all races), could have myriad AP classes with one, or zero, African American or Hispanic students enrolled in them. Even though she knew the answer—and even though the College Board is aware of racial disparities in AP enrollments and claims to have made strides to address these—it makes the question no less necessary to voice, even as it is the case for families who are less financially fortunate or less educated on the perils of credit by exemption than ours that the pitfalls that I outline above are far outweighed by the perceived savings down the road in tuition dollars.

Indeed, cost-saving is at the heart of how many Gen Ed college courses are exempted, as well as central to parents' and students' concerns about the "repeat" work that they believe General Education curricula represent in relation to one's high school studies. Just as placement and tracking are critical to understanding how General Education and for-credit pre-college options operate as a linked system, one could easily argue that the history of General Education is also a history of labor struggles in academe justified by framing Gen Ed as a set of courses typically enrolled by lower-ability (read: without prior credit), marginalized students who do not "need" expensive instruction offered by tenure-stream faculty, at least not in massively enrolled courses like first-year writing and first-year math. As noted above, first-year writing programs at large universities are staffed significantly or exclusively by contingent faculty or graduate students. Lower-level math courses suffer the same annexed and contingent labor-based fate, while other Gen Ed courses in the sciences and social sciences that require less 1:1 instruction and scaffolding may be taught in massive lectures of hundreds of students, led by one faculty member but "sectioned" for discussions into smaller groups led by teaching assistants. It is only at the smallest colleges, and those without substantial graduate programs, that Gen Ed coursework is regularly and reliably taught by permanent faculty. And in many cases, those courses, especially in first-year writing, are rhetorically reframed as "seminars" that are topics-based and interdisciplinary (or what I like to call "fake comp").

Indeed, in 1946, then Dean of Liberal Arts at the University of Iowa and Gen Ed advocate and pioneer Earl James McGrath cited a proclamation by

James Bryant Conant himself that includes this key observation about the mechanics of teaching Gen Ed courses—focused on the sciences, secondary to Conant's training as a chemist: "To attempt in the same courses to instruct those who are *interested in science* as part of a General Education is almost a hopeless undertaking from the start. What seems to be needed here are new types of courses given out by the departments of physics or chemistry or biology, but undertaken by *a special staff* who will be concerned entirely with the problems of teaching science at the college level as part of a General Education" (qtd. in "General Education Movement" 7; emphases mine).

Two key points noted above continue to pervade General Education instruction today: first, that those who are "interested" in subjects (i.e., students majoring in said subject) should be segregated from those who do not share such core interests, and second, that those teaching the "interested" students aren't the right faculty to teach the uninterested. On the first point, Conant's early vision of Gen Ed required a buy-in on the part of faculty that students would be educated in *general* principles of the subject at hand, yet with equal ability to succeed through the trajectory of the course. Having students with higher-level interests and abilities makes teaching students without those in the same classroom understandably difficult, and is a phenomenon not completely avoidable in any classroom, but still a core principle for Gen Ed.

While this vision of separating students by interest *and ability* lies at the core of early Gen Ed principles, Conant's vision for General Education was both revolutionary in terms of its social aims and inextricable ties to democracy and the greater good, and also limited by his own views on structural hierarchies, both good and bad, in American secondary and postsecondary education. It is further true that Conant's version of General Education was a (fairly impatient) response to the increasing specialization that American universities were prioritizing in adoption of the German postsecondary teaching model, which we might simply summarize here as the rise of graduate teaching and the rejection of generalized instruction in favor of faculty choice and specialization in teaching assignments, which has led to the operational principles of American research-intensive institutions today.

Despite these historical truths about labor, testing, economics, and curriculum, the key position that first-year writing plays in the rise and subsequent downfall of General Education as an American enterprise, and the corresponding rhetorical import of the Gen Ed movement throughout the past eight pivotal decades of its existence, has yet to be part of our national narrative. But it needs to be. Simply put, we cannot tell the story of General Education without including how it is *sold*—by testing corporations who hope families loathe it enough to avoid it via pre-college exemption; by universities who tout its benefits weakheartedly but advertise its various virtues come enrollment planning time; and by the general public, who increasingly demonize General Education, as noted above. We also cannot tell the story of first-year writing without recognizing its segmented place into Gen Ed and the constraints this place creates on the course's public and institutional value. These two stories of General Education are complex, intertwined, and interdependent.

About This Book

Across the following four chapters, I tell the eighty-year story of Gen Ed in roughly chronological order. Readers might thus divide this book into two conjoined stories: one about shared histories (chapters 1 and 2) and one about current controversies and problems (chapters 3 and 4), capped off by a reflection about the future of higher education itself (conclusion). In connecting the present to the past, I hope that readers might be introduced to both new texts and new ways of looking at what they see as familiar ones. Above all, I want you to come away from this book with a more complex—if less comfortable—understanding of what General Education has been, is, and ultimately could be.

Chapter 1 starts the story by situating the history of Gen Ed as one driven in part by the variable of student choices and curricular responses to those choices. It demonstrates the slow evolution of Gen Ed offerings and choices over time by undertaking a close reading of the first volume of two influential journals that emerged just three and a half years apart in the postwar era: *The Journal of General Education*, in October 1946, and *College Composition and Communication*, in March 1950. These journals illustrate the early story of the Gen Ed movement as it pervaded professional discourse in higher education, and in the field of rhetoric and writing studies. The first volume of *JGE* followed on the Redbook's aims, giving further voice to members of and consultants for the Harvard group as well as prominent proponents of the Redbook at other institutions and in public office. It also provided a platform for advancing Conant's ideals and served as a primer for his three books on higher education that would follow during the 1950s, at roughly five-year intervals. This chapter also shows how closely tied first-year writing instruction was to discourse about Gen Ed. Both *JGE* and *CCC* articulate their separate but allied aims for Gen Ed, and both take seriously the position of college faculty (and high school teachers) in the pursuit of Gen Ed teaching—in *JGE*'s case, across multiple subjects. Yet they existed in parallel but not entirely overlapping rhetorical spaces in higher education. Their history is thus an important starting place for subsequent tales about the original intentions of Gen Ed, and where first-year writing fit into those intentions, past and present, and also sets up your reading of subsequent chapters that show how we have both emulated and rejected the Harvard group's proposals.

Chapter 2 moves from a story of two journals to a story of state policies and politics and how they affect the ways General Education does or does not serve students, using archives on higher education reform at the University System of Georgia (USG) and the twenty-six colleges and universities that currently make up that system. Because the USG has, since 1967, employed a common core curricula and since 1997, a common course-numbering system, its various institutions are linked together in a manner that differentiates it from many other public university state systems in the United States. This chapter examines the reasons why the USG's past and current revisions of its Gen Ed requirements came to be, and how these reflect interpretative leveling of what "core" coursework means for students studying at vastly different educational institutions. It also discusses similar initiatives at two other equally large and diverse university systems (University of Texas and University of Florida) as comparative and anchoring examples.

Chapter 2 ultimately argues that no state is immune to such policies, and that all citizens need to understand the mechanisms of General Education and higher education at the state level. It tells the story of the overarching aims of the USG Gen Ed program as it evolved (or failed to evolve) at three significant mile markers: 1954, 1961, and 1997—as well as current (2025) efforts to reframe the curriculum for public consumption across the system. Throughout this narrative, it spotlights USG's actions during segregation in the South, and how some decisions further marginalized Black students and also nullified local differences in pedagogy and curricular design. Plainly put, this chapter shows that the (hi)story of Gen Ed in the USG cannot be separated from contextual histories of segregationist practices.

Chapter 3 moves chronologically forward to tell national stories about General Education's current debates and controversies, which pit, as a core-credit program exemplar, Advanced Placement against Gen Ed's overall ideology, use value, and civic benefit. It argues that AP curricula in American high schools are propelled by rhetoric promoting uplift and economic advancement, including addressing the public's fears of Gen Ed in college taking up valuable time and money. Focusing in part on first-year writing courses, this chapter divides the rhetoric surrounding pre-college credit by examination from the College Board into those of *competition, remediation,* and *efficiency*. While chapter 3 presents some data that may already be familiar to readers who follow such current debates, my focus on the rhetorical strategies of these initiatives and the fears and insecurities they play upon in American households, and in university strategic decisions, should be new to many others. As with the overall purpose of this book, I aim in chapter 3 to take what we think we already know and place it in the context of rhetorics regarding first-year writing, which is also increasingly seen as remedial and disproportionately enrolls first-generation students and students of color.

Chapter 4 takes the story of rhetorical strategies in promoting pre-college credit programming to a deeper disciplinary level, as a key factor in the evolution of the rhetoric of first-year writing over the last four decades. It argues that the disciplinary growth of rhetoric and writing studies has failed to consistently promote the value of first-year writing on college campuses. I situate this need for advocacy against the rise of dual enrollment / dual credit (DE/DC) nationwide, and the risk it poses to the sustainability of college writing programs as a whole. I compare the structurally equitable notions of General Education to the constructions of one local DE/DC program, OnRamps, in the University of Texas system. Questioning the ultimate value of the first-year course as serving one of two competing purposes—as a means of intellectual liberation for new college writers, versus a simple "sorting" and inoculation mechanism for "content" coursework that can be done through DE/DC outsourcing—in this chapter, I ask whether the story of public, rhetorical valuations of first-year college writing is being persuasively told. I further argue this rhetoric sidesteps public concerns about college writing as a central site for remediation or duplication within the overall Gen Ed curriculum.

Finally, my conclusion offers some contemplative observations on whether General Education, as a socioeducational movement, can still do the work that Conant and the Harvard group originally envisioned, given its primary function as keyed to "workforce development" in many states, and the general populace's mixed feelings about the value of a college degree in volatile political times. This chapter also highlights ongoing perceptions of how well colleges have historically addressed inequities in social class, especially following explosive college enrollments post–World War II. Finally, it spotlights the newly emerging story of the so-called paper ceiling and its allied nonprofit and corporate sponsorship, which speaks to anxieties about career trajectories for current (Gen Z) students. And it outlines what new stories about Gen Ed might be pathways for the future, including a brief examination of one progressive local model that explicitly espouses the core values of Gen Ed, and aims to publicize those for greater uptake.

A Final Note About Process (and Stories)

Throughout this book I have provided links to information, reports, and studies publicly available online, and have also leaned on current news regarding General Education's histories and futures. This is a book whose topic is somewhat of a moving target, given that American colleges and universities—and the structures that support them—can change, consolidate, and disappear altogether in a moment, along with their Gen Ed enrollments, all in the name of financial solvency. So in order to represent the rhetorics guiding these changes, and tell a dynamic story, I need to be as current in my sources as possible. As such, I rely heavily on web-based reports and studies that offer up-to-the minute data. I realize that given the limitations of print genres, even more will happen with General Education, possibly good but mostly bad, while this book is going to press. I ask readers to therefore use my arguments here as a springboard for telling and retelling stories of Gen Ed on their own. My story is necessarily frozen in time, but the fragile life of Gen Ed marches on, especially for the students who have been made to believe that the substitutes, surrogates, and tests created to destroy it are actually designed to benefit their educational journeys and their lives beyond college.

Now, let's begin our story, a cautionary tale that has been heretofore relegated to the shadows of American history but is actually best told in the cold, bracing light of day.

1
Educating the Great Community

Postwar Gen Ed Philosophies and the Variable of Student Choice

> A general education movement is under way. It is moving across the educational landscape with speed and force. It will sweep away many conventional forms of high school and college education. It will cause major modifications in professional and technical education. It will radically change requirements for graduate degrees. It will profoundly affect the thinking and the lives of our people.
> —Earl James McGrath, "The General Education Movement," 1946

If we want to understand the rhetoric of General Education today, we have to understand its beginnings some eighty years ago. Building on the brief overview of the Harvard Committee's Redbook that I provided in my introduction, in this chapter I focus on Gen Ed philosophies in two journals that emerged right after the Redbook: *The Journal of General Education* (JGE) and *College Composition and Communication* (CCC). Each promoted as well as debated the Redbook's principles of Gen Ed in the context of the United States' educational concerns at the start of what would eventually be termed the "Long Fifties" (1945–1964). Taken as a pairing, *JGE* and *CCC* serve to bookend the fledgling relationship between first-year writing and General Education, with each holding similar pedagogical ideals and each championing a new, professionalized way of thinking about teaching "average" college students within a class-based, and occasionally meritocratic, American society.

They further highlight some of the issues endemic to higher education discussions in the immediate postwar years, including programming for so-called gifted high school and college students, the place of vocational education in a booming economy, and ability level–centered instruction in English and math. This postwar rhetoric of Gen Ed is worth recovering, as it illustrates the widespread national uptake of Conant's original aims of equalizing and democratizing higher education. It also contains principles behind Gen Ed as a curriculum and a *movement*, as noted in the epigraph to this chapter, which still resonate in our current socioeconomic times as we work to help all students become educated toward participation in our civic democracy.

To get us settled into this micro archival history, especially for readers who are not historians themselves, I first put these histories of Gen Ed in pragmatic and contemporary context as dependent upon student predilections and behaviors. Even though the earliest proponents of Gen Ed viewed it as a holistic endeavor, with similarly broad outcomes to match, students instead tend to see Gen Ed as a menu of individual course *choices*, rather than an articulated whole. This is part of the challenge of advancing the value of Gen Ed: how to effectively persuade students (and parents) that the end actually does justify the means.

While such persuasion regarding Gen Ed's intrinsic value is the overall purpose of this book, a metaphor at this junction might be useful in anchoring our forthcoming discussions of Gen Ed, both past and present. If we think of Gen Ed as a meal in a restaurant, on some campuses today, that meal is prix fixe in nature. On other campuses, it is a multistation buffet. Throughout history, this restaurant where Gen Ed is served has had many owners—some more generous or far-reaching with the construction of their meal options than others. And to stay profitable, and socially current, these owners have continued to offer the most popular dishes in the greatest quantities while taking others off the menu entirely. Yet, with few exceptions, each of these owners have been consistently concerned with two things: high-quality ingredients and overall nutritional value. Its customers, however, are only interested in their individual dining experiences, positive or negative, with each dish or food item. And so the restaurant and its customers operate in what appears to be a unified purpose, but actually are interacting with the same food toward very different ends.

Using this paradigm, we might think of the Harvard group as the original restaurateur, which at its grand opening had only the highest-quality goals for service and patron experiences, and which invited customers from around the nation to sample and make suggestions for its offerings (soups and salads, appetizers, mains, desserts, drinks)—without intent to promote any specific food items within these categories. To move from metaphor back to history in action, when Harvard debuted its plan in 1945, it did not make judgments as to how capacious or specific the range of Gen Ed course offerings should be, instead focusing on philosophical aims for the curriculum as a whole across several core disciplines.

In other words, unlike the operational realities of many Gen Ed programs today—those subsequent restaurants around the country—the Redbook only articulated the *vision* for the curriculum, not the specific curriculum itself. As Michael Roth has noted, the committee "did not try to argue that some works are obviously superior to others, only that Western society had recognized particular works as part of its tradition for a long time . . . it argued that the books traditionally read by the educated elite should be the books we learn to read together" (*Beyond the University* 131). Exposure to these works, as well as foundational lessons in core academic subjects, would help develop "traits of mind" that would generate "a liberal outlook" in the students themselves (133).

To return to my metaphor, the Harvard group hoped that eating from the Gen Ed menu provided—regardless of the campus-restaurant where it was located—would inculcate in students a lifelong value of nutrition and dietary quality, and an appreciation for good company and lively debate about food, and other things, when dining with those unlike themselves. Readers will see these values, in terms relevant to democracy and liberal education, represented in essays from both *JGE* and *CCC*, which showcase arguments for how different parts of the overall curriculum benefit students in myriad intellectual and personal ways.

As readers of the history in this chapter, and also the next, you are thus encouraged to see your way past local or even regional curricular specifics, that is, the items on the menu—as important as they may be for individual colleges' and universities' operations—and focus instead on the broader goals and philosophies that have brought together Gen Ed initiatives across various institutions and also have made Gen Ed a unification tool for larger political ends, as I will discuss in chapter 2. These goals and philosophies, toward student uplift and enrichment, are what I argue we have lost, but which we could renew, with significant education of students, faculty, and the public about the true value of Gen Ed teachings. Even as the Harvard group was not as diverse as our students (or our US population) today, we can still apply their proposal to a wide range of Gen Ed programs that speak to that diversity—of choice, of taste, and of values—in all its forms.

Courses and Choices: Where Are We Going and Where Have We Been?

As academic administrators (and parents also) know, we can never fully understand why a student chooses *not* to do something—such as enroll in a particular course—especially if they don't explain it to us at the time. It's much like voting; few people are honest about why they *don't* cast a ballot in a presidential election, and others never give a reason at all. Students are influenced by various factors at course registration time, including what their friends are taking or would recommend, the time and day a course is offered, whether an instructor is popular, whether a topic sounds interesting (or easy), and the big one—whether they *need this course to graduate*. If a course does not meet a graduation requirement of some kind, or speak to a specific career aspiration that the student holds, the chances go down dramatically that a student will enroll in it. And of course, if a student already received credit for the course topic or requirement in high school, then they definitely won't take it (again).

Students rarely think of their courses as a cohesive set of goals and values that the college or university wants them to achieve. Indeed, there is little consensus on whether students understand Gen Ed's positive educational intentions at all (Vander Schee; Thompson et al.).[1] Despite our outcomes-driven atmosphere in higher education—which students often welcome, as it clearly outlines what is *expected* of them in a course—the philosophical and whole-person outcomes of General Education that Harvard first promoted are far more fuzzy or invisible to students as a whole today. Thus, while some faculty and other Gen Ed proponents have advocated for a narrowing of course choices in Gen Ed, in order to force various threads or perspectives or subjects against too *much* choice (or push the "specials" over the lesser-priced entrees, in menu terms), the reality is (undergraduate) life finds a way, driven by the above logics. One might argue that *how* Gen Ed is thus constructed on a particular campus is less important than *why* it is constructed as it is—and whether that logic can be translated for students in ways that mean something to them.

Individual choices are tough to chart, and even tougher to use as the basis for a larger argument. Human behavior is too reliant upon positionalities of all kinds, especially across social demographics whose views differ toward education as a significant financial investment. But a sample comparison of aggregated choices made over time—as was done in a January 2025 feature in *The Pennsylvania Gazette*, the alumni magazine for the University of Pennsylvania (aka Penn)—can reveal interesting trends in student enrollments in Gen Ed that evince a utilitarian decision-making process by students, one also recognized by the institution itself.

The *Gazette* article, "Course Corrections," reflects on the sixty-five-year history of Penn's course guide, tracking both the most popular classes by academic year as well as overall subject trends across decades (Popp). In 1959–1960, or about fifteen years after the publication of *General Education in a Free Society*, the three most popular (i.e., highly enrolled) courses at Penn were English Composition I and II, and Introduction to Literature (Prose), followed by General Biology, General Psychology, History of American Democracy, Art and Civilization, Intro to Literature (Poetry); Europe Since 1815; Calculus and Analytical Geometry; Fundamentals of Math I, Shakespeare, and General Chemistry. Rounding out the list were a dozen or so business-related courses offered by Penn's top-ranked Wharton School of Business. As the article summarizes, these 1959–1960 rankings were due in part to "Wharton's liberal arts requirements [which] had an outsized impact on overall course enrollments" due to the school's size (26).

Compare these with the three most popular courses at Penn in spring and fall 2023, which were Intro to Microeconomics, Calculus II, and Intro to Psychology, followed by Calculus I, Intro to Macroeconomics, General Chemistry I, Organic Chemistry I, Ensemble Performance (Music), Calculus III, and Intro to Society, plus fifteen other Wharton-offered business and finance courses (Popp 33). Now, let's compare the trends between 1959 and 2023 by broader course categories: In fall 1959, there were 1,688 students enrolled in History courses; in fall 2023, that number was 898. In fall 1964, there were 385 students enrolled in Corporate Finance; in fall 2023, there were 824. The most popular course in humanities departments overall in 2023 was History of American Law to 1877, which enrolled 288 students. An outlier was the relatively stable enrollments of Philosophy courses, which numbered 1,469 in 1959 and 1,290 in 2023.[2]

Students' needs are clearly changing, as are their career goals. In a 2023 Penn Career Services survey, nearly half of the class of 2022 (across all schools and majors) reported securing a job in either finance or consulting (Popp 34), which tracks with the kind of courses students are currently choosing in these areas. Institutional context is also important. The University of Pennsylvania is a private, Ivy League university ranked number 10 for "US National Universities" by *US News and World Report* that for fall 2024 only accepted 6 percent of all applicants, and enrolled just over 2,300 first-year students. But it is also surprisingly diverse: 20 percent of the class of 2028 qualified for Pell grants, and as the *Gazette* article notes, "even students who receive relatively generous financial aid packages [toward the $87,860 annual cost of attendance] are excruciatingly aware of the sacrifices their families make to send them to college" (35). Further, 19 percent of that class's admitted Penn students were first-generation, and 57 percent identified as students of color. These students are also highly qualified, with middle 50 percent SAT scores between 1510 and 1560.[3] And as I will discuss later in this book, students with those kind of qualifications are the most likely to be exempted from multiple, if not all, Gen Ed courses prior to college admission.

These trends in Gen Ed enrollments might thus be viewed, in historical context, as a bellwether for the rapid decline of General Education as *liberal education*, a moniker that runs throughout the pages of *JGE* as synonymous with the Harvard plan. Whereas the original intentions of the Harvard group were to specifically provide courses and programming for the "average" student, they were not to be to the *exclusion* of the exceptional student, as liberal education was to be education for all. Also, the Harvard group did not mean Gen Ed to be for *only* the disadvantaged or non-elite student; rather it was *also* for the elite population. To examine the course enrollment trends at Penn is to therefore offer two hypotheses. First, that students' career interests by 2023 had considerably narrowed, causing them to move away from many Gen Ed subjects, especially in the humanities, and toward more business-oriented courses that better served their professional aspirations. And second, that Penn students are earning credit prior to enrollment in *other* Gen Ed subjects at rates far eclipsing those of 1959–1960, and thus are taking more specialized coursework, predominantly in business. The latter hypothesis is simply a truth; as I will show in chapter 3, the rise of AP, IB, and DE/DC only began to skyrocket in the last thirty or so years, that is, since about 1990. Students in 1959–1960 had no such widespread opportunities and were also admitted at a much higher rate overall via less selective processes than the students in 2023 (~40 percent versus 6 percent).

But there is a third hypotheses that is even simpler to pose: that students in some majors *choose* not to earn a liberal education anymore, and that Penn's leaders recognize, if do not agree with, that choice. As Peter Struck, then-Dean of the College of Arts and Sciences at Penn and a Classical Studies professor, comments in the *Gazette* article, students who come from lower-income backgrounds at Penn are likely to worry that "things are well taken care of financially with respect to [their] parents and everyone that [they] love and people that are investing deeply in [them] to do this thing . . . that pressure was different 20 years ago, when the students were more likely to be from very well-heeled backgrounds and in fact their futures *were* going to be secure" (35). At the same time, Struck is an advocate for a liberal education that covers all subjects in Gen Ed, as "it's important that you [the student] be numerate—that you understand data and how it works, and you understand the sciences ... but you're going to be at a great disadvantage if you're not also literate" because "when problems come your way, they don't look like problem sets ... lots of them are going to require you to understand culture and its legacy and its history and where people are embedded" (34).

Certainly General Education, like all of higher education, has had to morph and shift with the changing social, political, and economic times. There should be no expectation that what students wanted or needed seventy years ago at Penn, or at any American college or university, is exactly what they need today. But that expectation is not my argument. My argument is that *student choice itself*, historically, *is never an independent variable*; it is dependent upon what they are presented with, and how the choices are made meaningful to their personal and professional goals in education. Further, *not all students get to make the same choices*—not about the courses they take, the colleges they go to, or the running start they may or may not get on Gen Ed curricula before they even graduate high school. And when the values and beliefs that academics and the public alike espouse about General Education no longer correspond, rhetorically, to the good reasons that students use for making the choices that they do—despite the advocacy of high-profile deans like Struck—that's when we have a problem with the future of Gen Ed as an enterprise.

Taking these points about choice into consideration, let's now rewind back to 1946 to see where the values Struck espouses first took hold nationwide, to remind ourselves of their own good reasons, and how we might carry them more forcefully forward into Gen Ed today and seek to better influence (or at least inform) both student choices and the rhetoric of Gen Ed curricula.

Gen Ed in the Postwar Era: Democracy, Citizenry, and the Greater Good

The modern organizational principles of General Education were designed to shape students' minds and ways of being toward engaged civic participation in a democracy, as backed by the tenets of humanistic inquiry.[4] The General Education movement promoted a middle ground between the polarized options of elite and professional education for advanced training in specific white-collar careers, and vocational education for work in trades, service, and blue-collar positions. It was rooted in a philosophy of teaching and learning intended to stem the perceived tide of overspecialization in schooling and help students lacking familial or other legacy advantages obtain a meaningful education—one that pedagogical approaches and social stratification in high schools and colleges at that time did not adequately provide.[5] As framed by Harvard, postwar Gen Ed was an equitable inoculation of the nation's masses against destructive sociopolitical conditions on the horizon, should society refuse its collective civic responsibilities.

Today's Gen Ed follows a curricular taxonomy that founding voices of the movement would find familiar. It also includes periodic curricular improvements on individual campuses, and larger guidance by the AAC&U, that reflect broader values of equity and inclusion in twenty-first-century America, for example the addition of courses in cultural understanding, globalization, and information literacy. Such amendments remind us that the postwar movement did not center on inclusion of minoritized or marginalized populations. The historical framing of civic participation was admittedly informed by a dominant, white, male ideology that focused heavily on social class but generally avoided discussions of race, disability, sexuality, or other differences.[6]

Yet despite recent paradigmatic interventions such as these, and calls for a holistic revival of the humanities overall,[7] the prevailing rhetorical import of General Education nationwide could be altered if it took up the rhetorical framings of the postwar era and rejected the impulses of what Chris Gallagher regards as the "unbundling" movement in higher education (35). Gen Ed on our local campuses often focuses on improving *structures* but is often less attentive to broad *messaging* and is also generally ahistorical. The Gen Ed movement of the 1940s, in contrast, envisioned the humanities, social sciences, and also mathematics and the sciences as urgently and equally ideologically necessary, since "science and technology had advanced faster than the understanding of the social and moral challenges posed," which left unchecked would lead to consequences for national peace and security (Smith and Bender 3).

Deborah Brandt has reflected, if more cynically, on the adoption of literacy in particular as a national asset when she argued that "During World War II, reading, writing, and ciphering became dramatically more valuable as media for producing or handling the new. Soldiers were tested not for what they learned in school, but how fast they could be expected to learn. What mattered was the capacity to absorb innovation faster and better than the enemy" ("Drafting US Literacy" 499). The rise of Gen Ed is to my mind also part and parcel of Brandt's contention that "mass literacy created mass schooling" (496) in the United States. English studies, however, did less to engage directly with this cause; as Richard Ohmann has argued, "English and its neighbors struck an ambivalent posture of disengagement from and antagonism toward the postwar project of untrammeled capitalist development and U.S. dominance in the world" (77). He further argued for thus "locating English, through the 1950s and early 1960s, in a safe eddy of postwar development, and also in a latent contradiction with respect to the main current" (80).

To bring this stance to the present day, advocates of the postwar Gen Ed movement were focused on the holistic *why* of Gen Ed as a way to strengthening democracy and civic responsibility, with the humanities benefiting from this national patronage via increased foci on the importance and relevance of its inclusive academic subjects. This advocacy was significantly informed by both the need to preserve American ideals (and security) through mass education of the future workforce, and to equitably (and morally) educate increasing numbers of new, socioeconomically diverse students who would soon assume key responsibilities that required informed moral judgments about science and technology, humanity, and the greater good. Advocates of Gen Ed believed these lessons could only be reliably found in dedicated curricula designed for this larger purpose.

Gen Ed in the twenty-first century has been effectively operationalized to benefit the bottom line of colleges and universities, as it is usually maintained via one of two economically infused paradigms. At the institutional level, and as reflected in the historical course enrollments at Penn outlined above, Gen Ed course development is used to fight against rapidly rising enrollments in high-paying career fields, which many students flock to in response to postgraduation employment insecurities that haunt them.[8] This results in budget-centered course creation both inside and outside the liberal arts that can bend or break the principles of Gen Ed core values and disciplinary expertise.[9] At the advising level, Gen Ed requirements appear to students as generic area requirements to be satisfied, if possible, *before* college.

Both of these paradigms, which operate as codependent variables influencing how students complete their education, construct Gen Ed as an economically charged enterprise of capital gains and losses for institutions, rather than an edifying program offering benefits of mind and being.[10] Gen Ed as work perceived to be "done" in high school and as expensive requirements to complete are equally powerful rhetorical points in ghettoizing the marginalized students who lack socioeconomic privilege and who are statistically less likely to come to college with multiple college requirements already completed through various means.[11] In today's Gen Ed paradigm, these students lacking double-digit credit hours upon admission are marked as effectively *remedial* in relation to their credit-bearing peers.¹² But that is the opposite of what the Harvard group wanted them to be, and also opposed to what *JGE* and *CCC* authors believed Gen Ed could achieve for the most vulnerable among us.

Higher Education in the "Quiet Years"

General Education as a uniquely American concept appeared at a time of immense change, and great potential prosperity. The "Long Fifties" is regarded as one of the most economically advancing periods of the twentieth century, marked by expansion of leisure-focused and time-saving technologies, and the average citizen's access to them; the growth of suburban and other regionally planned communities; and an overall population explosion, aka the Baby Boom, the likes of which have not been matched since.¹³ Unlike other European allies who faced massive reconstruction efforts after World War II, the US comparatively faced shortages of materials (metal, rubber, and paper) and some foods and household goods (hence the Victory Gardens movement).¹⁴

America also faced the social reintegration of the returning servicemen and -women and the roles they would play in the booming postwar economy, including how they would become part of the growing population yet to be educated. When *JGE* published its inaugural issue in October 1946, contributors Dwight D. Eisenhower, Chester W. Nimitz, and A. A. Vandegrift characterized this time as "the interim period" or "the quiet years," indicating contemporary conditions of peacetime without guaranteed permanence.¹⁵ The postwar period was also a time in which the middle classes faced a choice "to move forward with the large social majority or *without* it," including in higher education reform (Newfield 31).

To ensure that returning US veterans would be able to secure gainful employment and make meaningful contributions to society, on June 2, 1944, President Roosevelt signed the GI Bill (Servicemen's Readjustment Act), which included both educational benefits as well as on-the-job training for veterans returning to civilian life.¹⁶ This act had immediate positive effects on overall college enrollment nationwide, an effect which would continue for at least three more decades, even though the original bill itself expired in 1956. This act, along with the subsequent Truman Commission Report of 1947, also created an inextricable tie between the power of education and the preservation of democracy in the United States.¹⁷

Such ties are readily on view in issue no. 1 of *JGE*, as Virgil Hancher—then president of the University of Iowa—argued in his lead essay, "We stand in awe of the atomic bomb, but its destruction may be quick and clean in comparison with the destructive power of deterioration by frustration resulting from our inability to relate the vastness of our knowledge to the meaning of life" (12). Similarly, in his *JGE* essay, W. K. Jordan, then president of Radcliffe College, posited that the social sciences existed at the philosophical core of General Education postwar, for their ability to help us understand our new postwar reality, in that

> A terrible war and the nihilistic forces that by so scant margin we mastered have compelled us to address ourselves to a careful examination of the destiny of man.... Do we as political scientists really understand that the very concept of sovereignty was destroyed simultaneously with Hiroshima; do we as historians fully realize that the virtues of nationalism were on that day consumed? (75)

During and after the war, both public and private colleges and universities were fast becoming an educational home for the masses, contrary to the gatekeeping processes in place at private institutions pre-1945. Prior to World War II, college had been primarily an avenue for the privileged—specifically white (Protestant) men (Thelin; Karabel; Synnott). With the war's mass casualties, however, colleges faced enrollment declines that promised to damage their bottom line. The GI Bill opened college and university doors to a far wider group of students, some of whom might otherwise have gone into skilled trades or unskilled labor, or would find themselves with no viable work at all. At the time of *JGE*'s initial publication in October 1946, 75 percent of all male college students age 18 to 29 were veterans. Of the 250,000 persons enrolled in college and also age 25 to 29, the "great majority" were veterans, including 90 percent of all male students (*Current Population Reports*). October 1946 was also just past the midway point of a decade of overall meteoric rise in the number of individuals in the US completing a four-year college degree. In 1939–1940, there were 186,500 college degrees granted nationwide. By 1949–1950, that number was 230 percent higher, at 432,058 (NCES, *120 Years*). Yet despite these efforts focused on educating returning military personnel, college was still not an option or choice for the majority of youth—a trend that continues today, notwithstanding the popular perception that "everyone" goes to college.[18] In fall 1946, 12.5 percent of the population age 18 to 24 was enrolled in a college or university; in fall 2021, the most recent available semester and year charted by the NCES (National Center for Education Statistics), this figure was 38 percent.[19]

This change in who would take college courses also came with changes in student preparation. No longer could faculty rely on students with patrician training from either selective public high schools or exclusive private ones. No longer were courses being taken solely by white men born into upper economic strata or so-called legacy families. In short, no longer could the college curriculum—and its intended outcomes—be designed and reserved for the "advanced" student, born of various paths to inherited cultural capital, a sentiment echoed at the start of this chapter by Dean Struck. The need for these non-elite men and women to engage in a reasonable alternative to *vocational* education and training, which would be specifically for entrance into skilled trades and other blue-collar occupations, was—and still is—at hand. Enter the national discourse on the Gen Ed movement as promoted and disseminated by *JGE*.

Soul and Self: Articulating General Education's Values

Even as the above national conditions are accepted as a predecessor to higher education today, the place of General Education as a facilitator of such national goals and as a site for resolving prewar inequities is less so. Like the students making course choices at Penn, the audiences for *JGE* were wide-ranging, and thus the essays in the journal's pages were prominent utterances made on a rapidly changing educational landscape. They mark not only the start of a national scholarly discourse on General Education, but also set the stage for a subsequent decade of publications by individuals from the Harvard group. These included 1953's *General Education in School and College* and two of Conant's own books, *Education in a Divided World* (1948) and *The American High School Today* (1959), which illustrate his evolving take on public schools and the American educational system.

The work of *JGE* also began a national discussion on the need for more streamlined curricula, governed by set standards, for exceptional students across high schools and colleges, which eventually became the Advanced Placement Program. This rise in discourse surrounding General Education also not-so-coincidentally occurs in the same decade as the advent of one of rhetoric and writing studies' flagship journals, *College Composition and Communication*, which launched its first issue in March 1950, less than three years after the emergence of *JGE*. Throughout the first decade of its publication, *CCC* reflected on the ideas of the Harvard group and its inheritors, starting with the committee reports in the second volume (May 1950) on the centrality of college composition (and communication) in General Education.

JGE emerged at a time when academia was just starting to restructure itself to handle mass enrollments, and when a parallel increase in faculty research expectations, designed to make sure the US remained highly competitive on the international stage, was just coming into view. As a result, academic faculty positions in the mid-1940s were not yet as highly specialized as today. Though current faculty work tends to be based on research specialization, up through the early 1990s, some tenure-track faculty positions in English departments were still being advertised as "generalists." These positions, often at institutions with higher standard teaching loads (i.e., 4/4 or 5/5) and concomitant lower research expectations, typically included responsibilities in first-year writing, introduction to literature or other related areas, and one advanced upper-division undergraduate course per semester. Prior to the US adoption of the German model in the 1950s, many universities today classified as Carnegie Research 1 institutions required faculty to teach higher course loads; this included Ivy League as well as elite public universities. Today, these lower-level Gen Ed courses have been widely reassigned to contingent labor and graduate student workers, with resulting inequities.

This burgeoning distinction postwar between specialized and general teaching was critical to proponents of the General Education movement. Arthur B. Mays, then professor of Industrial Arts at the University of Illinois, articulated how General Education served the postwar growing population in *JGE* volume 2, number 2 (1948), noting that American schooling practices had been designed to include "school subjects needed by all as the minimum knowledge one must have to attend to his [sic] ordinary affairs effectively" versus private schools designed to train "those destined for the professions" (156). As he further notes while cataloging these histories, it was especially difficult to "visualize a close relationship in the schools between vocational and cultural education" given the few students who attended high school (158). Such thinking stands in contrast to current concepts of education, as Mays saw school as a place to grow "physically, intellectually, morally, spiritually, aesthetically, and vocationally, and to achieve in all these areas as far as one desires and is able to achieve. It means not identical opportunities, but *equal* opportunities" (159–160).

Earl James McGrath, the inaugural editor of *JGE* at the helm of the journal from 1946 to 1948, was highly sympathetic to the view that the university should fight specialization and embrace teaching at all levels in order to responsibly serve this fast-growing population. As then dean of the University of Iowa College of Liberal Arts (1945–1948), McGrath began his editorial work at a time when the US faced skyrocketing birth rates toward a future explosion in K–12 enrollments. McGrath was a strong proponent of the generalist principle, more specifically the elevation of the teaching mission over the research mission that leads to specialized coursework that, in his view, benefits only select students and focuses too strongly on what he termed "cognitive learning." In a 1977 interview reviewing his life and work as the US commissioner of education (1949 to 1953) under Presidents Harry S Truman and Dwight D. Eisenhower,[20] McGrath comments that he objected to

> the notion come by from the German university that the educational process ought to concern itself only with cognitive learning, that it has no responsibility for the private lives of individuals ... we ought to say, "This is the nature of our society. These are the problems and the concerns with which citizens of that society might have to deal, now or in the future. These are the disciplines that bear on those problems or concerns, and therefore these ought to be the components of liberal education." (Kiester 28)

These democratizing principles for both teaching and learning undergird the early issues of *JGE*. They highlight philosophical debates about topics allied to the mission of General Education, such as the civic responsibilities of youth; teaching and technology; the place of written and oral communication in the curriculum; the socializing functions of core curricula; and specific treatises on core subjects in Gen Ed, such as mathematics and the social sciences—the latter a hot topic, given its home to fields such as political science and psychology, whose teachings were seen as key to postwar student development.

McGrath made no small plans in launching *JGE* with a slate of high-powered contributors whose voices would elevate the role of Gen Ed in improving students' intellectual and personal growth, and in creating an educated citizenry. These contributors included deans, presidents, and other leading figures in higher education, plus US military figures and even a US Supreme Court justice. Across eleven brief essays, issue 1 of *JGE* articulated a deep-seated, patriotic equivalency between education and democracy as the recipe for both an extended time of peace and a strong preparation for future conflicts. This first issue also set out to define what General Education is, and could be, in US colleges and universities—and with what associated impacts for curricular shifts in US secondary schools.

JGE made clear from its start that higher education in the US should take General Education seriously as a plan of study, and as a revolution in how to reify the purposes of secondary and postsecondary schooling. McGrath's impassioned introduction to the volume, and to the journal itself, argued that General Education

> prepares the individual for a full and satisfying life as member of a family, as a worker, as a citizen, and as an integrated and purposeful human being. It does not overlook differences in talent, interest, and purpose. Nor does it attempt to form everyone in a single mental and spiritual matrix. It seeks to make possible the maximum development of the individual consistent with the general good . . . general education rests on the principle that deviations in thought or in act must be based upon understanding rather than ignorance of the purposes, standards, and values of society. ("General Education" 3)

McGrath goes on to delineate the "salient feature" of the General Education movement as a "revolt against specialism" and also a "reaction against vocationalism" (4–5). He argued that "many new units of college instruction are composed of materials of interest to only a small percentage of advanced students" and that "even elementary courses" are focused on the individual pursuits of faculty scholars, such that most students have been "prevented from gaining the broad outlook on life and the intellectual tastes which should characterize those who have had the advantages of liberal education" (4–5). General Education would provide, in contrast, an effort to "integrate the subject matter of related disciplines" and in the process, make clear connections between a student's life and the subject matter through instruction around "life situations" as well as the elementary principles proceeding from "concrete to the abstract and the known to the unknown" (6). Citing the Redbook, McGrath notes that the four major objectives of General Education are all "described in functional terms directly related to the behavior of human beings—the ability to think, to communicate, to make valid judgments, and to evaluate moral situations," which today we would recognize as also the tenets of many humanities courses (7).

McGrath's overview is explicitly tied to General Education as a *movement*—against specialized learning, education for the elite student only, and the separation of a student's life from their studies. He closes his introduction by declaring that *JGE* will thus "serve as a medium for the expression of ideas related to this movement," which may include "conflicting educational philosophies" (8). Thus, *JGE* was designed not as an information-only site about this new curriculum—as neither a newsletter, nor a compendium for how-to essays on teaching. It was a venue for debate, discussion, and evaluation of experimental ideas related to General Education and its "philosophical and social implications" (8). As such, McGrath sets up General Education overall to be taken equally as seriously as analysis of any single topic in the university or any current socioeducational problem facing institutions in the postwar era.

Other contents of *JGE* issue 1 support McGrath's vision of the journal's purposes. Virgil Hancher's opening essay, noted above, focused on the "Components of General Education," setting forth the question that would vex academics for decades to come: "What is general education and what are its objectives" (9)? He asks, "Is there a minimum body of basic and fundamental knowledge which should be the possession of every college graduate? Or, to put the question in another fashion: Is there anything that the college graduate needs to know" (10)? Hancher thereafter outlines what has become the classical Gen Ed paradigm: understanding of the physical and biological worlds, the "development of western civilization," the great texts of literature, and "human relationships and moral values" (10). Hancher quickly comments that these subjects contrast with the Harvard report and its "more modest" recommendations of "three non-departmental courses, to be supplemented by one or more elective departmental courses of general character in each of the three divisions of the college—the humanities, the social sciences, and the natural sciences" (10).

This gentle criticism of the Harvard report is more strongly voiced in Walter T. Fisher's 1947 (vol. 1, no. 3) *JGE* essay on the "Lopsided Harvard Report," which illustrates the journal's appetite and capacity for debate regarding General Education. Fisher comments that the report shows "*what to teach* is the favorite, *how to teach it* is slighted" (195) and that methods of teaching are ignored overall, questioning "why did these professors of education allow themselves to be pushed to the sidelines, instead of insisting that at least one of the six chapters be on the general principles and philosophy of how to teach" (198)? Such a question has haunting resonance with today's Gen Ed curricula, as putting the "heart of the subject, the curriculum" (qtd. in Fisher 195) on display *as* Gen Ed, rather than the pedagogies and student-faculty interactions that bring it alive, is one means of sustaining the checklist coverage models dominant on college campuses.

For Hancher, having students simply *take* a course just to say they have been introduced to a given subject is not enough. Rather, the economic complexity of living in a democracy requires such baseline knowledge *across* multiple areas of the university and its teachings, backed by the belief that "a society whose tax structure precludes the survival of a public spirited leisure class ... must rely on a broad base of understanding among its citizenry if there is to be an intelligent direction of affairs in the body politic" (13). Hancher further saw beyond the undergraduate degree and into the future of the graduate school–bound student (who, in his paradigm, now could come from a broader group than before the advent of the movement). He regarded this student as deficient without baseline General Education teachings, and was against such a student simply acquiring further narrow specialized knowledge, resulting in the "richness and depth sometimes lacking in graduate work" (14).[21] As Hancher declares in valuing broad-based education equally to specialized learning at the upper undergraduate and graduate levels, "interpretation and synthesis are no less important than discovery" (14). He closes his essay by arguing that education cannot "afford to remain outside the great processes of our time and maintain an ethical neutrality" if it is to serve a rapidly evolving democratic society.

This "greater good" argument is picked up by W. H. Cowley, then professor of higher education at Stanford, in his *JGE* essay "Education for the Great Community." Cowley spends his first few pages addressing critics of General Education more broadly, including an unnamed colleague who termed publications such as *Education for All American Youth*, by the Educational Policies Commission, "a Walt Disney type of treatise on education," and someone who "did not like the Harvard Report, either," due to their perception that General Education would dilute the teachings of the university (22). But Cowley pushes back, stating that the movement's purposes are more far-reaching than intellectual disputes about curricular purity:

> when people assert that education must fend the disasters that face the world, they obviously do not mean education which will produce better bakers, businessmen, carpenters, mechanics, lawyers, and physicians *as such*. Rather, they mean better men and women *regardless of their occupations*. In brief, they mean *general* and not vocational education . . . the core of the problem resides in the education of youth as *people* rather than merely as workers . . . we are men and women first, and education must start and end with this often-neglected fact as its pole star. (23)

Cowley emphasizes how the whole-person approach to education is incompatible with our current arguments about course competencies or even the separation of levels of instruction across the university. Rather, Cowley is concerned with "Soul and Self," a concept borrowed from the field of philosophy. He states that this concept "distinguishes each individual from every other individual but which, at the same time, constitutes the unit of associations of individuals" (24). It is from this basis that Cowley further argues for both physical and social activity as part of Gen Ed, the former of which became the "PE" requirement in schools and some universities. Cowley notably asserts within his whole-self argument that Gen Ed students are unlike the faculty who teaches them. Without using the label "First-Generation," as such was not yet a term of art, Cowley describes such students as coming from "homes in which books and ideas have never been valued" and who cannot be "whittled down to fit the dehumanized ideals of the intellectuals who assert that the college is nothing more than a place of the mind" and a site for the "genteel tradition" (28, 31). Specifically, he charges that to help students

> climb from such drab circumstances to cultivated interests and preceptions requires patience and sympathy and devotion which only the rare professor is willing to expend—if, indeed, he himself possesses cultivated interests and sympathies. The great majority of professors have their scientific experiments to complete, their journal articles to produce, their textbooks to finish. They have no time for students. (28–29)

Such arguments, which continue to be leveled at faculty who value research over teaching today (and at the elite institutions who employ them), go to the heart of General Education's designs to liberate as well as educate—and to the importance of faculty involvement at the most fundamental levels of instruction.[22] Cowley later provides a succinct analysis of the problem with General Education as a self-guided movement by students, based on economics and efficiency, when he argues "most college students take courses which predominantly emphasize occupational efficiency and financial success and which give little if any attention to the student's need for depth of understanding of the world at large and even less attention to his moral responsibilities thereto" (30).

A similar argument is echoed in Paul F. Roach's 1948 *JGE* essay (vol. 2, no. 3), "The Social Function of General Education," where he posits that

> the student of an age which may later be termed either "postwar" or "between-war" ... is primarily interested in a broad perspective on the problems of our time. The questions of ageless truth and absolute standards of good and bad are of little interest simply because they appear to have little immediate bearing on the resolution of present, insistent contradictions. (248)

Following such a paradigm, it is highly unlikely that Cowley, Roach, or any of the authors in the early volumes of *JGE* would support the dual credit programs of today that allow students as young as fourteen years old to enroll in college-level courses. In fact, none of the *JGE* authors anticipate or advocate for such *college-level* work being done in the high schools. While Conant and the Harvard Committee make clear that scaffolded General Education should *begin* in the high schools, to avoid the early bifurcation of vocational versus elite instruction, all discussions in *JGE* of college curriculum are about work taking place *in college*, where it is expected that "education must associate students with the past, present, and the future . . . it must lift students out of a narrow and selfish what's-in-it-for-me conception of self-realization to a devotion to the Great Community" (32).

Another *JGE* author, W. W. Charters, professor of education and an architect of the Payne Fund Studies (1928–1932), was deeply invested in external social phenomena that could affect children's education. Charters thus puts assertions about student interests in a slightly differently way in his essay, "Patterns of Courses in General Education." Charters bluntly states that "General Education is concerned with what its students need rather than merely with what they happen to be interested in" (59), arguing for clarity in structure at the institutional level that accounts for developmental needs while also accounting for needs of particular learning groups (for which he spotlights Stephens College, his then employer, as an example). This sets up Charters's observations of how General Education was already operating in various institutions, using either models of "subject patterns" or "need patterns," the latter of which included individual, social, and a combination of the two (60, 62). Charters reminds readers that "The number of subjects is enormous and for mastery, years of study would be required, while the student is expected to complete this general education in sixty semester hours or less" (60), setting forth the common timeline of study for students to satisfy Gen Ed requirements in their first two years of college.

Such a mission for the secondary schools in relation to colleges and universities—and graduate and adult education—was further explicitly addressed in Gordon N. Mackenzie and Hubert Evans's 1946 *JGE* essay, "The Challenge of General Education for the Secondary Schools." They propose that "every secondary school must develop its own General Education program with its indigenous characteristics" (64), in order to follow their beliefs that

> General Education should be viewed as a continuous program of life experiences for all children, youth, and adults; life experiences that focus on common needs, common interests, common problems. . . . "Common" does not mean identical nor does it imply the same learnings, the same achievements for all. It suggests common desirable directions of development for the welfare of the individual and the citizen in a democracy. (67)

Mackenzie and Evans go on to argue that General Education "must be developed with reference to the social, economic, and political problems that pervade the lives of children and youth" (71) and be responsive to developmental needs of those children and youth along the way, throughout the stages of General Education being offered. Indeed, they highlight the problem of terminology in General Education that further complicates its standardized teachings across levels—asking "how can a stranger or even a worker in general education make sense out of the synonymous use of such terms as core curriculum, basic education, common learnings, general education—particularly when the meaning of each term varies with the person using it?" (66).

Such arguments for developmentally centered, divisible levels of General Education rooted in humanistic inquiry and development are also in evidence in James Bryant Conant's 1959 book *The American High School Today*, aka the "Conant Report," which was based on his survey of numerous high schools nationwide and advocates for twenty-one specific improvements to American high schools, among these a standard set of high school courses across subjects, including extensive preparation in English composition. Conant observed that "it is impossible to relate the details of a high school course of study to the subsequent work of a student in a college or university" because "uniform standards for admission to college are impossible in the United States" (60–61).

Conant ultimately contends that "the idea is completely illusory that the high school curriculum might be stiffened by agreement as to entrance requirements on the part of colleges and universities" (61). Further still, Conant calls out the Advanced Placement Program (in which he held a leadership role) as being only for the "3 percent of the student population" who might be labeled "highly gifted." Conant envisioned such students in AP courses in the twelfth grade *only*, making no nods to the present concept of "early college" or dual enrollment. In today's terms, Conant viewed General Education's principles and teachings as *scaffolded* rather than compressed within interchangeable educational venues and formats.

The impassioned arguments put forth by Conant and the Harvard Committee are further bookended in *JGE* issue 1 by two other Harvard faculty members, Byron Hollingshead and Robert J. Havighurst. Havighurst's *JGE* essay on the "Emotional Outcomes of General Education" takes a bold leap by opening with this declarative paragraph:

> The two basic processes of general education are knowing and loving. Knowing consists of a range of *intellectual* activities, such as observing,

remembering, forming concepts, generalizing, and reasoning. Loving consists of a range of *emotional* activities, such as desiring, appreciating, liking, admiring, enjoying, tolerating, and sympathizing. General education may be thought of as the development of these two broad categories of activities under supervision of persons assigned for the task by society. (39)

One might observe that both the "knowing" and "loving" attributes often work in consort in humanities instruction—for example, reasoning while also appreciating arguments and points of view, and generalizing while also sympathizing with historical events and their actors. Though today most if not all humanists would resist the categories of "intellectual" versus "emotional" as a learning paradigm, Havighurst defends this taxonomy by arguing against the primacy of reason over emotion at all costs. In his view, "there is no room in general education for the negative view of the emotions which considers reason and knowledge as their natural enemy" nor a curriculum that considers "the task of education the expansion of the empire of reason at the expense of the domain of emotion," for general education at the postsecondary level should more closely resemble the attention to the student as a person already on view at the secondary level, and thus, "the emotions should be allies, not enemies" (42).

For Havighurst, General Education in its best forms provides a curriculum intertwined with what we would today call "well-being" efforts, for example the (then) new student union at the University of Minnesota—also a public institutional pioneer in General Education—as a center of work-and-play philosophy in action (41). In Havighurst's paradigm, General Education and its associated programming is the vehicle for promoting the "process of binding an individual to his [sic] social group [which] goes on from birth" (43), a view that does not take into account social uplift as a possible byproduct of a college education, but rather promotes education across all so-called birth classes in America, including those higher education was doomed to forget prior to the GI Bill. Such echoes Byron S. Hollingshead's closing essay in *JGE* issue 1, which sums up the core goal of General Education: to develop what he calls "social solidarity" (76). This means a recognition that no one model of education truly fits all, and that General Education in itself will not answer the calls for "social mobility by specialism" that the American educational system aims to offer, given that meritocracies exist alongside hierarchies, and schooling is only one part of a vast socioeconomic fabric.

Such an utterance might be seen as an early argument *against* the concept of liberatory pedagogy that emerged some two to three decades later in principles of first-year writing instruction, though the overall principles of the Harvard Committee were clearly rooted in John Dewey's education-as-uplift principles as a whole. Indeed, Hollingshead contends that "from the teaching of these subjects, we want to get the cultivated citizen . . . what we are seeking may be classified under intellectual qualities, personal qualities, and qualities prized in a democratic society" (77). Such instruction "is not in the direction of 'getting in' general education during a particular period" (80). His concept of General Education resists today's compartmentalized, or "packaged" instructional models. Instead, he and the other contributors to *JGE* favor thoughtful and purposeful learning founded in intellectual and moral development, a task uniquely keyed to humanistic inquiry. Such arguments intersected with the rise of a new discipline that would also have its own journal, in the pages of which similar discussions of how to teach writing to a "general" population, and with what pedagogical intentions, would emerge.

CCC: The Echoes of General Education as Liberation

While *JGE* set out to reach a wide range of readers in academia, *CCC* (*College Composition and Communication*) set out to reach a more targeted group: college writing teachers in English and communication departments. Yet both journals had a clear investment in the emerging Gen Ed movement and how it would shape current and future disciplinary pedagogical discourse. The intersecting historical missions of, and contributors to, *CCC* and *JGE* are concisely documented in James Beasley's article, "*The Journal of General Education* and an Institutional Return to Rhetoric," which explains that the creation of *JGE* functioned as a forum for University of Chicago faculty to advocate for their conceptions of General Education as they had envisioned it on their own campus prior to the emergence of the Harvard model. *JGE* also served as a platform for encouraging a return to classical rhetoric in English studies, by scholars such as Richard Weaver (Beasley 126). This position on the primacy of rhetoric was later echoed in a 1952 *JGE* article on composition and logic by Henry W. Sams, also an editorial board member for the journal, who would in 1954 publish an article in *CCC* entitled "Fields of Research in Rhetoric" (Beasley 130). Beasley further contends that the 1952 *College English* article by Weaver and colleagues, "Looking for an Argument," was "more of a response to [a previous article in *JGE*] on logic and semantics in the composition course" than the first freestanding call for rhetoric as a component of the composition course, as James Berlin had previously argued (Beasley 134).

In addition to his study of these crossovers between *JGE* and the nascent field of composition studies, Beasley also characterizes the views of *JGE*'s early contributors as believing that "the gap between the topics a student already knew and the large-scale topics that a novice writer could possibly not know would constitute the province of general education" (128). Beasley further argues that *JGE* offered an important forum for discussing the broader intersections of academic writing (and rhetoric) and the changing shape of higher education and its students. He notes that prior to the appearance of *College Composition and Communication*, English studies, including the flagship journal of NCTE (National Council of Teachers of English), *College English*, was falling behind in addressing how writing instruction was rapidly changing to meet postwar societal demands. Beasley observes that unlike during the height of belles-lettres pedagogy, "General Education no longer meant adherence to a canon, and an argument that the teacher expected, but could focus on using research to solve real-world problems for which no one had the answers. The field of English was not quite ready for such 'workday' pursuits" (130).

Indeed, insofar as the early volumes of *JGE* under Earl McGrath would lean on the Harvard Committee's recommendations as a liberating middle ground for the vast number of students entering college, the early volumes of *CCC* under editor Charles Roberts would use its pages to debate what writing instruction should be in the context of General Education, especially as the discipline emerged from long-standing principles central to English studies as a whole. As writing (née composition) studies began to form, contributors to pieces published in *CCC* openly questioned the future of writing instruction, particularly in relation to new and existing mediums (television, radio) and the general belief that teaching students to engage in clear and persuasive discourse was critical to a democratic society.

The concern over social and intellectual integration of masses of returning veterans into college writing courses is reflected in the rise of postwar field conversations about topics such as "Zero English" (i.e., basic writing) as well as honors or gifted English, each designed to segment student writers across course types appropriate to both age and experience. Emergent were also "water cooler" exchanges in publications such as *Illinois English Bulletin*, NCTE's *English Journal* and *College English* (which in the 1940s featured essays on the place of the humanities in wartime and the role of teaching returning servicemen) and of course *CCC*, which launched in 1950 as the publication of the new Conference on College Composition and Communication.

As Lisa Lebduska notes in "Composing in the Wake of War," though there was "an initial desire on the part of faculty and veteran alike to downplay the effects of war and the differentness of the veteran population, once significant numbers of veterans began enrolling, the impact of their differentness had to be acknowledged" (70). This followed on more general fears by faculty that "the GI presence would further contribute to the demise of liberal education," in the service of more technical teachings tailored to older and often less-prepared students (70). The mixed consequences of this new student population in writing and other courses also revealed a student body more committed to connecting its education to the goals of democracy. As Lebduska explains,

> The shift to connect literature to individual experience paralleled the move to increase student discussion and participation-classroom engagement that went beyond the chalk and talk lecture. Additionally, this move to recognize individual connections to literature helped foster the democratic classroom. The GI student classroom participants were yet another instance of what Mettler describes as "citizen soldiers"—a civic-minded generation of veterans committed to participatory democracy. (75)

Amidst this postwar conversation about equity and democracy, a new field was born, memorialized in *CCC*, whose beginnings were admittedly smaller than *JGE*. As Charles Roberts comments in his first editorial in March 1950, "The bulletin is starting modestly and with limited means. We can promise quarterly publication of a sixteen page issue. Eventually our membership may grow sufficiently large to support the more frequent publication of a thicker bulletin" ("Editorial Comment," vol. 1, no. 1, 13). John C. Gerber, then chairman of the Conference on College Composition and Communication (CCCC) reinforces Roberts's aims and message in his statement, also published in *CCC* in March 1950. Gerber explains that

> Someone has estimated that there are at least nine thousand of us teaching in college courses in composition and communication. Faced with many of the same problems, concerned certainly with the same general objectives, we have for the most part gone our separate ways.... Occasionally we have heard that a new kind of course is working well.... But we rarely get the facts. We have had no systematic way of exchanging views and information quickly. Certainly we have had no means of developing a coordinated research program. To meet such obvious needs, the Conference on College Composition and Communication has been formed.... We believe that the activities of this new organization are aimed at practical needs in the profession, that the standards of the profession will be raised because of them. ("Conference" 12)

Gerber's declaration of intent signals the beginning of the discipline, with research aims, and the beginning of informed exchange about teaching writing in a scholarly space—parallel in mission to *JGE*, but with smaller goals. It also marks an effort at nationwide communication about issues critical to the teaching of writing, which we may see as parallel to *JGE*'s intentions regarding General Education. Of course, Gerber's prediction regarding the growth and membership of the organization would play out over the course of its now eighty-plus years of existence, with *CCC* growing to become a highly selective, flagship journal and CCCC growing to become the parent organization for thousands of writing studies scholars. Roberts commented on the incremental progress toward this future after just one year of the journal's publication, in December 1950, "We approach our second year of publication with higher hopes and fewer misgivings . . . buoyed up by a growing subscription list, a greater influx of contributors, and, more mounting evidence that some people are actually reading our publication" ("Editorial Comment," vol. 1, no. 4, 16).[23]

While *CCC* symbolized the formal beginning of a discipline, its structural beginnings—in comparison with the scope and contents of *JGE*—were as a newsletter-style publication of about thirty-two pages designed for sharing and exchanging views on teaching writing, primarily to first-year students, including those labeled "remedial" or "developmental," as well as articles on teaching communication—including its important interactions with television, radio, and other media.[24] As such, its initial, brief articles were in two genres: those that transmitted local pedagogical results of a particular approach in the writing classroom or the writing program, and those that expressed global views on the state of teaching writing. None of these would be considered "research" articles by today's standards, but neither are they devoid of larger observations about where and how writing fit into the college curriculum, including General Education curricula.

In particular, the second issue of *CCC* (May 1950) focused entirely on the "Workshop Reports" of the first CCCC meeting, which took place March 24–25, 1950. These thirteen reports of one to two pages each dove into a variety of current issues in composition and communication instruction, including the use of a writing laboratory and a reading clinic, the grading of "themes," and administration of both types of courses at the department level. As Roberts notes in his foreword to the reports, "The reader will note . . . that some ideas run like a refrain through reports from groups working ostensibly on quite different topics. It is in these that we may detect a philosophy of freshman English emerging" (3). The first two workshops summarized were "The Function of the Composition Course in General Education" and "The Function of the Communication Course in General Education." In each of these, there are strong echoes of the Harvard Committee's principles regarding General Education, as well the formation of an approach to teaching writing and communication that is directly responsive to those principles.

For example, the workshop members outlined at the start of their brief report the following objectives of General Education that "should govern the organization of the composition course":

1. To cultivate the ability to think logically.
2. To cultivate respect for human worth despite accidents of class, color, culture, or other decisive circumstances.
3. To develop taste.
4. To develop the ability to discipline emotions and to arrive at reasonable judgments.
5. To develop intellectual competence.
6. To cultivate a belief in the necessity for ethical behavior. (5)

What is striking about these six objectives is that only the first is explicitly connected to the teaching of writing on an instrumental basis, whereas the other five are in-process outcomes of students becoming effective and thoughtful *writers*. Such are far from the technical operations measured today in credit by examination. In framing the composition course as emblematic of these values, workshop participants agreed upon several methods for achieving the above objectives of General Education. Among these was "reading works drawn from world literature to inform the student of differences among men [and] requiring the student to study his own ideas and behavior in comparison with that of others" (3). Also among the goals were reading materials "that enable the student to achieve a better understanding of human nature; requiring of compositions on controversial topics the qualities of clarity and fairness" (3).

Such valuations are taken up in the "Report of Workshop No. 3" on "Objectives and Organization of the Composition Course," which made two important assertions about the scope and import of the teaching of writing in postwar classrooms, namely:

> the course will *not by itself* bear responsibility within its institution for producing Graduates who can meet the normal non-professional requirements of writing without Embarrassment to the institution granting them degrees.

> Nor will it *by itself* assume Responsibility for developing in its students an acceptance of humanistic values. (9)

Critical in these declarations are three prevailing assumptions. First, that writing instruction *begins* in the first-year composition course but does not end there; it is to be integrated across a student's whole education, and other departments and disciplines should be equally responsible for such development. Second, that students should meet "normal, non-professional" requirements of writing, which echoes the fundamental principles of General Education against specialization and hyperfocused professional aims, in all subjects. And third, that the writing course is important to students developing "an acceptance of humanistic values," but not the only place such work must be done.

Further examples of the organization's intersecting conversations on General Education may be found in other early issues of *CCC*. For example, Kenneth Oliver's article, "The One-Legged, Wingless Bird of Freshman English," directly comments on the March 1950 workshops and their focus on the "immediate social purposes" of language study in the writing classroom, which emphasizes interpretation of newspaper and radio messages and their potential danger as propaganda and, to his mind, de-emphasizes the study of composing itself and of personal expression. He argues:

> To assume that there is no general need for the teaching of expression of personal experiences and convictions to college students in the only course required of them where such teaching might reasonably be done, is to deny the importance of man as an individual capable of his own response to his total environment.... Expression: vigorous, effective, sincere personal expression may lead to that maturity of thought which can prevent persuasion from developing Hitlers and Politburos at too tragic a rate among us. (5)

A similar tension between the critical study of media and the teaching of personal expression is evident in another article in this same issue, "After Communications, You Can't Go Home Again," by Rhodes R. Stabley, who outlines a sequence of lessons in the first-year communication course (on a trimester schedule). This includes four units: "The World of the Senses and of Nature; Personal Relations, Arts, Science; three units for the second semester—the Good Life, Religion, Role of Education, Ideas of Liberty and Democracy; three units for the third semester—Challenge of Democracy, War and Peace, World of Tomorrow" (8). These are each designed to develop in students "a greater understanding of the interrelationship of the communicative arts, and greater appreciation of their role in a democratic society" (8).

Such lessons are made even more explicit in the article that follows Stabley's, "The Need for the 'Permissive' in Basic Communications." Here, Arnold E. Needham grounds his argument in questions of structure and purpose in the freshman course: "Where are the student's needs in all this? Where is his readiness for these studies? Come to think of it, where is the student? For where he is, there, surely, should we be also" (13). He thus advocates for a course guided at least in part by "student-selected, student-planned, individually planned, activities in communications, as distinct from committee-planned and committee-imposed assignments" (13). He further makes what now seems a prescient observation about how students would come to perceive the value and purposes of college, and toward the issues of student choice discussed in the start of this chapter:

> As long as students enter college and universities solely in response to social and economic pressures, with no desire for general education or self-development, there will be many who will take advantage of anything to get by with as little effort as possible. . . . It wouldn't matter what methods you used. (16)

Each of the above articles zeroes in on the modern purposes of so-called freshman English, namely, something closer to a whole-person educational pedagogy than a skills-based, test-driven course. This is not to say that such whole-person teachings were not present prior to World War II; certainly we can find progressive writing curricula at many colleges and universities before the 1940s, especially in women's colleges. But it is in these first issues of *CCC* that we see such lessons openly put into dialogue with the larger principles of General Education, and framed as critical to democracy (even as some authors, such as Stabley, felt the push for civic lessons outweighed the importance of creative expression). It is here we also see the *centrality* of the first-year writing course as it bears much of the weight of the General Education curricula as a whole. Such is a point that writing studies as a field needs to return to, to do its part in reviving Gen Ed as a movement.

In the 1951–1952 issues of *CCC*, we begin to see these questions of purpose and structure positioned in terms of specific institutional types—namely across three articles that tackle the problem of freshman English in the professional school (which we might today better term the technical college or institute), in the liberal arts college, and in the university.[25] C. Harold Gray's focus on the professional school includes a warning about the errors of history in educational design, with strong critical undertones regarding General

Education's purpose to create "citizens" writ large—in his case, in an engineering college (Rensselaer Polytechnic Institute)–as well as the value of "segregating" technical students into composition classes away from those studying other fields. Gray argues that "when we began to shape curricula for all kinds of students, we fell into the error of failing to take into account the backgrounds and professional interests on which had been based a more effective curriculum in earlier days. We began to think we were dealing with that abstraction, the 'human being' or that other abstraction, 'the citizen'" (5–6). Such arguments for separate writing classes for engineering or technical students prefigure these on campuses today—which Gray contends allow faculty to focus on the specific interests of these students, with arguably different learning needs, as doing so will "perpetuate and mature them" (5).[26]

Such calls to divide and conquer the core writing course within General Education also have reverberated across institutions since the founding of CCCC; whether or not that separation is valid is for each local campus ultimately to decide. But what Gray's commentary surfaces—again, presciently—is the current state of first-year writing as uniformly transferable, generic, and not specific to any particular population. If Gray were alive today, it seems doubtful that his valuation of specialized writing curricula for engineers and other science-minded students would fit with the vision of the College Board's AP English exams for universal first-year writing credit, or similar generically offered dual credit options in high schools.

These early workshops and articles that followed in *CCC*, appearing on the heels of *JGE*'s first issues and during the early stages of the Gen Ed movement, serve as a keen reminder that not only is writing instruction *indivisible* from other parts of a student's intellectual and civic education, it also cannot be an isolated "skills" course divorced from other subjects, or separate from whole-person learning in General Education across and *beyond* the curriculum.

Curricular Efficiency in a Divided World

As James Bryant Conant interrogated in *Education in a Divided World* (1948), nowhere are Americans more hopeful that our class divisions might be eradicated than through higher education. As Conant also observed, however, the US is a hierarchy built upon a prevailing "caste system," which drives citizens to be upwardly mobile, often without sufficient opportunity. Conant argued that "What we are concerned with . . . is the way in which the educational system of a nation reflects the degree of 'class consciousness' of the country" (61), which includes how to provide opportunities for students who suffer from prejudice as "a handicap [sic] to education and employment" (68). If we take his words, including his declaration of prejudice (construed as racial but also class-based), and review them for accuracy based on present conditions, I submit that they do not need amendments. As we consider enrollment trends across different institutional types as relevant to numerous factors that further marginalize students and create lost educational opportunities, higher education still struggles with workable mechanisms for equity, both inside and outside curricular structures. And as illustrated with my opening discussion of historical course enrollments at Penn, even on high-achieving, diverse college campuses, liberal education is trending away from the center of student choice.

The foundations of learning that would make such transformation more *likely* to happen reside in the General Education programming that we push aside—to the high schools, to the testing companies, to methods of double- and triple-counted graduation requirements—in order to make this critical component of college faster, cheaper, and (we think) *smarter* in its design. Yet as I have argued here, we have not evolved enough as a nation since 1945 such that we no longer need to worry about the democratizing principles of Gen Ed, and its roots in humanistic inquiry that helps students to become ethical and reasoned beings. Even as we take into account factors not all foreseen by the Harvard Committee—for example, the lower levels of state funding at many majority-minority institutions; the historical problems of segregated K–12 schools; and the admissions challenges faced by women and underserved populations at elite institutions all the way through the mid-1970s—we can still look to the democratizing principles of the General Education movement and gain perspective on the *why*, if not the instrumental *how*, of its implementation and dissemination.

To argue persuasively for a return to postwar views of Gen Ed, however, we must rethink not only curricular but also labor models. Earl McGrath had great hopes for General Education in his last *JGE* editorial in July 1948. He observed a shift from survey courses requiring broad swaths of memorization to more narrowly defined courses exploring philosophical questions in depth. But he remained concerned that the after-effects of General Education were not being felt strongly enough, particularly in graduate education and in teacher training. He was further concerned that teaching General Education *well* meant a singular focus and purpose that heavy teaching loads did little to enable. We see similar issues today, especially for contingent faculty assigned to Gen Ed courses who lack institutional supports, and graduate students who may be intellectually suited to the job but who still lack McGrath's proposed wider educational background in the philosophical principles of General Education.

McGrath added that to do the kind of intellectual training that General Education was designed to offer, the assessment of such work would be difficult to design. In his words,

> it is relatively easy to evaluate the learning and the retention of factual material. To appraise the student's ability to think critically or to exercise the skills... is, however, a much more difficult task. Until such tests are available it will not be possible to determine the extent to which the objectives of general education are actually being achieved. ("General Education," 276)

Though in 1948, assessment in higher education was still decades away from becoming a field of study, McGrath's concerns were prescient.[27] To assess and thereby value what students learn in humanistic-driven work requires time and space, and reflective mechanisms that are not found in all curricular paradigms today—or are divorced from the Gen Ed curriculum as a whole. What we need to address today is how to better incorporate such holistic assessment into our Gen Ed courses in order to prioritize humanistic inquiry *and* make its value known beyond mantras such as "employers value communication skills" or "critical thinking is important in all fields."

In other words, we must go beyond having the humanities serve as a handmaiden to professional fields and postgraduate workforce demands, and pay keen attention to how the democratizing rhetoric of the past might influence the Gen Ed choices that students make in the future. We must resist the primacy of specialization in favor of the general—not an empty signifier, but that which serves the greater good. And in doing so, we must recall the above histories of General Education that gave us the very arguments we need.

In the next chapter, I will continue this historical examination of Gen Ed rhetorics by going local, into the example of the (public) University System of Georgia and its uptake of General Education since the 1950s. In doing so, I argue that *what* and *why* Gen Ed is always will be in conversation with who our students are, and the rhetorical choices of policymakers that reveal how we do or do not value these students equally across diverse populations.

2
"The Interests of the State"

Curricular Sameness and Public University Systems

> The question is simply this: Should not the sorting process which education is always making be applied more vigorously before the student comes to college instead of being delayed until after he comes? It would not diminish the number of students; it might check the rate of increase.
> —University System of Georgia Chancellor Steadman V. Sanford, September 1935

Many of us think about college only in terms of what happens on our local campuses. As discussed in chapter 1, students often lack the wider worldview of Gen Ed as a curriculum. Similarly, students, parents, and faculty alike often concern themselves with only their own university's initiatives and priorities over time. But to identify and reclaim the rhetorics of General Education, as this book aims to do, requires us to also learn the stories of national ecosystems of higher education. As such, this chapter narrates the histories of Gen Ed past and present in three US states with both large and diverse student populations and complicated political histories, just as the next chapter analyzes pre-college testing and its detrimental impacts on the enterprise of General Education curricula in all fifty states.

Understanding how Gen Ed works at the state level is an important part of deciphering and repurposing the rhetorics of Gen Ed, since many public universities require that an appropriately high percentage of their student body—usually 60 to 75 percent—are state residents. This is a requirement for receiving appropriations toward important items such as student financial aid, and operating expenditures. In 2020, about 75 percent of all college students nationwide attended an institution in their home state—down from a twenty-year peak of about 83 percent in 2008.[1] That means it is (far) more likely than not that a high school senior you know will next year attend a two- or four-year college near their home. As a result, state university systems are primarily (and logically) focused on how they can advance the educational goals of their own state residents, which are secondary to the economy of the state as a whole. General Education, as part of that overall education, is an important element of how well these residents are prepared to execute on the state's overall goals, as citizens of a national democracy and global economy.

Despite these goals at the state level, it's also true that educational ecosystems can prevent these same colleges and universities from addressing their students' own local needs. At public universities, decisions about budgets, space, personnel, and also curricula are ultimately beholden to overarching rules and regulations set forth by boards of regents, trustees, or governors—for example, the ratio of in-state to out-of-state students noted above. Often these board members have no experience working in higher education. Such rules thus may not always be in harmony or dialogue with the guidelines of campus stakeholders, nor do they always follow best practices in academic fields of study. They do, however, still heavily inform the rhetorics of General Education, as I illustrate below.

Given the low value placed on General Education as well as higher education in our public discourse, it is unsurprising that states such as Georgia have created additional measures to standardize their operations toward more generic, interchangeable purposes across diverse institutions. Such decisions can have consequences, however, that highlight inequities across institutional type and populations served.[2] Even so, system budgets and organizational structures are designed, first and foremost, to look *collectively inward* and attempt to keep students from leaving the state for college, or to embark on future careers—akin to the international concept of "brain drain." In the State of Georgia, such efficiency principles also made future educational consolidation plans far more logical—and possible—including the advent of the Core curriculum, and thirty years later, Common Course Numbering (CCN).[3]

Below, I examine one of the particular ecosystems affecting General Education in the University System of Georgia (USG), which I use as a case study about the comparative rhetorics of Gen Ed. I argue that the centralized control of the system itself over the past ninety years, leading eventually to the establishment of a common "core" curriculum and later, CCN, led to a General Education curriculum governed by promises of efficiency for students, improvement of state budgets, and educational sameness. To situate CCN and its rhetorical emphases in Georgia, this chapter also examines CCN in two other US states, Texas and Florida, that, like Georgia, are anchored by a massive university system or systems with multiple campuses or branches.

The story of the USG Core curriculum and CCN can be found in a few archival locations: the State of Georgia Archives, the archives of the University of Georgia and Georgia Tech, and archived public news databases. The past and present messaging of the system, including institutional reports, also promotes efficiency rhetorics regarding college completion for Georgia's citizens, despite concerns from educators and other policymakers on the ground. These state-level decisions and resulting actions illustrate the competing rhetorics of student success, state collective identities, and financial and operational efficiencies, and their battle-scarred consequences for marginalized students, including students of color. At the same time, CCN provided little allowance for the original spirit of scaffolded diversity, curiosity, and individuality set forth by the Redbook. Racial prejudice and segregation, even after *Brown v. Board of Education*, played a central role in the Georgia system decisions about consolidation of educational identities, including in relation to the majority-minority and HBCU (historically Black colleges and universities) campuses across the state.

Though you, the reader, may not live in Georgia, or in the other two states profiled in this chapter, the lessons I'll provide about local curricular choices and control, the role of politics in higher education, and the effects on equality in education for students across populations, are not specific to these states by any means. Further, terms like *common course numbering*, *seamless transfer*, and *articulation agreements* are rarely heard or understood in public conversations about General Education. This chapter brings the knowledge and implications of those concepts into the light. In these precarious times, every citizen of every state needs to understand how public higher education works, and how General Education curricula, within higher education structures *and* strictures, struggles to be equal for all, when hampered by measures that would seem to promote equality but in fact contradict Gen Ed's original principles and its intrinsic aims.

In reading the intersecting stories of Gen Ed in Georgia, Florida, and Texas, you will see that the factors controlling and shaping it were neither born overnight nor into a vacuum. They were and are part and parcel of massive, bureaucratic structures within which Gen Ed must exist as a massive educational initiative. Just as students make choices that we as parents, faculty, and administrators cannot always control, as discussed in chapter 1, so too are rules made by state boards and politicians that local institutions can neither alter nor control. What we *can* do is recognize their aggregate affects and, in doing so, guard against the historical mistakes that they have caused, as we build a better rhetorical future for Gen Ed in each of our own home states and collectively nationwide.

Let's begin these stories with facts about public higher education in Georgia—its size and scope and brief developmental history over time—and then move on to what CCN is and how it works in practice.

The USG and Origins of Efficiency Logics, 1929–1935

The University of Georgia System—or the USG, as all employees and citizens of Georgia call it—is one of the largest systems of public higher education in the United States and includes my current employer, the Georgia Institute of Technology. It encompasses twenty-six colleges and universities, which in spring 2024 enrolled a total of 326,385 students. This figure includes, on one end of the educational spectrum, 72,306 graduate, professional, and medical resident students and, on the other, 2,653 high school students participating in dual enrollment programs.

A further 3,373 enrollees were so-called transient students—which the USG defines as someone "who takes courses temporarily in another college or university (their host institution) with the intention of transferring the course credit back to their home institution" and who may live in-state or out-of-state (https://www.usg.edu/student_affairs/prospective_students/transient). Such is a common strategy undertaken by students home for the summer from an out-of-state college who want to take a Gen Ed course nearby and for less money. As noted above, the majority of students at large public universities already live in-state, but they may not live close to the specific institution where they are enrolled during the academic year. Such is a phenomenon important to recall later when we are discussing state system measures designed explicitly for transfer convenience between USG institutions. The aggregated enrollment statistics for the USG found online do not reflect the number of students who have transferred from one USG school to another during this, or any, semester.

Of these total students enrolled across all categories in the USG in 2024, and across levels of instruction, 43.6 percent were white, 24.9 percent were Black or African American, 13.6 percent were Asian, 11.5 percent were Hispanic, 4.0 percent were two or more races, 0.1 percent were American Indian or Alaskan Native, and 0.1 percent were Native Hawai'ian or Pacific Islander. Of the total students enrolled, 56.1 percent were women.[4] These demographics are roughly reflective of the overall racial diversity of the state of Georgia, which as recorded in the 2020 census was 51.9 percent white, 12.4 percent Black or African American, 6.0 percent Asian, 18.7 percent Hispanic, 10.2 percent two or more races, 1.1 percent American Indian or Alaskan Native, and 0.2 percent Native Hawai'ian or Pacific Islander, as well as 8.4 percent reporting as "some other race alone." These figures show nearly twice as much enrollment of Black or African American and Asian students in the USG system versus population figures for these groups in the state. But we also need to account for the fact that while a significant 78 percent (44,019) of total USG students are residents of Georgia, aligning with the national average observed at the start of this chapter, another 13.4 percent (22,911) of students are residents of other US states, and a further 7.6 percent (24,911) reside outside the United States. Of these total international students, a large amount—14,795, or 59 percent—were concentrated at Georgia Tech.[5]

The USG, by any measure of accounting, is therefore a large and diverse machine of higher education operating within an equally diverse southern state, one that includes a major metropolitan area (Atlanta) that is home to more than fifteen public and private colleges and universities, including several HBCUs, and also a large college town (Athens), home to the flagship UGA (University of Georgia). Such have been the geographic and demographic conditions of the USG since its official formation under the auspices of the State of Georgia Board of Regents on January 1, 1932, who declared in its charter document, aka the "Reorganization Act"—that

> The twenty-six institutions comprising the University System should no longer function as separate, independent, and unrelated entities competing with each other for patronage and financial support. The manifest purpose of the Act creating the Board of Regents is to unify and coordinate the work of these institutions so that the educational program of each shall be integrated with that of every other institution and with the system as a whole. The result aimed at is a correlated, harmonious, and symmetrical structure free from wasteful duplications, but promoting the maximum of educational opportunity to the students and the State. In short, the emphasis has been

shifted from the interests of particular institutions to the interests of the State.[6]

The emphasis on "the interests of the state" and the goal of decrying "wasteful duplications" were precursors for many other large-scale efficiency operations yet to come to higher education. There is no default nationwide requirement that all state (public) institutions be governed under one umbrella; such is instead an efficiency method that installs a board to oversee the collective of campuses, and an agency to whom those campuses' presidents ultimately report. The efficiency principle reigns supreme in board decisions. For example, it is standard for public university systems to approve or deny new degree programs based on clauses that prohibit the duplication of those that may closely resemble, mirror, or match others at fellow in-state universities. In the Texas state system, this is known as the "50 mile" rule. The assumption behind these clauses is that students will be willing to travel to enroll in the program they seek to attend, wherever it is available within the state.[7]

The further presumption of duplication clauses is that students do not need to have multiple choices for a particular kind of program, and that secondarily, state system institutions should not internally compete to provide the "best" program of a kind. It is, instead, in the interests of the state to conserve resources toward other new programs that also serve the state as a whole.[8] Of course, such presumptions raise many questions about local student needs and mobility, and may drive some students to *leave* the state in order to enroll in a program that better suits their personal or professional needs. Such processes also typically benefit research universities, which have the most resources to mount a program, and to do so first, before others can also create similar degrees. This is but one way that it is commonplace for a system budget to reflect a centralized set of state priorities rather than the diverse needs of individual campuses, with better-resourced institutions coming out on top.

Despite critical differences in mission and population across its many institutional locations, the USG's system-wide Gen Ed program, or the "Core," was established in January 1967 and was constructed to be used at all Georgia state colleges and universities to, perhaps paradoxically, offer a sameness across Gen Ed curricula in ways not allowed by degree program duplication guards, above. As described in March 1986 by then Chancellor H. Dean Propst, the Core was developed "as a joint effort between the Committee on Transfer of Credit and the several academic committees [and] approved by the Advisory

Council on January 17, 1967," with all system institutions putting their curricula in place by fall 1969. A subsequent revision to the Core was implemented in 1980 (Propst 1).

The Core's design required up to 60 (quarter system) credits of six General Education course areas and 30 (quarter system) credits of lower division major-specific requirements, with each campus designating its own courses that would fulfill area requirements. The original version of the plan divided these into three areas that generally matched those outlined in the Redbook: humanities, mathematics and the natural sciences, and social sciences. The revised areas numbered five: Written Communications and Mathematics (Area A); Institutional Foundations (Area B); Humanities, Fine Arts, and World Languages (Area C); Natural and Computational Sciences (Area D); and Social Sciences (Area E). In 2012, select courses from the thirteen subject rubrics within the Core, including English, also became transferable to and from the Technical College System of Georgia, or TCSG.[9] As I discuss at the end of this chapter, in 2024, the Core was transformed yet again, in rhetorical import and in relation to so-called national and local workforce development.

In constructing its statewide General Education requirements in this unified manner, the USG's Core differed from other statewide curricula elsewhere, in its uniformity of design and in its attachment of Gen Ed coursework to major fields of study within one combined credit paradigm to be followed by all USG institutions. This structure is reflected in Chancellor Propst's further description of the Core's "three primary purposes":

> First, it establishes the principle that general education is the foundation of all baccalaureate degree programs. Second, the Core encourages each institution to develop a superior program of general education, reflecting its mission. The guidelines of the Core require demonstrated achievement in some specific areas, but also allow for the inclusion of other areas of achievement deemed desirable by each institution. Third, the Core guarantees students and their parents that full credit for courses satisfactorily completed at one institution will be accepted by all other System institutions. This guarantee affirms the integrity of credits offered throughout the University System. (Propst)

Even though the Core promised these three interrelated outcomes, the second promise, of mission-specific areas within a "superior program," was later complicated by CCN, which promised that any particular course within the Core would be the "same" at all institutions, for transfer purposes. CCN was itself a measure of further efficiency toward student mobility and a test of "integrity" of the system itself when it began in 1997, thirty years after the Core was established, when it became instrumental to the Core's curricular organizational principles.[10] As I describe below, the Core was followed as outlined above on all campuses *except* the University of Georgia (UGA)—a point to remember in historical discussions of segregation, which often centered on the unfettered status of UGA as the system's (all-white) flagship institution.[11]

The 1932 action establishing the Board of Regents made clear that the public colleges and universities of Georgia, including the flagship UGA in Athens, would hereafter function as a centrally controlled system—in educational operations, in financial decision-making, and in collective public identity. Other large public collectives made similar consolidating moves post–World War II, for example the State University of New York (1948), the California State Colleges (1961), the University of North Carolina System (1972), the University of Wisconsin System (1974), and the Pennsylvania State System of Higher Education, also known as PASSHE (1983).[12] Yet the USG was a pioneer in this efficiency- and publicity-minded effort to bring together its various educational institutions under one controlled roof.[13] Rather than have its colleges and universities serve as local institutions operating under purely local and situational conditions, respondent to local student and community needs, following the 1932 decree, the institutions within the USG would now operate as *one*, with a further amendment in 1943, following a battle between the USG and the governor of Georgia in 1941, detailed later in this chapter, that ended with the USG having "constitutional status."[14]

Equally important to the 1932 consolidation is the decree that individual college and university budgets would now be uniformly controlled at the level of state government, in the form of a lump sum held by the USG, and allocated to the institutions annually in relation to overall state priorities. This practice continues today in Georgia and elsewhere, with institutional budgets allocated in proportion to their mission, enrollment growth, and completion of other metrics that advance the system as a whole—often as articulated in strategic plans. Such arrangements almost always advantage larger, research-driven institutions with demonstrated growth potential and the means for income through external grants and contracts, and large endowments. These arrangements negatively impact smaller colleges, or those whose missions or student bodies do not make significant growth feasible, or even necessarily desirable.[15]

Additional archival documents leading up to the 1932 consolidation further articulate its systematic aims. In the 1929 report of the Georgia Legislature, article 8, the USG is defined by twenty-two "branches," including five (white)

Agricultural and Mechanical Schools, three (African American) schools, one state college of Agricultural and Mechanical Arts, and one Agricultural College; Georgia State College for Women (two campuses); the State Normal School; Georgia Normal College; the Medical College of UGA; two normal schools for African American teachers; Middle Georgia College; South Georgia Junior College; Georgia Institute of Technology; Georgia Experiment Station at Griffin; and Georgia Coastal Plains Experiment Station ("Georgia Legislature 1929 Session Report"). These various campuses were representative of southern higher education at the time, with segregated campuses for African American men and women, and also separate campuses for white women,[16] plus state normal schools for teachers, and a heavy emphasis on agricultural education, all of which were reflective of the Georgia state economy and social educational standards pre-*Brown v. Board of Education*. But they also represent an aggregation of very different institutions, serving very different populations, that prior to the 1932 declaration all carried the University of Georgia (hereafter UGA) "brand."[17]

In this same document, under section 88, the "several boards of trustees or directors for each of the schools, colleges, institutions and stations named [above], and designated as branches of the University of Georgia, are abolished." Further, in article 9, section 97, "there is hereby created a Department of Education" who would work under a superintendent of education elected by the people of Georgia. Such was part of a larger proposal that year to bring all aspects of the state operations under better organizational and financial control "in order to secure better service and through co-ordination and consolidation to promote economy and efficiency in the work of the government."

A 1939 brief written by the Georgia House Committee on Economy and Efficiency summarized these past actions following an appearance before the committee by the Board of Regents chairman, secretary, and chancellor, who reported that "Sections XIII and XIV of the charter of the University of Georgia enacted by the General Assembly of 1785 clearly provided for a coordinated system of state education, extending from the primary grades through the high schools, up to and including its crown, the university, all under the supervision of the latter" ("University System of Georgia"). As I discuss later in this chapter, today we would call this "K–16" education. In fact, some literature on dual enrollment / dual credit programs, as well as postwar studies of General Education, explicitly invokes grades 13 and 14 to represent the two years that typically constitute high school-to-college credit overlap, as well as two-year college enrollments and the students enrolled at such colleges who do not seek a four-year degree.[18] These are important rhetorical formations that undercut autonomous teaching and learning at each developmental stage of a student's education, and also seek to unify these disparate sites by a common mission and purpose.

The 1939 brief goes on to further argue that rather than centralizing all higher education in Athens, GA, these schools were located in strategic geographic centers across the state but still would be "in fact and in law parts of the university." However, the growth of the USG thereafter created problems:

> It was pointed out that the multiplication of the branches of the University continued so fast that it was not halted until there was fastened upon the state an educational monstrosity of twenty-six branches, bearing the misnomer, the University of Georgia. It was a group of unrelated institutions. Reorganization was badly needed. It came. So intelligently were plans drawn and a program outlined that at present the University system is attracting national attention, if not assuming national leadership. It can be frankly stated that no reform has been conceived or carried forward with the vision and thoroughness of the University system since the passage of the Reorganization Act of January 1, 1932. ("University System of Georgia")

The notion of a "misnomer" is critical here in separating out individual institutional identities, including those of the HBCUs, none of which were to be considered UGA-related in name or mission. As illustrated in this House statement, the need for efficiency of purpose and clarity of naming were key drivers in the consolidation plan, whose intention was to achieve "national attention, if not national leadership." There is also a clear vision in this reorganization separating out the UGA as divisible from other USG institutions, a move that a decade later became a keen symbolic site of widespread national attention, whereby Georgia politicians sought to extinguish any hint of desegregation efforts within the USG.

One might argue that a basic logic exists in this explanation: What qualifies as a "branch" campus of a state university anyway, even some ninety-nine years hence? Such campuses may vary widely in size and scope, as well as student population. At the same time, in designating a campus to be a "branch," there is also a business plan related to the rhetorical strategy of *branding*. In today's economy, there often exists a positive (competitive) association for selling students on the institution, as less selective branches may still be considered part of the more selective flagship campus—and so students who are disappointed to be denied admission to the flagship campus may still have "University of X" on their transcripts (and diplomas).

Continuing my own metaphorical constructions from chapters past, we might think of branch campus affiliations as akin to the high-fashion labels that have branched out to department and discount stores, with lower-cost but same-named products. Consumers can purchase these items for far less than those seen on the runway, while still feeling the status (and perceived quality) of brand recognition. Along these same branding lines, some universities will also offer admission to a branch campus if a student is denied admission to the flagship, as what some may see as a consolation prize (parallel, perhaps, to brand affordability and selectivity in a cross-customer fashion brand's base) that still allows enrollment within the state system, with potential transfer to the flagship at a later date. Such agreements systematize the process of upward transfer that students might otherwise undertake individually on their own, and of course are facilitated by streamlined Gen Ed requirements and agreements as well.

The University System of Georgia's current process, called "Transfer Pathways," is described on the UGA website as "an invitation only program offered to a small cohort of students" with clear undertones of high selectivity that correspond to the university's flagship status in the state system.[19] At Georgia Tech, an equally elite R1 institution, the Transfer Pathways program is comparatively described as "an alternative route to the traditional transfer application process for qualified students" and includes eight different options, designed for specific transfer populations.[20] In each case, the R1 campus is rhetorically framed as the *destination* campus for students who start elsewhere in the USG, with each university hailing the methods by which it chooses to consider such students.

Supporting mechanisms such as the Core and CCN allow these transfer pathways to operate even more seamlessly, yet do not guarantee students will follow them, per student choice considerations discussed in chapter 1. Nor do they guarantee that students will feel that they are in fact a welcome part of the destination campus once they arrive.[21] Other students might be hampered in their transfer choices by what philosopher Jennifer M. Morton calls the "ethical costs of upward mobility," which can influence student "strivers" who are highly qualified for entry to elite or more expensive colleges but choose to stay close to home, or attend lower-cost institutions, out of guilt related to family cost burdens (155). Statistically speaking, Transfer Pathways as a route to a four-year degree in the USG is historically not as successful as it might be, especially for nonprivileged students. In data tracked for the student cohort graduating in 2015, only 4 percent of white students and 5 percent of Black students of all genders entered a Georgia public four-year institution through Transfer

Pathways, and only 27 percent of low-income transfer students completed a four-year degree within four years, versus the national average of 52 percent.[22]

There are also other instances of branch campuses of flagship universities today operating as specifically structured admission centers for certain students who are characterized as "not ready" for studies on the four-year campus, for academic or other reasons. Transfer agreements also are at the center of these programs. But rhetorical framings at elite private universities with such campuses are increasingly creative and financially beneficial, as such campuses may be in the United States or located internationally in a study abroad program and thus may also impact their first-time student admission statistics for national reporting purposes, which typically only "count" students studying on campus.[23] In the case of the USG, however, such associated marking of other campuses carrying the UGA brand was clearly at the time of decision-making an intentional dilution of the brand itself. The dissolution of branch designations meant that the Board of Regents would keep control over the perceived lesser institutions in the system (women's colleges, African American male and female colleges, and normal schools) but remove from them the imprimatur of the University of Georgia.

It is not difficult to read these decisions as historically motivated in some tangible part by segregation principles. Chancellor Steadman V. Sanford's 1935 address to the University of Georgia audience in Athens was delivered just prior to what would be the start of his ten-year term leading the USG, which ended with his sudden death in 1945 (Sanford, "Ladies and Gentlemen" 1935). This address revealed some of Sanford's deeper-held beliefs about access and equality, which were reflected in state politics and would serve as a preamble to fierce fights over integration of colleges and universities post-1954 (*Brown v. Board of Education*) within the USG. In his speech, Chancellor Sanford—who had been a high school teacher and administrator prior to serving as a professor and then Dean of Liberal Arts at UGA, but who did not hold any advanced degrees—follows on his statement made in the epigraph to this chapter. Therein, he questioned whether educational "sorting"—to employ the same term that James Bryant Conant would use three years later, as precursor to the start of the Gen Ed movement—should start in or before college, the latter being his preference. He bases this in part on rapid enrollment growth at UGA, which he questions as being reflective of who ought to go to college at all. Sanford explains further:

> In the United States more than 50% of the youth who reach high school age enter high school; in Germany, France, England, only 7%. Europe has the

studied exclusion plan; America has the compulsory inclusion plan—an open door policy. This open door policy is based on the proposition that the masses should become educated because they are the men and women with unlimited capacities and on the belief that the people perish for lack of knowledge. Can we call a halt? No, if we believe in the principle of equal educational opportunities for every child. Yes, if we believe in the principle of education adopted by England, France, and Germany—the selective plan.

Maybe this statement—which goes on to argue for the "selective" plan—would be less alarming to my ears, if, first, Georgia were not a highly segregated state which in 1935 only saw 1 *percent* of all its citizens attending college (as noted earlier in this very same speech), and second, if this comparison with European countries, including Germany, did not come two years into Hitler's reign, with all its associated human rights horrors.[24] Of course, this statement also came six years before the United States entered World War II, and ten years before the Harvard group published the Redbook. But Sanford's question, in the context of the reorganization of the USG to separate UGA's identity from other Georgia institutions, cannot help but be heard in segregationist as well as classist terms as relevant to the continuing education and well-being of Georgia's citizenry.

One wonders if Professor Jonathan J. Westfall, Chair of the Botany Department at the University of Georgia from 1938 to 1951, was on hand to hear Chancellor Sanford's speech. If so, he likely would have taken note of the points on increased selectivity. On February 13, 1945, Dr. Westfall sent a letter and attached document, "The General Education of Teachers and of All Others," by W. E. Peik, then Dean of the College of Education at the University of Minnesota, to all members of the Georgia AAUP (American Association of University Professors), both of which are now in the UGA archives. This was in response to a reference in a previous AAUP meeting to said document. In his letter of transmittal, Westfall states that "[Peik's] outline may easily serve as a basis of further discussion and reading. It is not introduced as a defense for any preconceived notion of what the curriculum in General Education at the University of Georgia should be, but is regarded as an unusually clear and direct series of statements, criticisms, and suggestions based on years of direct experience and thoughtful curriculum evaluation."

Among the many recommendations and observations in Peik's outline—based upon close study of Gen Ed initiatives at several universities, including at Harvard and also at fellow public, the University of Minnesota—is that a common characteristic among these plans is a "broadened concept of the function and aims of education" and "variable scholastic standards according to ability" (5) as well as the following foundational principles, which include instruction for students at *all* levels, not just those at the top of the ability spectrum:

> General Education for the complete and good life is the principal function of secondary and junior college education. Terminal, vocational, and professional education are also important but secondary to general education always.... Current higher education over-emphasizes knowledge as an end rather than a means to an end such as the ability, inclination, and habit to do critical or creative thinking.... Current higher education tends to emphasize rigid subject matter mastery standards with high selection of students rather than the optimal amount of higher education that can be adjusted to the capacity and needs of all, including the superior, the average, and the slow learning. (1)

Such principles, as discussed earlier, were designed as an outgrowth of the Harvard plan to educate *all* students, and in a manner as equal as possible, in order to meet the needs of a functioning democracy. In other archived publications regarding General Education's post-1932 consolidation, these principles are also present: for example, in the 1954 "Aims and Objectives of the Georgia Institute of Technology" report, which outlined the importance of technical knowledge as well as liberal arts training and therein hailed the "recognizable virtues" of a liberal education that "prepare the individual for a full, rich, and satisfying life ... as a well-integrated human being" (18).[25]

Yet these principles become complicated in university system operations that take the idea of "equal manner" to an extreme through curricular designs such as CCN, such that local pedagogies are diminished and course content per se becomes virtually immaterial. In such systems, there is also no guarantee that "equal" course options function as such across racially and socioeconomically divided campuses, as was the case in the years before and after *Brown v. Board of Education*, when Georgia politicians were advocating for racial segregation not only on college campuses but also in K–12 schools. These race-based historical policies would radiate out over the latter half of the twentieth century in Georgia higher education and tell a tale of segregation rather than unification, undercutting the mission and purpose of Gen Ed as designed for a diverse nation inclusive of all learners.

The USG and Gen Ed: Unequal and Yet the Same, 1938–1967

A leveling of Gen Ed requirements is the inevitable outcome of the marginalization of General Education as a movement. While Georgia is just one of several states with policies such as CCN, it also has a storied history of General Education reform and revisions done in the context of segregation and, later, integration of Black students into its public colleges and universities, beginning with the 1932 consolidation narrative noted above. This was due to, among other impulses, part of what Joy Ann Williamson-Lott observes were "racial anxieties about the erosion of white supremacy and rapid changes in racial relationships, politics, and the economy" in the South in the second half of the twentieth century, which "compromised the ability of institutions to upgrade" (2), built upon a foundation of "legal segregation, the ethno-religious homogeneity of southern whites, a one-party political system, an agricultural economy built on hard labor, and required practices of racial deference" (7). Each of these conditions is evident in the archives of practice and policy of the USG; it is likely readers would find similar conditions in archives of other southern institutions during this period as well.

The recovery of these histories in the context of General Education is critically important, as Gen Ed curricula courses increasingly and disproportionately still serve students who do not have the means or opportunity to take advantage of pre-college exemption mechanisms. These include students of color, first-generation students, low-income students, and other students from underserved geographies and communities—namely, those with lesser-resourced K–12 school systems and less access to advanced coursework in high schools, as I discuss further in chapter 3. Such unequal opportunities and the enrollment statistics that result allow pundits to characterize Gen Ed curricula as remedial versus a broad curriculum designed for *all* students, not just those lacking privilege. While CCN and its predecessor, the Core curriculum, may thus be argued as equalizing administrative measures for students of various backgrounds, each operates on the ground as a glossing-over of differences between and among student bodies, including those most impacted by Gen Ed itself, with little regard for institutional mission or how students came to study at one college or university instead of another.

The most recent and extensive history of how segregation impacted particular literacy practices and policies in Georgia is Annie Mendenhall's 2022 book *Desegregation State: College Writing Programs After the Civil Rights Movement*, which focuses on two USG campuses, Savannah State and Armstrong State, and the federal enforcement of desegregation in Georgia post–*Brown v. Board of Education* (1954).²⁶ As Mendenhall outlines, the state of Georgia refused to comply with *Brown v. Board of Education* until January 1961, when two Black students (Hamilton Holmes and Charlayne Hunter) and later a third (Mary Frances Early) were admitted to the University of Georgia after a legal battle. At the other two largest universities in the USG, Georgia Tech integrated Black students voluntarily (i.e., without a court order) in 1961 and Georgia State followed suit in 1962. Women were also admitted to previously all-male campuses during this time period, though still with notable divided educational opportunities therein.²⁷ These moves coincided with the desegregation in August 1961 of the Atlanta Public Schools, the first district in the State of Georgia to desegregate after *Brown v. Board of Education*. Mendenhall's book studies the effects of these broader moves on literacy instruction and racialized literacy politics in the USG system, specifically at HBCUs.

Mendenhall's study reinforces several important points about higher education in the 1960s, 1970s, and 1980s in the state of Georgia. Those are (1) how the USG's remedial courses and a literacy competency test (which later became the Regents' Exam) that began in 1967—the same year, not coincidentally, that the Core curriculum was put into place—was developed in response to calls for increased enrollment and retention of African American students and quickly morphed into "Special Studies" programs across USG campuses, which significantly disadvantaged and marginalized African American students in the system; (2) how such efforts led to a system whereby "desegregation became about the student demographics of a school or college rather than the transformation of racist institutional structures" (20); and (3) how state and national politics surrounding remediation, literacy, and students' right to their own language (SRTOL, in writing studies field terms) clouded and weaponized, and continue today to obfuscate, true justice measures for African American students in higher education.

These historical conditions are key to recall in discussions of CCN and Core curricula in the USG, as each initiative assumes that students can *and will* move between institutions and thus need seamless transfer mechanisms to do so. Yet in practice, the racially charged histories of the USG as a whole provide neither the foundational expectations that such students would be welcomed at predominantly white institutions (PWIs), nor the equitable measures to allow students unfettered opportunities to move among and between institutions, except for those already studying at four-year campuses. This includes students at R1 universities who use CCN as a means of taking Gen Ed requirements online or in the summers at two-year colleges near their home, for lower costs, and transferring in those credits thereafter. In short, seamless transfer does not mean *increased opportunities* for transfer. Neither does it encourage students to do all their requirements in one place—which would allow them to reap the intended benefits of a scaffolded curriculum that starts with Gen Ed and ends with specialized work in a major field of study, all on one campus. In the USG, Gen Ed courses are instead framed as *products* that can move across institutions generically, absent of local values reflected in local pedagogies.

In the State of Georgia Archives, there is at once evidence that USG leaders supported the fundamental idea of liberal education, as noted above, and also a litany of documentation illustrating the state's defense of segregation of students receiving that liberal education, framed as resistance to incorporating African American students post–*Brown v. Board of Education*. In his 1938 speech entitled "Dangers," Chancellor Sanford writes that leaders at USG institutions were "building up a strong case for a system of forced cooperation and remote control," in part because they are allowing students to "acquire many accomplishments but no education" (1–2). He later asks, "why should not at least two years of college work—liberal education—be required for admission to all our professional schools . . . [in the form of] at least graduation from a junior college or two years of college work?" (3). These calls for a broad introduction to General Education, aka liberal education, would seem to prefigure the later advent of the 1967 Core but also make sweeping judgments about education that avoid the creation of "two classes of men," in Sanford's words—those who are deeply *and* broadly educated and those who are not (2), which would only be applicable within the operations of segregated USG campuses.

The racially segregated USG also had to answer to external agencies during this time. In 1943, Chancellor Sanford wrote a letter to A. R. Mann, head of the General Education board in New York City, to report on the state's efforts to improve and support Black schools in the state. Note that this board is not the same "General Education" as I focus on here, but rather an organization of coincidentally the same name, operating from 1903 to 1960 and designed to "support higher education and medical schools in the United States, to help rural white and black schools in the South, and to modernize farming practices in the South." It was founded in New York City in February 1902 and chartered by the United States Congress on January 12, 1903, its object being the promotion of education throughout the United States, without distinction as to race, sex or creed, and which eventually became part of the Rockefeller Foundation.[28]

The State of Georgia Archives contain numerous samples of correspondence with leaders of this group, notably updates on how Georgia was advancing efforts to educate African American students—updates upon which future funding decisions from the General Education Board were made.

In this vein, Sanford's 1943 letter to Mann confidently declares that Georgia has "made great progress in our effort to give the negroes[29] substantially equal educational opportunities as the whites, both on the undergraduate and the graduate level, and eventually we shall do so." This comes after Sanford outlines the various segregated institutions in Georgia, and also after his statement about land grant missions. He makes clear, however, that further creation of segregated campuses based on student ability and need—particularly in fields outside the traditionally sanctioned areas of study for Black students—is not in the state's plan:

> The Georgia State College, Savannah, the land grant college for negroes is the oldest of the three institutions. It should have as its objective what the Morrill Act of 1862 prescribes, on the junior level and later on the senior level, or its equivalent by purchase—engineering and agriculture on the college level, the training of vocational teachers in agriculture, home economics, and industrial arts; county agents and home demonstration agents, and trades for adults and those unprepared for college. Trades will not meet the Morrill Act. It is absurd to think that Georgia should be asked to maintain another Georgia School of Technology for less than a dozen negroes.

This declaration against a technical institute for Black students is important in the context of General Education, as it signals the continued subdivision of educational pathways based on race. It would seem to also contradict Sanford's assertion that students in the professional schools should receive liberal education training. Yet such a statement neatly mirrors the directive in the 1943–1944 annual report of the USG, which declares that "The Constitution of Georgia properly and wisely provides that there shall never be coeducation of whites and Negroes in any public institution in Georgia. This is a policy that our people will always follow" (11). The Georgia School of Technology would later become the Georgia Institute of Technology, which would integrate a full eighteen years after this 1943 letter was written, in which Sanford also promises that Georgia "intend[s] to comply with the fourteenth amendment to the United States Constitution as quickly as possible," itself of course ratified in 1868.[30]

Various sleight-of-hand descriptions of segregated USG enrollments continued to abound in subsequent decades, for example, in a December 18, 1963, letter from USG Chancellor Harmon Caldwell to Mr. Howard W. Rogerson of the US Commission on Civil Rights, written in response to a request from November 25, 1963, for verification of institutional admission policies based on race. Caldwell asserts that the Commission's reporting is not correct, as "all institutions of the University System are operated by the Board of Regents under a policy that forbids any discrimination in the admission of applicants on the grounds of race. Some institutions have received applications from members of one race only and their students, therefore, are members of one race only." These included all institutions *except* UGA, Georgia Tech, Georgia State, West Georgia, Valdosta State, Columbus Junior College, Armstrong College, and Savannah State—with of course the first three of these institutions only integrating one to two years prior and the latter two still serving as majority-minority Black institutions. Indeed, a full plan for desegregating the USG was not filed with the Department of Health, Education, and Welfare (HEW) until June 11, 1973; a revised plan was submitted in May 1974, and found unacceptable by a US District Court, as it was not deemed to meet the aims of Title IV of the Civil Rights Act of 1964. This led to final implementation of the plan in 1977 (Board of Regents, "Brief History" 15).[31]

Other prior actions at the state level, fueled by the governor, would also belie the claim that all possible was being done for African American students. On May 30, 1941, the USG Board of Regents met to discuss several agenda items, the final being the "non-re-election" of Walter D. Cocking, Dean of the College of Education at the University of Georgia. This motion was made by then Governor Eugene Talmadge, who was told by an unnamed source that Dean Cocking had "made a statement that he wanted to see the time when a school for negroes would be established at Athens so that negroes and white boys and girls could associate together." The Board of Regents minutes state that "the governor said that he would remove any person in the University System advocating communism or racial equality." Talmadge's motion was seconded and voted through, 8 to 4 in favor of the removal of Dean Cocking. They also state that Dean Cocking "shall be informed that he was not re-elected Dean... because of his alleged communistic and racial equality utterances" and would be invited to a June hearing on the subject.[32]

After the conclusion of the hearing, and with support of fellow UGA faculty, including UGA President Harmon Coldwell, Cocking was reinstated, but not without Talmadge demanding resignations from three of the four board members who voted against terminating Cocking, in order to appoint regents sympathetic to Talmadge's opinions in their place. Such controversies would be memorialized as the "Cocking Affair" and would lead to the temporary loss of SACS (Southern Association of Schools and Colleges) accreditation for all of Georgia's state-supported colleges for white students (later restored), and also the voting out of Talmadge in 1943.[33]

These and other actions by Talmadge were topics of attention in Atlanta's greater Black community, as demonstrated in pieces published in the *Atlanta Daily World*, founded in 1928 and one of the oldest Black newspapers still in circulation today. For example, a July 30, 1941, *Atlanta Daily World* article references an SACS investigation to determine "to what extent 'political interference' had eaten into the integrity of the Georgia University system," as well as a possible withdrawal of funding support from the General Education Board, as noted above.[34] Another earlier editorial (January 6, 1939) from the paper outlines the creation of Fort Valley State Normal and Industrial College as a "senior college for Negroes" moving in location from Forsyth, Georgia, which would be welcome in part because the Forsyth location was "so far away from the center of our mass population."

The paper's staff go on to point out, however, that in 1936–1937, "of the slightly more than 1700 liberal arts graduates among Negroes, seventy-five percent completed their education at private colleges in the state. And this is another way of saying that the state has given over the main portion of its education of Negroes in the higher brackets to private institutions," referencing a study that happened to be conducted by Walter Cocking himself. Finally, the editorial calls for more opportunities for graduate education for Black students, forecasting "what is likely to happen sooner or later ... as is being done in other commonwealths": admission onto white graduate campuses.[35] Such stories written for Atlanta (and other Georgia) citizens not part of the USG would have been an important backdrop for discussions in Black families about how hospitable the USG might be to their own college-bound children.

Indeed, Chancellor Sanford himself would appear to have been acutely aware of the negative publicity abound in the Black community in the years immediately following this scandal and in the context of ongoing segregation of K–16 Georgia schools. In a letter to the Board of Regents Committee on Education, dated April 17, 1943, to recommend the new or reappointed heads of the USG institutions for the coming year, rename the Georgia Normal and Agricultural College at Albany to Albany State College, and focus the objectives of the Georgia State College, a segregated Black college, primarily on vocational and General Education, Sanford comments,

While such a plan may not meet the letter or the spirit of the recent decision in the Gaines case, it will satisfy the better class of our Negroes. Such action if taken now will convince the Negroes that the Regents are their friends and as rapidly as possible are trying to give them equal educational opportunities. (3)[36]

While the Cocking Affair reverberated throughout the USG and the local Black community, and highlighted the dangers of centralized power from the governor in relation to higher education, the continued division of USG institutions based on subdivided missions informed by racial segregation and other stratifying measures marched on. In 1950, a document titled "Allocation of Functions" was generated by the USG, which outlined the purpose and programs of each of the components of the Georgia system. In this document, there are three important declarations of divisible USG missions, regarding general and specialized education, and racial segregation therein.

First, in describing "the junior colleges," the document states that these should be "dissociated from the University system and . . . administered by local boards of education." Yet until such transfer of administration could take place, the junior colleges shall provide "two-year terminal vocational courses" across various areas of agriculture, home economics, automobile mechanics, and other fields, and shall "offer courses in the arts and sciences preparing for transfer to the junior year of the senior institutions. The emphasis shall be on general education" (4A). Second, the University of Georgia—now a freestanding, flagship institution—would be the only one in the system "for white students" to provide programs in "law, veterinary medicine, pharmacy, agriculture on a four-year basis, forestry, or journalism" (3). The document also decrees that the Savannah State College and the Albany State College remain only for African American students studying industrial and business and arts and sciences, respectively (6).

An interesting window into the USG's consolidation of two- and four-year colleges that was released just prior to the 1950 "Allocations" document, and thus likely informed it, is in the so-called Strayer Report of 1949, or *A Report of the Survey of the University System of Georgia*. It was led by George Strayer, a professor at Columbia Teachers College and educational consultant who had previously written similarly comprehensive reports for schools in the City of Baltimore (1921), the City of Chicago (1932), and the states of West Virginia (1945), Washington (1946), and California (1948), and the District of Columbia (1948). The USG's "75 Years of Transforming Lives" publication notes that the Strayer Report "strongly supported the need to subordinate the competitive ambitions of individual institutions for the sake of advancement of the entire System," including increased resources for graduate education, and also "recommended distinctive missions for certain institutions, delineated roles for the historically black institutions and addressed the roles and functions of the state's junior colleges" (Board of Regents, "University System of Georgia"). While this characterization is true overall, the report also called special attention to the local role of General Education within the state system and as connected to secondary schools, with recommendations for reconstruction and reform thereof.

Chapter 2 of the Strayer Report, titled "The Program and Administration of the Junior Colleges," remarks on "the expansion of the program of secondary education to include the thirteenth and fourteenth years has gained wide acceptance throughout the United States" (81)—echoing terminology noted above signaling the first two years of college as an extension of the secondary schools. This chapter argued for measures to bring the junior colleges in Georgia under the umbrella not of the USG but, instead, the *K–12 school system*. The report argues that junior colleges—offering low-cost educational options for students in geographic areas close to their homes—should be viewed as local rather than state-controlled entities. It goes on to forcefully argue that the recommendations of the "earlier report," that is, the George Works Report of 1943 (Works, "Report"),[37] should be followed, specifically that

> the State of Georgia has been tardy in accepting the view that the junior college is a local institution. All of the publicly supported institutions of this type in the State, save one, are supported and administered by the State through the Board of Regents of the University System. This is so contrary to the trend in America with reference to secondary education that the Survey Committee does not hesitate to urge a change of policy in this matter. (86)

The report takes its argument one step further, to strongly recommend that—also in line with the Works report—"the junior colleges should be administered by the Board of Education in the district in which they are located or by a Board of Education recruited from a larger area which should constitute a junior college district" (Strayer 87). This is because, according to the survey committee, "the junior college including the eleventh to fourteenth years of the common school system has certain advantages," and that organizing a larger group of four-year junior colleges would also "reduce the per capita cost" of such education, contributing "to the wealth of the state" in cost savings as well as increased workforce development—a concept that would continue to be important to discussions of General Education over the next five decades in the USG. To this end, the Strayer survey committee specifically recommends in the report section titled "An Administrative Code for the University System of Georgia," that five of the USG colleges be taken out of the USG: Georgia Southeastern College at Americus, Middle Georgia College at Cochran, West Georgia College at Carrollton, and South Georgia College at Douglas, all of which were also so called "Colleges for Negroes" (230).

These recommendations raise several important observations about the value of Black junior colleges in the USG to the local communities in which they are located, and the local high school students who move into and through them, separate from the machinery of the USG as a whole. The report further calls into question the dividing line between general and specialized education (i.e., work in major fields of study), as it argues that "the two-year terminal vocational curricula should include a program of general education" to "contribute to personal development, to competence in human relationships, and to the acceptance of civic responsibility," each of which echoes the original principles of the Gen Ed movement as well as earlier (sometimes contradictory) assertions by Georgia leaders regarding the value of a liberal education (82).

The Strayer Report further recommends that the curricula students take in General Education in junior colleges should prepare them for transfer to four-year colleges and universities, even though "work in the liberal arts and sciences ... may not in a small college be sufficiently differentiated to meet all of the requirements for junior standing in the many specializations developed in four-year colleges and universities" (83). Such would seem to acknowledge the differences between institutional missions that make wholesale transfer of such credits problematic. It also puts significant emphasis on Gen Ed overall as "of greater importance for these [junior college students] than is preparation for specialization" in a major field of study.

The report also shines a useful spotlight on the limits of efficiency systems in the USG as relevant to segregated colleges, institutional mission(s), and meaningful General Education instruction. While it paves the way for actions taken nearly two decades later to provide seamless transfer for students from community colleges to four-year universities (and theoretically, vice versa), it does not espouse the same values as those behind either the Core curriculum or CCN, as it aligns junior colleges *downward* with high schools and sees General Education as a critical part of a student's education that is not to be viewed as an interchangeable product.

Further, the report views junior colleges as, on the one hand, a growth opportunity for some students who stop at "grade fourteen" in order to enter the workforce, and, on the other, as a site of rapid transfer growth benefiting four-year institutions, by students continuing their education toward a bachelor's degree. And as relevant to racial segregation, the Strayer Report sees the Black junior colleges—though not the Black four-year colleges (Savannah State, Fort Valley State, and Albany State)—as divisible from the USG system of otherwise all-white colleges and universities. Given the report's focus on two-year colleges *only*, it would seem that such a recommendation was less about further racial segregation of systems and more about differentiation of educational missions between two- and four-year colleges.[38]

Yet the recommendations to break the junior colleges out of the USG system were not subsequently followed, as also noted by Cameron Fincher in a 1984 paper.[39] Perhaps this was due to legislators' fears of breaking up a system that now bore state constitutional status, or to continue the USG control of all segregated higher education in Georgia, both in ideological and in economic terms, especially over valuable transfer credits. Either way, such is an interesting choice to recall as we fast-forward five years to 1954, when the Georgia Commission on Education voted to adopt the School Segregation Amendment to the Georgia Constitution, put to a public vote on November 2 of that year. Prior to this vote, on September 14, 1954, Governor Talmadge wrote to Georgia Attorney General Eugene Cook, to ask his opinion on the proposed amendment. Cook concluded that "there is no authority under the Georgia constitution of 1945 to establish mixed schools, tax for mixed schools, or expend funds for mixed schools. If the Supreme Court of the United States should strike down the requirement in Article VIII [Separate but Equal] . . . it would have abolished free public education in Georgia under the present Constitution of 1945" (8).

With Cook's opinion documented, and with a further declaration in the report of Georgia Commission on Education dated September 28, 1954, which said that the Supreme Court ruling was "contrary to the Constitution of Georgia and the wishes of the people, and should not be accepted" and that "under the Constitution of Georgia taxes may not be levied for mixed public schools, and public money cannot be spent for mixed public schools," the Commission provided a "GEA Release." This release included statements about the amendment itself, the rhetoric of which employs scare tactics highlighting the perceived power of the federal government over states' rights, including regulation of K–12 teachers, their salaries, and their pensions:

The people of Georgia prefer segregated free private schools to mixed public schools. The segregation amendment will make it possible to change the educational system in those localities in which existing schools are knocked out by the Federal Courts. Unless the amendment is ratified, in those localities in which the present schools are destroyed by the Federal Courts, there will be no schools at all, for the Georgia Constitution prohibits expenditures of public money for mixed schools. In counties and cities against which no Federal Court decree is entered, no change of the educational system will be necessary, and in those countries and cities the existing separate public schools will go on just as now. . . . The Georgia Commission on Education has recommended the segregation amendment to all the people because the passage of the amendment will make it possible for Georgia to carry on segregated schools, which will be well supported and regulated, with full protection to teachers and students. (4–5)[40]

The amendment was thereafter adopted and voted into law but was overturned in 1958 as a revised approach of "minimal compliance" with desegregation, as opposed to "massive resistance," was implemented, which "won the Atlanta Board of Education a one year delay from the district court in implementing an integration plan" (Georgia Advisory Committee).

In this environment that fiercely resisted anything that contradicted the "separate but equal" doctrine previously in place, the state of Georgia simultaneously went into high gear to publicize just how *equal* these segregated schools and colleges were—again, a move that would later allow for Core curricula to be promoted as equivalent across all USG institutions, including all-Black schools. This purported equality is represented in a multicolor publication in the State of Georgia Archives entitled *Education in Georgia: Nineteen Fifty-Five thru Nineteen Fifty-Eight*, which claims Governor Marvin Griffin as its author. This sixty-five-page booklet, replete with photos of students, teachers, classrooms, and USG campus buildings, is an astounding example of rhetoric rising to propaganda, designed to convince Georgia's citizens that efforts such as *Brown v. Board of Education* were not only unnecessary but potentially *harmful* to the K–16 education.

Testimonies regarding Griffin's effectiveness and excellence from the Georgia Superintendent of Schools, USG Chancellor Harmon Caldwell, and the presidents of UGA, Georgia Tech, and the Georgia State College of Business Administration (each accompanied by a photo of the leaders themselves) preface the contents, with assurances by higher ed leaders that "Governor Griffin's fine record . . . is proof of his personal appreciation of the challenges confronting the college students seeking an education at our state-supported institutions" (3). The superintendent of Georgia schools proclaims in this section of testimonies that Griffin "will be described in the history books as Education's friend" (3). Rhetorically speaking, this booklet presents a unified stance that both implicitly and explicitly celebrates segregated education across all levels and, further, highlights Griffin's role as governor in that segregation.

The booklet serves to further unify the segregated purposes of the K–12 and higher education systems as *one* for the citizens of Georgia—complete with several images to illustrate its points—including a section entitled "Good Schools for Georgia's Negroes." Here, Griffin proclaims that "some of Georgia's most beautiful schools and most modern classrooms are for Negro children" (24) and that "No state has done more to educate its Negro citizens and raise their standards of living. Negroes provide a very great potential source of trained labor here in Georgia" (25). The document also proclaims that "Trade training provides skills for jobs in industry and agricultural classes teach Negroes how to work on modern mechanized farms" (25). These statements are accompanied by statistics proclaiming that "54% of Georgia's investment in new school facilities has been for Negro children" and "All Georgia teachers are paid equal state salaries based on equal qualifications" (25). Beside these stats is a picture of a small group of Black children of middle school to high school age working in a home economics classroom.

There are scant references to Black students (or teachers) in the rest of the booklet, which is populated by photo after photo of white students and teachers wherever education is discussed. One exception is on page 33, which outlines "better services for blind children" and deaf children, where it is noted that one improvement project is a "new building for beauty culture and masonry classes (Negro Unit)" and "Home economics and woodworking shop building (Negro Unit)" under deaf education, as well as a building for "library and music department at the School for Negroes" under education for the blind (33). And of the thirty-plus pages that comprise the second half of the booklet, illustrating significant financial investments in new buildings and initiatives in the USG's institutions, all are at the four research universities, and none at the segregated colleges for Black (or women) students.

Such staunch defense of segregated schools at the end of the 1950s makes the decision to implement a Core curriculum across all USG campuses all the more baffling, if we take the Core as a move antithetical to the singular autonomy of different campuses serving different populations. But the USG did not actually see these campuses as fully autonomous, as a closer look at the bottom line of enrollments may help to reveal. In the aforementioned 1943–1944 annual report of the USG, there is a subsection titled "Too Many Courses," which summarizes the findings of Chancellor Caldwell at UGA, drawing also upon the fact that no USG institution at this time offered doctoral degrees (49):

> President Caldwell in his annual report is of the firm conviction that the university undertakes to offer too many courses. "I have, therefore, urged all the faculties to make careful studies of their academic offerings with a view to eliminating courses of doubtful value and to concentrating the efforts of the faculty and students on a smaller number of more worthwhile courses. If this is done, it will also mean that the ratio of faculty members to members of the student body will be smaller in the postwar period. With a given amount of money we will be in a position therefore, to pay somewhat better salaries to those who are employed and perhaps also to release more of the time of some of our faculty members for research work. The reduction in the number of courses should not impair the quality of our educational program." (Griffin, 37).

It is not hard to draw several interrelated conclusions from Caldwell's statement. First, that in offering fewer courses, resources might be conserved, leading to a smaller student-faculty ratio. Second, that more faculty might be released for research—an important imperative to come in the next decade as the German model came into full force, as noted earlier in this book.[41] And third, such reduction in courses could most easily happen within and across General Education, and could—in the future—be enabled by the Core curriculum (even UGA's own version of it)—which would provide for less duplication of effort in enrollments and more selectivity in who would be educated. To lay this groundwork, a Board of Regents policy was passed in 1959 to "tighten admission standards at all system institutions and admit only those students who, based on testing results, personal interviews, and academic and intellectual ability, were capable of successfully completing a program of study in higher education" (Davison 7). In 1964, and following a recommendation for system expansion (from the same 1959 study that raised USG admission standards), a plan for constructing a series of new junior colleges was also created (12).

Such efficiency in enrollments would allow UGA and other R1 USG institutions to better deploy their finances toward research as well as more selective educational programming. In 1953–1954, the academic year just prior to *Brown v. Board of Education*, the UGA enrolled 5,012 students; Georgia State (then known as the UGA Atlanta Division) enrolled 3,506; and Georgia Tech enrolled 3,900. Each of the other USG institutions enrolled between only 320 and 988 students each, or a fraction of the density found across the three research-related universities. Total enrollments in the USG were 19,669—down from 23,039 in 1952–1953, with the most significant enrollment losses at the three research universities. By 1959–1960, total USG enrollments were at 27,928, or a 21 percent increase in eight years, with enrollments at UGA, Georgia Tech, and Georgia State coming in at 7,255, 5,568, and 2,767, respectively, and all other USG institutions holding at between 397 and 1,300 students each ("University System of Georgia Equivalent Full-Time Enrollments"). In comparison, *national enrollments in all colleges and universities during the 1950s rose by 49 percent*, in part due to an increase in the college-age population (NCES, *120 Years* 66). So these USG enrollments were noticeably behind national trends post–World War II, trends that supported Gen Ed as a national movement for all.

Coupling these enrollment data in the USG with the increased concerns about both financial efficiency and quality of experience for students and faculty, it's not hard to see how a mechanism for seamless transfer across and into USG institutions would be desirable to create just about a decade later. Such would ultimately echo the 1932 Act in serving the proclaimed interests of the state. I submit that the Core curriculum was a natural outgrowth of the USG as a *system* with centralized control, and one that felt increased need to provide mobility for students across its campus—or at least those students who were *able* to have such mobility (i.e., white students). It was created to boost enrollments at the research campuses and curb students leaving the state. In this light, the advent of the Core makes much more sense. At the same time, the rise of HBCUs—and particularly the prominence of institutions such as Spelman, Clark Atlanta, and Morehouse in Atlanta—were available for students whom the USG did not welcome on its white campuses and who wanted a liberal education not possible at the agriculturally and vocationally focused campuses of the USG where they were allowed to enroll.

While I cannot prove that the USG was *only* interested in increasing white student transfer among and between its various institutions both before and after *Brown v. Board of Education*, it is true that the advent of HBCUs in the South over the first half of the twentieth century was a direct response to systemic segregation, and these institutions operated as networks for social mobility in African American communities who did not have full access to the mobility opportunities afforded to whites within more selective colleges and universities. As Richardson and Harris observed in their 2004 discussion of backlash litigation against HBCUs over the second half of the twentieth century, *Brown v. Board of Education*

> encouraged [traditionally white institutions] to consider the admission of students on the basis of race alone to be at least potentially unconstitutional. But college and university students function largely as consumers in an open marketplace exercising decisions based on a broader range of choices than lower schools have historically offered. Choice has become a volatile topic within the context of lower schools, but choice has been a given in higher education influenced by family legacy, regional and cost preferences, and the esoteric qualities of universities that attract students to apply and enroll. (366)

They also note that by 1954, "90% of Blacks attending college, or roughly 100,000 students, had matriculated at HBCUs" (371). It also continues to be the case that Black students at HBCUs have higher average earning power upon graduation than those who attend PWIs (Hammond et al.). Given these conditions, and the prevalence of more elite HBCUs in Atlanta, it is not difficult to imagine that the USG's interest in both internal student transfer and student mobility to seek college degrees outside the state of Georgia was significantly focused on white students during the mid-twentieth century. This would explain the lack of regard for stark differences in local Gen Ed curricular goals between, say, Abraham Baldwin Agricultural College and Georgia Tech when creating the Core curriculum and its transfer provisions in 1967. These HBCU students were not, theoretically speaking, ever going to transfer *at all*. But if they did, they would be disadvantaged further upon admission, and in many cases subject to the 1967 special studies remediation regulations noted above, in order to proceed to major-level requirements thereafter.

Indeed, archival documents on the Core's implementation illustrate the priorities of the system over the individual, as first articulated in 1932, even as the importance of General Education was upheld as part of this rhetorical framework. The creation of additional, integrated two-year (junior) colleges in 1966 in Albany, Gainesville, and Marietta, with a fourth to follow in Dalton, Georgia, in 1967, reinforced the financial and educational value of expanding enrollment opportunities across all sectors of the USG. As outlined in the July 1, 1965, Georgia Educational Improvement Council's "Status Report on Recommendations of the Governor's Commission to Improve Education," the "comprehensive community junior college is the primary means by which local area and community needs should be met for education beyond the high school"—a statement in line with the Strayer Report of 1949, except for the additional assurance that such colleges "such be integral and fully coordinated parts of the University System of higher education" (30). These two-year college campuses open to both white and Black students would make the USG greater in size and more ripe for centralized General Education sameness that would regulate and minimize any transfer issues resulting from local curricular requirements.

The Core curriculum's beginnings are outlined in a memo from M. J. Goglia, professor of Mechanical Engineering at Georgia Tech, to all academic chairmen and secretaries of the USG, dated January 23, 1967, which summarizes the report of the Committee on Transfer of Credit approved by the University System Advisory Council the week prior. Goglia states that "because of the increased attrition and enrollment at institutions of higher education, the expansion of junior colleges, and the increased mobility of the student population, transfer of college credit among institutions has become of critical importance in the efficient operation of the University System of Georgia."[42] The Commission had two charges: to identify specific courses across the system and recommend where they should be accepted as transfer credit, and to "analyze lower division courses by various senior units," note where they differed, and propose how they would transfer among state institutions. These resulted in a "general concept of course commonalities" that formed the basis for the proposed Core (1–2).[43]

It's important to highlight annotation number 4 in the summary memo, that "nothing in this core should be construed to mean that any specific courses must be required, but rather demonstrated achievement in the core area as determined by the institution where the core or the fractional part thereof is taken shall be the intent of this core curriculum." At the same time, per annotation number 7, "each institution is to determine whether its own students satisfy the core requirements. This determination shall then be honored by all other institutions as satisfying their requirements as well, if the core is completed" (4). These two statements in consort promise an almost limitless autonomy to decide what is "best" for an institution's students, including what courses are within each area.

Yet such a principle is only useful in relation to institutional autonomy when a student *never transfers* to another USG institution. Once a student transfers, that institutional autonomy is generally meaningless, as the first institution never sees the student through to graduation. And further, the institution accepting the Core credits as complete in full is beholden to whatever the student's previous institution felt was "best." There is zero guarantee that the receiving institution agrees, or that the Core as completed by the student matches up to the work they will do as a continuing student in any major at the receiving institution, or that their program of study will match others who started and finished their degree on that campus. As minutes from the Administrative Committee on the Transfer of Credit of the USG Advisory Council dated May 6, 1971 concede, "While [a student's record] might include the lower division subjects from the basic areas of the 'core,' the receiving faculty should realize that students meeting such requirements may lose some opportunities to take valuable electives" ("Minutes of the Meeting").

Of course, such problems can occur in any credit transfer situation. Institutional control at the course level is gone if a state has an articulation agreement between its community colleges and four-year public universities to accept all credits from an associate's degree, as thirty-five of fifty US states currently do, with some of the other fifteen states having further arrangements for credit transfer.[44] But the USG Core went beyond these common measures of transferability, to dictate *what* would be required across *all* USG campuses and *how* that would transfer in whole or in part. The Core thus paved the way for a further measure of sameness in the form of CCN, which would be adopted as part of Gen Ed principles at other university systems outside Georgia.

Making Gen Ed Maximally Efficient: Common Course Numbering

Such unification of identity and purpose in the 1932 creation of the USG system, and the ensuing complications it raised regarding social and racial stratification of educational resources, is also a hallmark of many other state university systems across the country today. Having the above histories as a backdrop to the current conditions of CCN in the USG is critical to understanding the evolution of views toward educating, and profiting from, Georgia's diverse citizenry. But these histories of today's USG and CCN are also fundamental to other state systems where CCN rules Gen Ed operations, in some cases with similar politics to what fueled the stratification of the USG system itself.

The USG, as noted above, is *one* complete system; in comparison, state systems in Illinois, Michigan, Connecticut, and California, to name just a few, instead choose to consolidate particular state colleges into a system linguistically marked by a school's relationship to the flagship, and then construct an additional second-tier system for the less-selective universities within the state. This organizational choice creates bifurcated state systems that privilege research universities and their marked satellite or branch campuses over regional comprehensive universities and other state colleges, which may also have histories of acquiring other campuses.

Common Course Numbering in Georgia covers the numerous introductory courses under the forty-five subject headings included in the USG CCN database. These courses on one campus carry the same number as that course offered at any other campus within the state.[45] CCN both limits any major individual college and university innovation and revision of key courses within a local Gen Ed curriculum as well as within the overall curriculum itself, and also prescribes a set of courses presumed to be the "same" across all institutions. The system of CCN is central to the USG's intention to be "a composite of diverse institutions that, in spite of their diversity, require System-wide coherence to facilitate success for transfer students."[46] This makes CCN both emblematic of larger operations and also much harder to defend in principle given the diversity of USG institutions, their populations, and their missions that it seeks to encompass, unless we abide by the convenient rhetoric that Gen Ed is Gen Ed, no matter where it is or who offers it.

Besides Georgia, fourteen other US states participate in CCN as of the time of this writing. An additional twelve states have a partial common numbering system, wherein some courses articulate while others do not, or there are shared course outcomes but not shared numbers in course catalogs. To put this another way: over half of the US states participate in some kind of articulation measures that allow what is called, in higher education industry terms, *seamless transfer* between public institutions of higher education that are within the boundaries of that state or that state's university system (Education Commission of the States).

This sameness that CCN provides sounds like a wonderful concept on its face, especially for students who are able to freely transfer between and among institutions without any credit loss—a significant concern particularly for limited-income individuals and their families.[47] Indeed, this is the primary rhetoric that supports CCN: one of maximal efficiency toward student success, avoiding the curricular "hurdles" that exist to delay progress. For Georgia residents, however, some of the financial concerns accompanying "lost" credits are abated by the HOPE Scholarship, which guarantees students receive "the maximum amount" for tuition each semester at any USG institution, so long as they maintain a 3.0 GPA, for up to ten years or 127 completed credits, whichever comes first. A similar scholarship is the Zell, which applies to higher-achieving students (3.7 GPA).[48]

This is not to say that there are not other associated costs that families must pay outside tuition. Additionally, neither scholarship program covers out-of-state students. But the HOPE and Zell are a *positive* example of USG's uniform policies that do help students from Georgia, even as previous research has shown that HOPE "decreased full-time enrollments and increased course withdrawals among resident freshmen" secondary to student concerns regarding the maintenance of the 3.0 GPA, and that few of the students who receive a HOPE scholarship are also low-income, Pell-eligible students (Kinsley and Goldrick-Rab 91).

In CCN, one might also assume there exists a theoretically shared vision for a course and its subject matter across institutions. CCN *should* lead to shared cross-institutional conversations and action about best practices, up-to-date teaching methods, and course revisions that stay abreast of student learning needs. This is *in theory*. In practice, CCN is a shorthand for declaring Gen Ed courses as one-size-fits-all, regardless of the school where they are offered, with little shared goals across campuses. This shorthand is implemented as a substitute for local pedagogy across the USG's diverse institutions, each with its own separate mission statement—an unusual rhetorical marker in itself—and each with its own embedded values and directives for streamlined dissemination to, and uptake by, prospective students, the public, and donors.[49]

Certainly, local campuses across the USG do their best to create learning outcomes that fit the particular needs of their students. Georgia Tech is cognizant that it is a technical institute, which guides the design and delivery of ENGL 1101 and 1102. But in principle, Georgia Tech is still offering courses under 1101 and 1102 that are by state definition "equivalent" to the same courses offered at, for example, Kennesaw State University, a regional comprehensive university less selective and less specialized than Georgia Tech. And it is still beholden to centralized descriptions of ENGL 1101 and 1102 that are monitored and enforceable by the USG. As noted above, in a system this large and institutionally diverse, the sum definition of "same" is nontrivial and not without consequences, as other states who participate in CCN have also found.

Recent scholarship is surprisingly scant regarding CCN and General Education outcomes per se; most of what does exist focuses on state-level studies of whether seamless transfer is living up to expectations.[50] Such literature emphasizes the importance of minimizing lost credits as students move between institutions (see, for example, Zimpher et al.; and Bringsjord et al., both of which discuss successes with seamless transfer and other student-centered alignment measures and supports within the SUNY system). Nearly all literature starts from the question, does CCN enable flexibility in transfer for students? The answer is almost always *yes*, but it is simply a fact-based question predicated on transcriptable credit outcomes. It is not a question about quality of experience, diversity of local offerings, or content of the individual courses themselves and their pedagogical applicability in a different institutional context. This is because a key component of seamless transfer is the portability of Gen Ed *credits*, with little regard for appropriate Gen Ed *content* across different institutions.

One national pilot on CCN and portable credits taken to the extreme was the "Interstate Passport" (IP) initiative, hailing from the Western Interstate Commission for Higher Education, or WICHE for short (https://interstatepassport.wiche.edu/). As McKay, Edwards, and Douglas (2022) discuss, the IP initiative was the result of "multi-state faculty developed learning outcomes and proficiency criteria instead of specific courses and credits" designed to alleviate lost credits as students moved between institutions in different states, and "dedicated to the block transfer of LDGE [lower-division General Education] attainment" ("Smoothing the Path" 74–75).

Interstate Passport's final cohort (2021–2022) included sixty-nine institutions, all in western states except a scattering in the Midwest and South. Its operations, phased out due to "grant funding ending and low recruitment," were based on nine knowledge and skill areas in AAC&U's LEAP (https://interstatepassport.wiche.edu/members/learn-more/faqs/). While the LEAP outcomes are widely respected and frequently at the core of General Education reforms on college and university campuses, the concept of CCN as a force in flattening the local value of Gen Ed in relation to particular student populations and faculty expertise is contradictory to such outcomes. This is due to seamless transfer's aims to make students' paths through college ultimately less recursive, a goal that could lead to another initiative such as Interstate Passport being attempted again in the United States.[51]

Georgia is thus not a unique state as far as Gen Ed policy is concerned, but it is a useful case study for how Gen Ed programs evolve when other competing forces are at play, and how no single campus is able to stem forces present at the state level. Georgia also has an especially complex local set of circumstances that resulted in its curricular content and import failing to always meet the needs of its diverse citizens, as one would have hoped following the Redbook. Such was also the case with the implementation of CCN in both Texas and Florida.

Common Numbers, Uncommon Practices: Texas and Florida

The policies and practices of CCN at two other US states help to illustrate the challenges posed by CCN beyond Georgia. I examine Texas and Florida because they are each bellwether states for controversial higher education reform that, like Georgia, are intwined with race and politics. This includes Texas's well-publicized reframing of US history in high school textbooks, which include reported political and racial biases in their lessons;[52] and Florida's 2023 rejection on political grounds of the new AP African American Studies course for college credit, as well as its revocation of DEI policies and offices at all state universities (a move also made by Texas) in that same year, via Senate Bill 266.[53] What further binds these two states together in terms of General Education is their participation in a large state university system whose central flagship campus policies are followed on all other regional or branch campuses within that system.

While CCN was implemented in the USG in 1997, its origins in the University of Texas system pre-date Georgia's by nearly two decades. Unlike Georgia's two state conglomerates, the state of Texas has *six* independent university systems, in part due to its massive size: the University of North Texas System, the University of Houston system, TAMU (Texas A&M), TSUS (Texas State), the Texas Tech System, and the University of Texas system, which is the largest of the group. The UT system also has a board of regents that is appointed by the governor and confirmed by the senate, established in 1881 with UT–Austin as its flagship campus. The UT system encompasses nine universities, at Arlington, Dallas, El Paso, Permian Basin, Rio Grande Valley, San Antonio, and Tyler, and also Austin State. All students on all UT campuses must complete the mandated UT forty-two-hour core curriculum, which began in the 1972–1973 academic year.[54]

TCCNS (Texas Common Course Numbering System) began with a study by the Texas Association of Collegiate Registrars and Admissions Officers in 1973 and grew into a basic course-numbering system used at nine colleges by 1989. By 1993, the project was a statewide agreement, with 137 total Texas institutions currently participating (including all two-year and four-year colleges and universities, and technical colleges, plus "21 private institutions and three health science institutions"). As the TCCNS website also proudly states, "Perhaps the most surprising aspect of the Texas Common Course Numbering System is that its origin cannot be traced back to a state government mandate. The TCCNS arose as a completely voluntary, grass-roots cooperative effort among junior/community colleges and universities," employing a rhetoric of *local control*, which one might observe is a hallmark of public communications regarding higher education, and other sociopolitical matters, in Texas as a state (https://www.tccns.org/about/).

A window into how Texas's CCN system has been viewed by other states, as well as how CCN's general benefits and drawbacks have been legislated, is in a

1995 study on common course numbering by the Academic Senate for California Community Colleges, using Texas, Florida, and Illinois as comparatives. The publicly available report opens with the advantages and disadvantages of CCN, one of the latter being elision of academic freedom and shared governance over curricula:

> The very structure of community colleges and their governance by locally elected boards with autonomous faculty has been a central defining tenet of the community college movement. Unlike regional or statewide systems, this structure has facilitated the expression of community needs in the programs and services of local colleges.
>
> The desire to standardize the path for transfer by enacting a common curriculum, often implied by advocates of the common course numbering approach, may endanger that unique responsiveness which has been a hallmark of the community college system.... The professional judgement and talent of faculty are expressed in their curricular offerings. Moves toward standardization jeopardize the historic academic freedoms central to the California model of higher education. As such, these moves are likely to be resisted. (2–3)

The report further notes that "if the goal is helping students, improving transfer rates, and saving taxpayers' money, one would have to raise the question as to whether a common course numbering system will, in fact, do these things" (2). It additionally points out that Senate Bill 450 was a "junk bill" that did not include due diligence with faculty and other stakeholders.

When examining the Texas CCN, the California report noted that it suffered from four widespread issues: (1) unresolved level problems (freshmen vs. sophomore), (2) varying number of credits and course expectations, (3) differing institutional philosophies and academic freedom, and (4) course inventory changes (8). Each of these concerns are widely applicable on a national scale. CCN requires ability levels to be agreed upon via course numbering, with the implication that 100- or 1,000-level is freshman, 200- or 2,000-level sophomore, and so on. But of course, students pay little attention to what course numbers mean, and sometimes such courses also count for other degree requirements. Credit variances are also important, as three-credit courses require roughly 43–45 hours of work, per Carnegie credit hour standards, and four credits, approximately 60 hours. A Gen Ed system that requires more time and thought within a course by making it four credits instead of three—not uncommon for writing or mathematics—creates problems if the rest of the CCN system requires them to be only three credits. And course inventory changes are particularly sticky in larger revisions to a local Gen Ed curriculum, or with the addition or subtraction of faculty and programs supporting a particular course.

As relevant to differences in institutional philosophies and also course-transfer navigation, a study by Schudde, Jabbar, and Hartman (2020) of student transfer issues faced by Texas Community College students, including common course numbering, reflects these problems, employing interviews with faculty and students as well as examinations of transfer mechanisms on the ground at two Texas campuses. The authors note that "The faculty council at the University of Texas at Austin elaborated their concerns about 'unintended consequences related to preparedness, certification, and accreditation' [and] 'faculty representatives argued that students who completed parallel coursework at other state institutions would be less prepared than students who took their own courses'" (70). They further detail the unequal amount of information that various stakeholders possess in the process, especially since the agreements between institutions "depends on which college and program students transfer from" and because also the "quality of these agreements varies widely" (68).

Such lacking information harms students rather than streamlines their process. Schudde and coauthors conclude that

> community college advisors struggle to navigate complex transfer information shaped by more powerful university actors, and they sometimes provide inaccurate and incomplete advice to students. Students believe their role is to curate a large volume of transfer information to attain their goals. Ultimately, the transfer field, which follows the priorities and rules of university actors, disadvantages transfer-intending community college students, expecting them to navigate bureaucratic hurdles. These political and ecological contexts are probably partially responsible for the low attainment of transfer aspirations by community college entrants. (80)

Differing institutional philosophies and academic freedom are also in the background of common course numbering and transfer credit in the state of Florida, especially given its rejection—and then reversal—of the AP African American History course in high schools, and by extension also its transfer credit into its Florida State University System.[55] CCN was first initiated in Florida on June 3, 1975, as part of HB 1972, approved 30–0 by the Florida State Senate.[56] The Florida Department of Education has a web page devoted to the components of its CCN system, which articulates CCN's structural purposes as "a key component of Florida's K–20 seamless system of articulation [for] postsecondary courses at public vocational-technical centers, community colleges, universities, and participating nonpublic institutions.... The assigned numbers describe course content to improve research, assist program planning, and facilitate the transfer of students" (https://flscns.fldoe.org/).

Here we see a framing of K–20 that goes beyond the aforementioned "thirteenth and fourteenth grades" rhetoric reflected in the 1949 Strayer Report, which linguistically tied the junior and senior years of high school to the first two years of college. Florida's K–20 framing includes not only all years of college but *also* four years of postgraduate study, in one state system. Though one wonders how graduate courses and curricula in Florida aim to fit into the (typical) undergraduate-focused paradigm of CCN, it is clear from the CCN reports on this site that in Florida, such numbering applies to graduate courses as well as undergraduate.

This idea for the K–20 education paradigm in Florida likely derives in part from an August 1975 report titled "Indicators and Costing of Florida's Education Goals," prepared by Dr. John S. Waggaman at Florida State University and conducted at "the invitation of the Florida Commission of Education, as one of four efforts at identifying indicators for public education in Florida" (2). Early in the report, Waggaman posits that "Florida is (or has) made a serious effort in the financial support of education. Whether the effort is (or was) sufficient to meet the educational needs of the Florida population is another question" (5). In 1975, education costs were over 60 percent of the Florida general state appropriation (6), which the report points out was composed "mainly of salary costs" (9). However, the other kind of "cost" examined in this financial analysis is to the student, as "it is not necessarily the tuition and fees paid to a college, but the income lost while working" that matters (11).

The report further argues that the "cost" of a student's program is not just what they take in their major, but also costs from other courses taken, including those in the Gen Ed curricula (15). Under "Educational Goals and Costs," Gen Ed is included as the second of seven goals, the other four being, listed in order of "priority of the goals," "basic skills" (i.e., communication skills); "vocational competencies"; "professional competencies"; and "advanced knowledge and skills"; "research and development"; and "recreation and leisure skills" (16–17). General Education here is described as something "necessary for participation in a democratic society" and as including "skills, attitudes, and knowledge for general problem-solving and survival, human relations and citizenship, moral and ethical conduct, mental and physical health, aesthetic, scientific and cultural appreciation, and environmental and economic understanding" (16).

As with other similar articulations of Gen Ed's value in Georgia and elsewhere, these components match well onto the tenets of the Redbook, which of course would have been only thirty years old at the time of this report. The report further notes that Gen Ed (or "Goal 2") should take place in grades 4–7 and 8–12 and in "adult high school, community-junior college (transfer), University (lower level undergraduate), University (upper level undergraduate, e.g., humanities and pre-professional)" (17). At this point, the report recommends that the "most desirable costing system conceivable . . . would be a combination of the K–12 and two post-secondary systems [community college and university]" (18).

Here is where we start to see the beginning of curricular efficiencies taking hold, as the report advocates for system combination and collaborations that would implicitly reduce labor costs. Why have a student take a course "twice" when they can be part of a system that integrates all seven goals for Florida students into one? Yet it also raises the issue of "mak[ing] visible the extreme variation in cost which may be found throughout the system" (23), even as, rather than reducing costs, in fact "costs may need to rise to insure a greater possibility of educational goal attainment" (24). These two observations, however, are complicated by a final recommendation near the end of the report, which proposes that

> there needs to be some way to identify precisely the genuinely duplicate programs and course offerings, i.e., those which the same students could take any of several locations with little or no added non-educational student expenses. . . . Perhaps Common Course Numbering will provide information about duplicate courses between and among the vo-tech centers, community colleges, and universities; if so perhaps [CCN] could be extended down through the high schools and include all adult education courses as well. (38)

The above report puts into words the true valuations of a consolidated system with CCN: avoiding *duplicate effort* across wildly different educational venues—including high school, which in turn *saves money*. Florida's is thus a sweeping, standardized system highly cognizant of cost efficiencies. It also unites *all* educational levels in a defined mission, designated and controlled by the state, including of course General Education curricula, and further aligns K–12 missions with public college and university missions. The K–20 framing implies that students can and *will* complete one coordinated path of education. This is a laudable goal, but the efficiency rhetoric that guides it elides many individual moments of agency along the way, on both the part of students and their families, and the institutions themselves.

On the CCN site for Florida, students and other members of the public can find the recent history of bills that amend requirements in the CCN system, or provide addenda to them.[57] Visitors can also read reports related to the courses themselves—including course descriptions across institutions. A keen example is the thirty-four-page report outlining all ENC-rubric (English Composition) labeled offerings, which includes individual institutional catalog titles for ENC 1101. These titles vary widely, depending upon the institution, including College Writing, English Composition I, Composition I, Freshman Communication Skills I, Freshman Composition I, Writing and Rhetoric I, and First-Year Composition and Rhetoric. The descriptions of each of the ENC 1101 courses vary, and often dramatically so, across institutions.

For example, ENC 1101 at the Florida Academy for Nursing and Health Occupations, a private two-year college, is described as offering students "a thorough understanding of the writing process and structure for college essays, reports, and summaries," whereas ENC 1101 at Broward College, a public two-year college, is described as "a university parallel course in which the student writes expository themes in various modes, research methods, and library skills are introduced, and a documented paper is required." ENC 1101 at Florida International University, a four-year public research university, is described as introducing "students to rhetorical concepts and audience-centered approaches to writing, including composing processes, language conventions and style, and critical analysis and engagement within written texts and other forms of communication." Yet the CCN system ensures—as it does in all states where it is used—that each of these will be transferred *equally* across institutions within the state.[58]

In Georgia, there is no such public accounting of how the USG's comparative course, ENGL 1101 (Composition I) is described across all USG institutions. Rather, there is a common course description in the USG Academic Affairs handbook that describes ENGL 1101 as "a composition course focusing on skills required for effective writing in a variety of contexts, with emphasis on exposition, analysis, and argumentation, and also including introductory use of a variety of research skills."[59] Yet on individual campuses, there exist more robust and site-specific descriptions that are more tailored to population and mission. For example, at Kennesaw State University, students in ENGL 1101 will learn to "employ writing process strategies for invention, arrangement, and revision; identify the audience, purpose, and context for their writing; develop a thesis and construct an argument; quote, paraphrase and summarize; and practice multiple types of writing, for example, journal, free writes, responses, reflections" among other skills and strategies.[60]

Comparatively, at Georgia Tech, ENGL 1101 "introduces rhetorical principles and multimodal composing. Supplementary texts can include all varieties of print and digital nonfiction . . . and other types of nonfiction artifacts."[61] The course further "teaches students communication and critical thinking skills that will prepare them to succeed academically at Georgia Tech and professionally in the work place."[62] And at Augusta University, a four-year university and also the site of the Augusta Medical Center, ENGL 1101 (called College Composition I) is described as "a writing-based course where students develop skills in analysis and how to use sources to support an argument. Students read and write in a variety of genres, culminating with a major source-based argument paper." Its course goals include a focus on Argument, Rhetorical Knowledge, Conventions, Use of Sources, and Writing Processes, roughly mirroring the core components of the Council of Writing Program Administrators (CWPA) 2011 Framework for Success in Postsecondary Writing.[63]

We might compare these differences in course descriptions on the local level to survey findings across USG institutions conducted in 1961, six years before the Core curriculum went into effect, as compiled by the USG Sub-Committee on Freshman English. The survey asked a number of questions about placement (including number of students required to take the course, and by what metrics), course requirements, texts employed, sequence of assignments, number of credits offered (at this time, under a quarter rather than semester system), and other course-specific attributes. Fifteen of the USG institutions responded. Some notable findings were wide variances in placement method; percentage of time spent on skill sets, including research writing; and final grade distribution. The 1961 survey makes clear that local pedagogies were important to each institution, and that they did not always allow for unified approaches across locations.

Though Georgia Tech's writing program representative(s) left responses to many individual questions blank in their return of the survey to the committee, they also wrote in extended answers to questions that did not ask for such. Two of these responses were free-form rationales for their course design(s), as follows:

> Two assumptions underlie the Georgia Tech freshman composition courses. A. That the high school graduate has studied and attained at least a fair competence of grammar, usage, punctuation, sentence structure,

paragraphing, [and] reading. B. That the skills of composition can be learned and improved . . . the Department of English does not seek to make professional writers of the Tech students; but we are extremely interested in helping them to write prose that is clear, sound in reasoning, logically organized, and effective—for these are major characteristics of the writing of educated men.

This 1961 survey, of course, was administered at a key time in Tech's history—as it began to integrate its student body to include African American men, and only nine years after it admitted its first woman student. Despite being a coed campus, the language of "educated men" remains part of the response, above, as well as an institutional philosophy. And the rhetorics of efficiency—to improve upon work that should *already* have been largely completed in high school before entering a highly selective university—is also present.

Still, first-year writing at Tech at this juncture is framed very much in the spirit of the institution itself: an institute constructed for and by (predominantly) white men who need to be "logically organized and effective" engineers. Such specific missions are unable to be fully executed when all writing courses, writing students, and by extension writing *programs*, are united by statewide metrics for transfer that pretend that they are, in fact, all the same. As the USG continues into the future, this sameness has remained, but with import shifts in the rhetoric used to sell students and their families on General Education as an enterprise.

IMPACTS, or, Rearranging the Gen Ed Deck Chairs for Workforce Development

Since CCN began in 1997, the USG has redrawn its institutional map a few times, in just the last ten years consolidating Albany State College and Darton State College (2015), Kennesaw State University and Southern Polytechnic State College (2015), and Georgia Perimeter College and Georgia State University (2016), as well as offering "specially tailored degrees and academic programs" across the "new" Georgia Southern University in Statesboro, GA (2017).[64] Throughout, CCN and the Core have remained as staples governing Gen Ed and intra-system transfer. But in 2024, the rhetorical framework of the Core curriculum was shifted to carry a new label, "Core IMPACTS." As the USG website detailing IMPACTS, directed to an audience of prospective and current USG students, explains:

Every student in the University System of Georgia engages in a General Education curriculum—Core IMPACTS—that provides a solid foundation for life, learning, and careers, and helps you build momentum to fulfill your academic, personal, and professional aspirations. Core IMPACTS introduces the different ways we have of knowing the world and connects you to the big questions that drive your future and provide the essential skills needed to succeed. The IMPACTS Core is structured across seven areas: Institutional Priority; Mathematics and Quantitative Skills; Political Science and U.S. History; Arts, Humanities and Ethics; Communicating in Writing; Technology, Mathematics and Sciences; Social Sciences.

It goes on to directly address the purposes of the new Core described above:

Students have often thought of General Education as a set of "boxes to check," but Core IMPACTS is not a random collection of courses to "get out of the way." Each one provides a key part of your intellectual, academic, personal, and professional growth. Together, Core IMPACTS provides a comprehensive grounding, fostering adaptability and resilience in your academic journey, while shaping you into an engaged and effective citizen and leader. (https://www.usg.edu/curriculum/core-impacts)

I want to applaud the USG for trying very hard here to both appeal to students and make Gen Ed sound like something far less utilitarian and far more progressive than it has been so far in the history of the system. It attempts to invoke the very principles of General Education that I have been advocating throughout this book, right down to hailing students as citizens and leaders. To also take on the "boxes to check" rhetoric of Gen Ed requirements is a very smart move, public relations–wise, in "selling" the Core to students. So Gen Ed advocates such as myself should be happy with this change, right?

If we look closely, however, at what has *really* changed in General Education as a result of this shift, and what still remains, it's clear that IMPACTS is not really so much a revision to what already exists in the Core as it is a renaming and reordering of areas A–F, with new emphasis on components such as "Technology." As a result, IMPACTS is a (potentially skillful) *rebranding* of General Education driven by a key concept on the rise in twenty-first-century higher education: workforce development. The website for IMPACTS calls this concept explicitly into focus when it notes how "the Core IMPACTS your future!":[65]

Core IMPACTS courses focus on developing skills and competencies crucial to your post-college success. Each Core IMPACTS course you take will include embedded Career-Ready Competencies—things like critical thinking, inquiry and analysis, persuasion, teamwork and problem solving—that help you build essential skills that are highly valued in the workforce and central to being prepared to lead in a complex, interconnected and changing world.

To support this workforce emphasis within Gen Ed, each USG institution must use the system-written statements about workforce skills in *all* syllabi for their courses within the IMPACTS Core. For example, in course syllabi for the Humanities and Ethics area, the required language to be included at the top of each syllabus is the following:

> **This is a Core IMPACTS course that is part of the Humanities area.**
> Core IMPACTS refers to the core curriculum, which provides students with essential knowledge in foundational academic areas. This course will help master course content, and support students' broad academic and career goals.
>
> **This course should direct students toward a broad Orienting Question:**
> - How do I interpret the human experience through creative, linguistic, and philosophical works?
>
> **Completion of this course should enable students to meet the following Learning Outcome:**
> - Students will effectively analyze and interpret the meaning, cultural significance, and ethical implications of literary/philosophical texts or of works in the visual/performing arts.
>
> **Course content, activities and exercises in this course should help students develop the following Career-Ready Competencies:**
> - Ethical Reasoning
> - Information Literacy
> - Intercultural Competence

The learning outcome was previously used for all Humanities courses in the existing Core, except at UGA. Units were instructed in late 2023 to add the above language to all course syllabi effective spring 2024, despite a lack of direction as to how "career-ready competencies" can or should be exhibited within individual courses in the Core. The rationale for the IMPACTS change was articulated in an email from then Executive Vice Chancellor of the USG, Dr. Ashwani Monga, in an email to USG Provosts (and shared down the line with other campus leaders) on September 27, 2023. His message read, in part:

> As you well know, the central issue is that many of our students see core areas A1, A2, etc., as boxes to be checked off. They mindlessly gulp down an

alphabet soup of the core before proceeding to the real meal of their major or, worse, are so disillusioned by the soup that they skip the meal altogether.... It is critical that we retain students by keeping them interested through the earliest courses that they take. It is critical that we help students graduate faster by removing obstacles to their progression. It is critical that we give them the foundation that enables them to do well in their major and eventual career. And it is critical that we make students have the learning and competencies that are fundamental to success in any career. The Core IMPACTS promises to move the needle on all these fronts.

Monga's use of a rhetorical device for emphasis, anaphora ("it is critical"), neatly underscores the four principles behind IMPACTS: retaining students, decreasing time to degree, providing a "foundation" for future learning, and providing "competencies" for their careers. His "check the boxes" metaphor is one we see later on the IMPACTS page itself, as noted above, and one that explicitly acknowledges General Education as a set of requirements that lack deeper meaning for students. On this latter point, sadly, he is generally not wrong. But the impetus for IMPACTS as framed *both* to faculty and administrative stakeholders and students is not to make Gen Ed itself *better*, such that students can appreciate it *more*. Rather, it is to make Gen Ed *sound* better so that students will stay in the USG to finish their degrees rather than "skip the meal altogether" as a result of Gen Ed being *distasteful*. Incomplete degrees equals lost revenue. So the *rhetoric* of Gen Ed must change, even if the components and values of it will not.

Additionally, the emphasis on workforce development—a concept I will return to in this book's conclusion—is clear throughout all aspects of this messaging, including the required syllabi language. How does a course, for example, in lyric poetry help develop "workforce" skills? How about one in nineteenth-century British literature? I doubt readers know these answers, because Gen Ed does not serve, in any measure, as preparation for careers *down to the individual course levels*, as the framing of IMPACTS would have us believe—and which, when presented to students, sets up unrealistic or just unbelievable expectations for learning. These further exacerbate, in turn, students' usual one-course-at-a-time approach to college, as discussed in chapter 1. Rather, a *holistic* preparation in textual analysis benefits students who can use such skills going into careers, just as a holistic preparation in principles of history and political science can help students in their lives as workers and citizens. Asking faculty to pledge that their specific course will meet specific workforce goals is taking Gen Ed to its ludicrous instrumental ends. It is not improving the student experience, and it is not making Gen Ed better.

The impact of IMPACTS—pun absolutely intended—remains to be seen. But its emergence nearly one hundred years after the initial USG consolidation in 1932 brings us full circle to education-as-efficiency in a large state system that has many of the same struggles as other similar systems in the United States. Again, Georgia is *not* unique; it is an example of where Gen Ed has gone and can go wrong anywhere in the United States. This is why we need to pay attention to it, including its latest pivot to promoting General Education as a digestible set of competencies that we as faculty and administrators must sell to students in order to save ourselves. In my next chapter, I'll narrate how national testing companies also promote efficiency, and its associated benefits toward cost savings and professional advancement of students, to a dangerous extreme, in the process putting a target on the back of Gen Ed courses and curricula on college campuses.

3
To AP or Not to AP

Advanced Placement and the Rhetorics of Exemption

This chapter continues the story of how student choice, policy agents, and local institutional actors all play a part in the rhetorics of Gen Ed. Now that we've discussed both the national and local histories of Gen Ed, in theory and in practice, since 1945, in this chapter I move more firmly into the present day with an examination of Advanced Placement (AP), one of the highest-enrolled, and well-known, pre-college credit programs in the United States. If General Education has an enemy, its name is Advanced Placement.

The College Board, which runs AP, has become the primary interlocutor in what I am calling the *rhetoric of exemption*, which argues for the reduction and eventual demise of General Education as a program of study on college and university campuses. Such rhetoric, as relevant to AP due to its massive scale of subject-matter offerings and widespread uptake in thousands of American high schools today, persuades the public that Gen Ed college coursework can be accomplished just as well while still in high school, and that students can prove their mastery of it through the two-hour AP tests administered by the College Board each May.

Further, since AP courses fulfill high school requirements *and* may lead to college credit, they are the ultimate example of the so-called (and highly valued) double-count credits in academia. The rhetoric of exemption is an aggregation of three other layered rhetorics at work across AP audiences, or customers: the rhetoric of *competition* in the high schools, of *remediation* in the colleges, and of *efficiency* in how the exams are evaluated and credits awarded. In this chapter, I show how each of these rhetorics creates the overarching rhetoric of exemption, which is the backbone of Advanced Placement as an industry in the United States.

AP and its close cousins that also provide exemption opportunities for particular groups of students at smaller scales, namely the College-Level Examination Program (CLEP, also administered by the College Board),[1] designed mostly for returning adults. Separate from these programs, and operating on an international scale, is the International Baccalaureate (IB) program,[2] designed for high-performing students and only offered at select high schools. Each of these are extremely powerful forces in the public and institutional discourse on General Education, as are dual credit / dual enrollment programs, which I discuss further in chapter 4.[3] But it is AP that most forcefully contradicts the inherent value of General Education as a campus-based, locally structured, and universally taught curriculum, and it is by far the loudest, largest, and most consequential voice for promoting the value of credit by examination.

I say this because AP, unlike, for example, dual credit programs, has a nationally organized rhetorical center in the College Board. DE/DC programs, in contrast, are dependent upon local high school and university partnerships and networks that vary from state to state in size and scope, even as they have a generally accepted purpose nationwide that positions higher education as failing. As Tyler Branson argues, DE programs are "an extension of accountability-based education reform initiatives that prioritize *student choice, time-to-degree,* and modes of education seen to be *efficient* and *cost-effective*" and that frame colleges and universities as "broken institutions" (*Policy Regimes* 102). DE/DC is also worthy of strong attention when discussing General Education and also first-year writing's position within it, since—as Christine Denecker and Casie Moreland further note, in the introduction to their collection *The Dual Enrollment Kaleidoscope* (2022)—"In terms of first-year composition (FYC), DE has the complexity of a kaleidoscope's refractions: it is here, there, and everywhere" (11).

The rhetorical import of AP promotes a wide menu of anti–Gen Ed student options: from a one-off for students to try to gain credit in a particular subject in which they feel they are proficient, to a massive double-digit credit endeavor for the student trying to bypass Gen Ed requirements altogether. The rhetoric of AP thus has both a micro and macro focus, depending upon how and where students want to use AP credit to compete with others. It thus differs significantly from IB, which requires students to engage in a fully articulated curriculum over multiple years in high school. IB programs are far more selective in their enrollments than either AP or DC/DE, and are offered far more sparingly in the US, given their international scope not keyed onto American economic systems or rhetorics of higher education. Though IB programs may be used for college credit, the IB mission statement stands in stark contrast to AP in that it "develops inquiring, knowledgeable and caring young people who help to create a better and more peaceful world through education that builds intercultural understanding and respect" (https://www.ibo.org/about-the-ib/mission/), a mission that coincidentally also strongly resembles the original aims of General Education itself.

Nowhere does the College Board state openly that AP as a program in the high schools *should* or *will* eventually replace offerings of General Education curricula on college campuses nationwide. But it is not hard to imagine that eventuality, as Gen Ed drifts further from its original democratizing goals and principles, as I discussed in chapter 1, or as common course numbering systems continue to flatten Gen Ed's purpose on local campuses within large state systems, as I discussed in chapter 2. Of course, most critical in the demise of Gen Ed's public value is its role as part of college's unaffordable price tag for many students, given the number of credits a full General Education program typically requires. Such economic anxiety is a key part of the rhetoric of exemption, as the price of the AP exam is far less than the price of a college course.[4] As I will discuss in my conclusion, in order to revive and embrace the original purposes of General Education, including tuning out and destabilizing the rhetoric of its various opponents—ensuring Gen Ed once again can become an equitable, liberating force for all students—we must openly acknowledge the possibility of colleges and universities ceasing to offer Gen Ed curricula *altogether*, and recognize how this would forever change the meaning of a college degree and perhaps the purpose of higher education itself.

This chapter is not designed to be simply a rehearsal of how massive the AP industry and other testing mechanisms have become, however, as those data may be found through various means online. I know, however, that the rhetoric of AP is one that each citizen encounters through what Kenneth Burke termed their own *terministic screen*—or how they perceive an event, phenomena, or action based on their own experiences and life situation. This means some readers may never have thought about AP in anything other than positive terms. My purpose, therefore, is to tell a different story: of the rhetorical import of AP, its uptake on college campuses, and its effect on students and parents, especially given the College Board's claims that AP is a tool for democratizing education and providing unequaled opportunities to students least able to afford college. In my storytelling, I argue against the College Board's claims, by highlighting the inherent contradictions in the rhetoric of AP in practice and illustrating how, in order to be effective as a business enterprise, AP must negate the value of its competition, that is, General Education courses on college campuses. I also discuss a specific example of the rhetoric of AP in assessing and granting credit for the AP Language and Composition exam—which, along with the AP Literature and Composition exam, makes up the two most frequently taken AP subjects, and also where students achieve some of the highest passing, credit-bearing scores.

I'll start this story with a personal one that I hope illustrates the on-the-ground effects of AP on students' ways of thinking about General Education, and college.

"Just Give Me the Test": AP and Student Choice

This story of student choices—to continue the theme from chapter 1—and Gen Ed exemption comes from my life as an academic administrator. From January 2016 to June 2017, I served as the faculty director of a quality enhancement project (QEP) on General Education, as a Faculty Fellow in the Provost's office at the University of Illinois Urbana-Champaign.[5] A QEP is a "special" focused project, usually related to student success, that colleges and universities have to do as part of their ten-year cycle of reaccreditation, which is still currently required by the federal government for institutions to receive federal financial aid, amongst other necessary services. This position gave me a first-row seat for Gen Ed conversations at the local and national levels, and campus challenges in making Gen Ed curricula both relevant to students and an enterprise that the public values.

Our QEP was called Grand Challenge Learning—so named after the "grand challenges" initiative promoted in higher education circles, particularly Engineering.[6] It was clustered around three Grand Challenge (GC) areas: Inequality and Cultural Understanding, Sustainability and the Environment, and Health and Wellness,[7] with small, interdisciplinary 100- and 200-level seminars that met one or more Gen Ed requirements across areas of study. Over my time directing the project, 373 students—mostly in their first or second year of college, and from majors all across our campus—completed one or more of these Grand Challenge courses for Gen Ed credit.

Thanks to a friendly collaboration with our campus admissions office, our program had a coveted booth at the university's annual summer orientation programs fair, wherein new students learn more about clubs, campus organizations, and in our case, Gen Ed course options, while visiting Urbana with their families to tour campus and register for their first-semester classes. If you have ever been to one of these fairs, you know that they are populated with curious (and sometimes nervous) students and parents who are often also overwhelmed by the machinery of college. At the GC booth, dressed in our best orange and blue Illini gear—to be intentionally casual and relentlessly friendly—we answered students' and parents' questions about what GC was and also what General Education was. As we did so, many parents would respond, "well [my child] has taken / will take that at our local community college, where it's cheaper" or "she/he has a lot of Gen Ed credit already," and then walk off with some GC and UIUC promotional swag. We also called out to students and parents passing by, an experience admittedly similar to selling wares in the center space of a shopping mall. My program assistant and I would ask, "Want to learn more about Grand Challenges?" or "Want to get involved in interdisciplinary learning?" or "Are you interested in completing your Gen Ed credits in a cool and different way?" This work was sales, certainly; however, the product was not a glitzy phone case or a radio-controlled stuffed dog but a thoughtfully designed program rooted in liberal education traditions.

One early June morning, a student walked up to our GC booth after hearing us call out our questions. But it soon became clear he wasn't interested in Grand Challenges, or even Gen Ed. He was interested in Gen Ed *exemption*. Our brief exchange went roughly like this:

ME: Hi! Can I tell you a little bit more about Grand Challenge Learning?

STUDENT: I have all my gen eds done already. I have AP credit.

ME: [keeping cheery] Well, that's great! But there are some course requirements at UIUC that aren't offered in the AP program, so you still have to complete them on campus.

STUDENT: No, I have all my gen eds done.

ME: Actually, you will still need to complete our cultural studies and our advanced composition requirements. Those don't have corresponding AP exams. We have GC courses that fulfill those. Want to learn more?

STUDENT: No. Just tell me where I can take the tests. I will take the tests. I've taken all the other tests. [moving closer to me now, and speaking emphatically] PLEASE GIVE ME THE TESTS.

ME: But there *are* no tests for those subjects, so...

STUDENT: I just want the tests [walking away, after scooping up a handful of swag].

Beyond the exchange above, what I also learned when meeting this student is that he was from one of our more affluent feeder suburban Chicago high schools where AP courses are widely taken, and that he had something in excess of 40 *credits* by exam coming into UIUC (or around fourteen AP subject exams, counting for 3 course credits each). This alone wasn't a surprise, since it was not uncommon while I was an associate dean of Liberal Arts, and while I was a WPA in the English department, to see transcripts of students who had amassed as much as 50 credits via AP, ACT/SAT, and dual credit / dual enrollment programs, which gave them junior standing upon admission.[8] What *was* surprising was this student's repeated insistence that *everything* had a test. His governing logic for higher education was to test out of everything you can, and enroll only in what you can't. And further, that Gen Ed was Gen Ed was Gen Ed, all of which is exemptible—so where was I hiding those other tests?

The import, if not the specifics, of my story may be familiar to readers who are also in higher education. My time as an academic administrator has taught me that rarely do our professional experiences exist in a vacuum; thus, it's important to share stories and use others' comparative tales to inform how we act locally in response. But I also believe such stories could not even be told if it were not for the omnipresence of AP curricula in American high schools, and the subsequent standardized tests that measure students' knowledge of this curricula, which in turn provides them with pre-college credit that reduces or in some cases eliminates entirely their Gen Ed requirements otherwise taken on our college campuses.[9]

The College Board is forthright in its transparency both about its curricula and the products that test students' knowledge of it, as well as the products' purported results, if slightly less so about their financial operations.[10] It has made a plethora of its testing data available to the public, some of which forms the basis for the statistical discussions in this chapter. Collectively, these data make various arguments for the unique, progressive nature of AP within today's higher education credit milieu. Thus, anyone with internet access can read about the various forty-seven AP subject exams currently being offered, the way these exams are generally structured and organized, the statistics on how many exams are taken annually and what scores are received, and the latest developments toward making the courses and exams more accessible to a variety of demographic groups in the US.

The College Board also does significant outreach to policymakers and university administrators, all designed to showcase current developments in AP, such as the development of improved subject exams or new research into student learning and testing that informs their practices. This outreach is designed to persuade curricular decision-makers to embrace and, wherever possible, expand their relationship with AP at their own institutions. Such sessions are also a means of opening the books on the operational and philosophical aspects of AP writ large. Having myself participated in two of these outreach sessions (in very different formats, led by different AP players) as well as one AP Language and Composition exam reading, I can confirm that they are also not designed for hearing open challenges to the AP system or its value. There is a very bandwagon-effect approach to AP's communications with the public, present in all aspects of the AP delivery chain: in exam scoring sessions held each June, in information and publicity for high school students and their parents, and in statewide legislative agreements and other published press, which is delivered by colleges and universities to prospective students.

To familiarize less knowledgeable readers with the *scope* of AP, however, I must briefly illustrate what kind of scale we are talking about when we talk about AP.

AP by the Numbers

As Dr. David Jolliffe, professor emeritus and former Brown Chair of Literacy at the University of Arkansas, used to famously say in his role as Chief Reader for the AP Language and Literature exams, from 2003 to 2007, "Advanced Placement is not Advanced Exemption."[11] This mantra echoes the original goals of AP, which when it was launched as a program in 1955 were to provide a rigorous set of courses for high school students at the highest end of the achievement scale. However, AP was also originally designed in part to "to avoid repetition in course work at the high school and college levels," a concept now taken to the extreme (College Board, "Brief History"). Hence, exemption rather than placement is how AP functions in wide practice some seventy years later, with hundreds of thousands of students each year taking exams that allow them to bypass core Gen Ed courses, often without placement into a higher-level college course in the same subject. For example, even as some students are exempted from Composition I and thus are able to move directly into Composition II in their first semester of college by virtue of a passing score on the AP Lit or Language exam, equally as many students may bypass Composition altogether if only one writing course is required on their campus, or if the AP credit on that campus is tied to the second-semester course. Such is the case especially when Composition I is framed as remedial, preparatory, or otherwise not designed for "well-prepared" incoming students.

For other college subject areas such as literature, history, psychology, or government, where sequenced required courses outside the major are more the exception than the norm, the entire subject area may be exempted by the relevant AP exam. This also applies to broad area Gen Ed requirements such as "Humanities" or "Social Sciences," wherein students have numerous options for credit, which is the more typical structure of Gen Ed programs today, and where students thus have choices in what they take within that requirement. AP credit often will come in tied to that broad area, not a course-specific one, as would also course-transfer credit from another institution. All such prior course credits are entered in this same section of a student's transcript, where they meet and intermingle as part of a student's overall academic record.[12] In my experience as an administrator explaining how credits transfer, many students have found such accounting confusing, and understandably so.

We also must remember that AP exams are open to *all* high school students of all ages, not just those who take AP courses, even though the College Board's mission statement regarding AP implies more self-selectivity: "The Advanced Placement® Program (AP) enables willing and academically prepared students to pursue college-level studies while still in high school." It further states that "The AP Program develops college-level courses that high schools can choose to offer," which are built on a set of standards created by AP, with individual teachers creating their own syllabi around those.[13] I note the rhetorical choice to specifically hail "willing" students as well as those who are "academically prepared," and to emphasize *choice* on the part of the high schools. This is not to mention the declaration that such courses are "college-level courses" by design, itself the critical selling point in making AP seem equivalent to Gen Ed courses offered on college campuses. As I will discuss, none of these stated conditions may be actually true, depending on the student, the high school, and the institutional pressures to offer and enroll as many students in AP courses as possible.

Though the majority of AP test-takers are, in fact, those who took the corresponding AP course in high school, other students who may be home-schooled, enrolled at high schools that do not offer AP, or who want to receive college credit for a specific AP subject not offered at their high school, may also take any AP exam without taking the corresponding course, so long as they pay the fee (which in 2024 ranged from $98 to $146, with $36 fee reductions available for students with "significant financial need").[14] Many states also subsidize AP exam fees for low-income students, paying those fees to the College Board directly. Moreover, there is no age limit for test-takers; students in their freshman year (ninth grade) of high school—who are as young as fourteen years old—can *and do* take AP exams, alongside high school juniors and seniors. This is because the College Board strongly suggests, though does not require, that students take the exam for the corresponding AP course immediately after completing it, and since courses such as AP Environmental Science are commonly offered in high schools in ninth grade, and AP World History, in tenth grade.[15]

This temporal span of test-takers is also important to remember in exemption debates, as it means some students will take AP tests that could exempt them from college-level work as much as *four years before* they enter college—during which time students' intellectual capacities are still (rapidly) growing and changing, as is their emotional and social development, like their corresponding abilities to appreciate and apply the concepts they are studying. This temporal problem is also equally relevant to math and scientific skills and other field-based knowledge that is part of a scaffolded curriculum, as students may be taking advanced coursework in these areas many years after they have "mastered" introductory levels of the same, resulting in a recognized acquisition gap that can negatively affect their academic performance.

The same problem of a knowledge gap could be argued for students who take AP Language or Literature in their junior year of high school (or earlier), are exempted by virtue of their exam score, and then do not take another writing-intensive course in college until sophomore or junior year (if at all). According to data from the College Board for the testing year 2022, 25,917 students nationwide took the AP Language and Composition exam in either ninth or tenth grade, and 78 students took the exam before ninth grade. Comparatively, 3,348 students took the AP Literature and Composition exam in ninth or tenth grade, with 9 students actually taking the exam before ninth grade. The majority of AP Literature exams were taken in twelfth grade (286,684) and AP Language exams in eleventh grade (453,442), matching the curricular schedule on which the courses are usually offered in high schools.[16]

Related to credit accounting, many students who took an AP course and did *not* take the corresponding exam, for whatever personal, financial, or logistical reasons, are also often confused as to why their A grade in an AP Language and Composition course, for example, did not give them college credit. When I was a WPA, I had to explain to these students that their grade alone was not enough for college credit, per the rules of the College Board. Such is a perplexing thing to students who, for example, also took another Gen Ed course at a community college campus, got a *passing* grade, and transferred that credit into their four-year university. In my experience, there are always some students who receive an A (or B) in the high school AP course and then receive a 1 or 2 on the exam and who argue (sometimes in tears, or in anger) that the course grade should "count." While I could not vouch for that course's quality or the student's knowledge as a result of it, I did accept that their course experience could have been positive, also resulting in a grade reflecting good to excellent academic work on their part—perhaps work that even prepared them in some measure for college writing. But my only response was always, AP is *exam-based*. Nothing means *anything* except the exam score.

To delve into a statistical snapshot about those exams, and the students who take them, here are some data from the College Board's most recent reporting (2023) across two publicly available spreadsheets: "AP Performance" and "AP Participation." Both of these may be downloaded from the College Board's AP site (whose website header or tagline is "Get the Most Out of AP," itself positing the program's maximal use value). In 2023, 19 percent of all high school students in grades 10, 11, and 12 in the United States took one or more AP exams. In real numbers, this was 2,471,209 test-takers (in that many students will take multiple exams, so "students" is not equivalent to "test-takers" in real numbers, only in percentages). A more specific, and contrasting—and hence important to highlight—set of statistics for the "Class of 2023" as provided by AP elsewhere on their site is summarized at https://reports.collegeboard.org/ap-program-results/class-of-2023. On this page, the figures for *public high school graduates* indicate 1,181,863 students took the exams, with 738,698 of those students receiving a 3 or higher on one or more exam, across "over 4.1 million tests taken" that year. This page also claims a total of 34.7 percent of all high school graduates took one or more exams in 2023, up from 31.5 percent in 2013. So, the differences in figures between these two reports appear to be measuring the full population of test-takers in 2023 versus just those who came from public high schools.

The "Class of 2023" page further states: "423,262 traditionally underrepresented students—including Black/African American, Hispanic/Latino, and American Indian/Alaska Native students—graduated in 2023 from US public high schools having taken at least 1 AP Exam, up 139,856 students from 2013." However, only in the "Performance" and "Participation" spreadsheets are specific student demographics laid out. These indicate that in 2023, 47 percent of test-takers identified as Asian or Asian American, 19 percent as white, 17 percent as Hispanic/Latino, 11 percent as Black or African American, 10 percent as Native American, 8 percent as Native Hawai'ian or other Pacific Islander, and 20 percent as identifying with "Two or More Races." These demographics have been fairly steady since 2013, with increases of 2 percent (white students) to 6 percent (Asian and Asian American students) across all racial groups, except those of two or more races, which was not tracked in 2013.[17]

The overall growth in the percentage of students nationwide taking AP exams between 2013 and 2023 was 29 percent. Per demographic group, the largest increase in test-takers has been Hispanic or Latino students (81 percent growth), followed by Asian and Asian American students (46 percent growth), and Black or African American students (25 percent). White student numbers have grown by 3 percent, and Native Hawai'ian or other Pacific Islander students have fallen by 4 percent (College Board, "AP Participation"). As an additional framework, the highest level of AP participation in 2023 by US state was Massachusetts, at 31.3 percent; the lowest, Mississippi, at 7.9 percent. For context, Massachusetts is ranked number 2 in the US for overall educational attainment by populace, whereas Mississippi is number 49.[18]

Measuring the number of test-takers is one data point for analysis. Measuring how well those students do on the exams is another. Again focusing on the ten-year period of 2013–2023, the mean score for all exams taken across *all* racial groups increased slightly during this period, from 2.82 in 2013 to 2.91 in 2023. Within each demographic group, Asian and Asian American students' scores have increased, from 3.17 to 3.41, followed by white students, from 2.99 to 3.07. For underrepresented groups, Black or African American students' scores increased from 1.99 to 2.12, and Hispanic or Latino students' scores increased from 2.38 to 2.42. Native American or Alaska Native students' mean scores have decreased slightly from 2.44 to 2.41, and Native Hawai'ian or other Pacific Islander students' mean scores have increased slightly from 2.36 to 2.40—though this statistic has only been tracked since 2018 (College Board, "AP Performance").

Take a moment to digest these numbers with me. First, they show that no underrepresented group taking the AP exams has an aggregate mean score at 3.0 or above across all exams, despite the College Board's various public statements outlining efforts to increase both participation and test results for such groups. Second, these data are compelling counterpoints to the whole-number data on AP scores, which on their own would seem to tell a different story about participation and success. For example, 832,422 students received a score of 3 on one or more AP exams in 2013, and 1,105,478 students similarly received a score of 3 in 2023—a 25 percent increase in the number of scores of 3 overall. However—as noted above from the two public reports—29 percent more students took the AP exam in 2023 versus 2013, and also, total tests taken increased from 3,370,563 in 2013 to 4,399,098. Thus, the number of chances for achieving a 3 also increased, in terms of overall test numbers. As I will discuss when outlining efficiency principles in AP, its reading process strongly encourages readers to grant scores of 3 or better on tests as much as possible, as the College Board is ever mindful of how its tests are perceived and valued if students do not "pass" them. You can't sell people a product that doesn't work.

Further, the percentage of students taking the exams is not the same as real numbers of individual test-takers. In the AP testing paradigm, subject tests cannot be retaken in the same year in which they were administered. Unlike the ACT or SAT, which can be taken multiple times in one year or season, AP exams may only be repeated the following May—which is also well after the student would have completed the course. As such, we can reasonably assume that the numbers above represent multiple tests either taken only once in that particular year by multiple individuals, with increases in number of test-takers rising as well as number of tests taken, or by students who took the test in a year prior and are now attempting to replace their score. We can also assume that each individual tracked took at least one exam, but we cannot know how many exams each individual took in total without delving into private student data for individual test-takers, which the College Board does not (and should not) provide.

Let's focus for a moment on AP exams and scores in Writing and Literature specifically, to look deeper into those aggregate numbers as specific to AP subject fields. In 2024, 54 percent of students taking the AP Language exam received a 3 or above (as compared with 56.1 percent in 2023); of those taking the AP Literature exams in 2024, 72 percent received a 3 or above (versus 77.2 percent in 2023). The total number of students who took each of these exams in 2024 was not available at the time of this writing, but in 2023, 356,000 students took the AP Language exam, and 562,000 students took the AP Literature exams.[19]

As noted above, a 3 is recommended as the cut score for college credit by AP exam. So at these rates, many thousands of students in 2023 were potentially exempted from at least one introductory writing or literature course—or from both, since it's not uncommon for institutions to give credit for *both* first-year writing and first-year literature on the basis of the AP Literature and Composition exam, likely because this was for many years the only one in English studies (and is still offered at more high schools than AP Lang). But statistically, the preponderance of students who received these exemptions were white or Asian American. It's also important to remember that a score of 3 is, in the calculations of AP, equivalent to a B-, C+, or C, which the College Board calls "qualified" (a 4, comparatively, is "well qualified," and a 5 is "extremely well qualified"; https://apstudents.collegeboard.org/about-ap-scores/ap-score-scale-table). The language of these scores is rooted in candidates meeting job requirements rather than measurements of intellectual accomplishment; I cannot imagine, for example, giving a student an A in a course and then declaring, "you are very well qualified, Sarah!"

It is also unlikely that WPAs, if given such authority, would allow a grade of C on "college-level" work done in high school to be enough to be exempted from the college writing course or courses on their own campuses. However, the College Board argues in response to this criticism (which I've heard its representatives say, firsthand) that courses transferred in from other postsecondary institutions for credit usually are accepted on a C-or-better (or D-or-better) basis, so a C on an AP exam should be considered using that same metric. Never mind that one metric is a two-hour exam and the other is a semester's worth of work on another college campus.

Further, many institutions are required to award credit for a score of 3, in compliance with statewide policies beyond their own local control (though in practice, some colleges exert local decision-making authority by only awarding free elective credit for a score of 3, and actual course-specific credit for a 4 or 5). Readers may see this as akin to policies for common course numbering and core curricula at the state level, as discussed in chapter 2. According to the College Board's online policy database, thirty-five of fifty US states have such policies, and "AP policies that grant credit for scores of 3 have grown 22% since 2015." The graphic provided on the AP website also shows how the other fifteen states have "institution-based credit policies" regarding AP, including common course numbering states such as Georgia.[20] In these instances, state lawmakers make the final decision on AP credit policies—not local campuses.[21] Campus stakeholders may be invited to such discussions, but once an agreement is struck, they are not able to countermand that entirely in their own institutional practices.

These agreements, as well as other decisions made by private institutions, result in significant exemption rates. For example, in 2024, there were 2,107 US colleges and universities that accepted the AP Literature and Composition exam for course credit; these included Ivy League institutions, large public flagship universities, private and public technical institutes, medium-sized and regional state colleges and universities, small private and public colleges, and two-year and community colleges—in other words, all institutional types. Of these total institutions, 37 required a score of 5 for credit (including Harvard, Yale, Princeton, Bard, Carnegie Mellon, and the University of Chicago), 493 required a score of 4, and the remaining 1,577 required a score of 3. In this same year, 2,058 US colleges and universities that encompassed the same diverse range of institutional types noted above accepted the AP Language and Composition exam for credit, with 34 requiring a minimum score of 5, 473 requiring a minimum score of 4, and the remaining 1,981 requiring a score of 3.[22]

What is less known is how many students nationwide enroll in AP courses but *do not* take the AP exams thereafter. There is just one such study, published in 2021, which examined students in metro Atlanta, Georgia, a large and highly diverse school district—which I would argue is statistically significant enough to extrapolate as representative of the nationwide patterns, for the purposes of this chapter.[23] Fazlul and coauthors found that 15 percent of these students who enrolled in AP courses did not take the corresponding exam. Their data indicate that the reasons include, first, the potential benefits of the exam not outweighing the fee to take the exam and, second, "a mountain of evidence on the behavioral and informational constraints that lead to undesirable educational outcomes on the path to and through college," as well as the fact that "some AP course enrollees may not know about college credit policies or how they can benefit from college credit, should they score high enough."

A more nefarious reason in addition to these might be that some high schools, seeing students' performance in the course, discourage them from taking the exam, as low test scores will bring down the school's AP average—which starting in 2023 is a metric rewarded by the College Board in the form of the AP Honor Roll for High Schools. This award goes to schools who have 40 percent or more of students enrolled in one or more AP class, but *also* 25 percent or more of students who receive a 3 or better on at least one exam. Also, as related to my point about the ages when students take AP exams in relation to their college entrance age, these award criteria further note that "At least 1 of those exams was taken [by the student] in 9th or 10th grade, so that students are spreading their AP experience across grades rather than feeling disproportionate pressure in any single year."[24] This remarkable rhetorical turn by the College Board both encourages AP enrollment *and* encourages testing at the earliest years of high school—purportedly to reduce pressure on students.

Each of these reasons, with whatever personal or political motivations behind them, track into further stratification of students in colleges and universities, economically and socially speaking, and result in the unequal measures of students who enroll in Gen Ed courses versus those who receive Gen Ed exemption credit. This is keenly illustrated by authors of the 2021 study above, who also examine the relationship between AP course enrollment and AP exams by student demographic in the metro Atlanta district, with these notable findings:

> Eighteen percent of the courses taken by students on FRL [free and reduced lunch] do not lead to an exam, compared to 15 percent for students not on FRL. Black students take an AP course but do not take the AP exam 23 percent of the time, compared to 10 and 13 percent for Asian students and White students, respectively [and] 18 and 15 percent for Hispanic students, respectively. (Fazlul et al.)

Using the above as a baseline set of data for understanding the scale and scope of AP in practice nationwide, let's now turn to how AP is marketed to (and by) high school students and their families in order to create a rhetoric of competition—one that enables if not dictates these socially stratified patterns in General Education, and that makes promises that are attended by lots of fine print, some of which is in invisible type.

AP in the High Schools: The Rhetoric of Competition

Just as General Education, as noted earlier in this book, is only as strong as the curriculum in which it is represented, the faculty who teach it, and the students who employ its lessons, so too is Advanced Placement as a national enterprise only as strong as its uptake in the high schools. Without students and parents being persuaded by, and willingly participating in, the competitive rhetoric regarding college placement and subsequent career success that AP promotes, its influence would be negligible. If you don't believe me, consider the precarity at present of the SAT and ACT exams as an enterprise as more and more selective US institutions drop these as requirements for college admissions.[25] Though students can take the AP exam without taking the corresponding course, as noted above, and though there exist a variety of prep resources, including individual AP exam practice books, available for students to study for the exam independently, AP is not a system that itself survives without the active partnership with American high schools (sometimes formed under duress) and the students who attend them.

It is key to again recall that *only the test matters* in the AP paradigm. As also noted earlier, taking an AP course may provide a student with so-called college-level work and may itself be the best option at a given high school for students who are college-bound. AP courses may also help students prepare for the rigors of college-level work even if they do not receive exam credit. As an added benefit, in many high school grading systems, AP courses are also weighted more heavily (on a special, weighted 5.0 versus a typical 4.0, grading scale) than other course subjects, meaning that a grade of A in an AP course will more positively affect a student's GPA than an A in a non-AP course.

But the course alone does not give a student corresponding college *credit*. Nor is the exam constructed as a formative assessment of a student's knowledge and ability; as I outline at the end of this chapter, the AP exam and its scoring are symbolic of the efficiency principles that rule overall College Board operations. With the exception of portfolio-based courses in AP Studio Art and AP Capstone and Research, the exams themselves are extremely truncated summative assessments of whatever the College Board and its various educational consultants believe are the key aspects of the AP course content that should be tested that year.[26]

As has been my observation throughout this book, the high cost of college is certainly one condition that fuels the money-saving rhetoric behind Gen Ed detractors, and is also one that AP espouses. As Kellie Sharp-Hoskins argues in her 2023 *Rhetoric in Debt* regarding student loans, debt itself "does not signify unilaterally as *immoral*. It is warranted, in part, when present cost is weighed against future benefit and the latter is deemed worthy. Thus, specific debts can signify as *investments* in the future, while others indicate poor decision-making" (54). Insofar as student loan debt starts with college enrollment, it's common to see arguments for saving money squarely focused on General Education coursework. The simple calculation is, if a student can do this work in high school, why should parents (or students) pay for them to do it in college? Such expenses, if we apply them to Sharp-Hoskins's argument, exhibit poor decision-making, even if many citizens agree that college is a sound—if expensive—investment.[27]

As Sharp-Hoskins argues further, though student loan debt began to be an accepted part of college costs in the 1980s, as state funding for higher education began to shrink, "the rhetoric of students did not ascend to crisis until it began effecting white, middle class Americans categorically" (58). We might say the same about the rhetorics opposing General Education; it's not perceived as a crisis for students of color and others from marginalized or economically disadvantaged populations to have to take Gen Ed courses (including those in writing and mathematics deemed "preparatory"). But it *is* a problem, rhetorically speaking, if the dominant classes also have to take such courses and pay for them. General Education is in this paradigm *remedial* and also race- and class-specific, as I argued in chapter 2 as well.

Financial exigence alone does not drive AP enrollments, as students from all economic strata enroll in AP courses and take AP exams, including those whose families are fortunate enough to be able to pay for their student's college costs in full. I count my own family among these; as I discussed in the introduction, my daughter earned multiple AP credits despite her understanding of our financial situation. What drives the enrollments in many families of means is the *perceived value* in undertaking those costs in lieu of using that tuition money for something else. AP simultaneously encourages students to use AP credit to shorten their time in college *and* to fill the freed-up credit-hour spaces they gain from Gen Ed exemption with other (implicitly more valuable) educational opportunities. Those other opportunities themselves also are the hallmarks of a competitive profile students may offer to employers upon graduation, or to graduate schools.

The rhetoric of AP is thus firmly rooted in competition, in setting oneself apart from the "others" who also vie for spots at top colleges and universities, and in American society more generally. This rhetoric of exemption used by AP attempts to engage multiple socioeconomically defined audiences at once, all the while purporting that the ultimate value of AP is universally applicable across entire diverse student bodies. Here, the baseline assumption is that "everyone" goes to college, come hell or high water. As noted in chapter 1, that is still far from the case, for both good and bad reasons.

This race to the top in college achievement is not one for which I blame AP alone; the increase in anxiety among college-age students over economic security, especially post-COVID but really traceable to the start of the twenty-first century, has led to unhealthy pursuits related to higher education. To very generally summarize current national conditions that characterize postsecondary education at the time of this writing, which I do not foresee changing any time soon: college applications are (way) up, admission rates at more selective colleges and universities are (way) down, college is (way) more expensive than ever due to reduced federal and state funding opportunities (which will only reach disaster proportions if the US Department of Education is actually dismantled),[28] and as a result, students are seeking any means necessary to secure a college degree, or the equivalent, to even be eligible for entry-level positions in their desired career fields (chiefly but not exclusively engineering, business, and computer science). AP reflects, and indeed is *dependent upon*, these wider socioeconomic conditions; in other words, the rise in AP programming and student participation, and AP's rhetoric of competition, is causation aided by correlation. AP is framed via an argument of competitive *value* for college-bound students who are shaping their academic records, admission packets, and financial futures.

Outwit, Out-Enroll, Outlast: AP as Competitive Advantage

The ultracompetitive conditions that enable the business model for pre-college credit programs have come under scrutiny by admissions experts in recent years, especially those who research student well-being. In 2013, Kretchmar and Farmer (University of North Carolina, Chapel Hill) contended that everyone involved in the process of college admissions has "perhaps lost sight of the original purpose of these [AP, IB, DE] programs, and high-school rigor has instead become less about preparing for college and more about comparing students to one another and using the comparison to decide who gets in" (29). They further noted that while "students who take at least five AP, IB or DE courses typically outperform those who don't take any . . . because the results are based on observational data—that is, students were not randomly assigned to take different numbers of college-level courses in high school—causal inferences cannot be made" (32). They argue that students who take a high number of AP courses bear a cost of lost opportunities in high school, as well as possibly lesser preparation for the rigor, and positive overall benefits, of college itself:

> Many students engage in the practice of extreme programming—taking 10, 15 and sometimes as many as 20 college-level courses during their high-school careers. To maximize the number of college-level courses they take, these students sometimes sacrifice other activities that might arguably make them better students and their lives more enjoyable and fulfilling. They can also come to their colleges and universities exhausted and unprepared for the challenges and opportunities they will face. (29)

Such cautions are also noted by a group of researchers at Stanford University who make up the advocacy group Challenge Success, whose 2013 brief asks several key questions about AP programming, including whether it increases a student's chances in college admissions. Acknowledging the amplified push by high schools to offer and enroll more and more students in AP courses, and as part of their overall analysis of AP's promised benefits, they warn that "the research isn't clear on whether AP experience alone increases the probability of college success" and that such metrics are "problematic from an equity standpoint, as students from rural, small, or lower socioeconomic status schools tend to have less access to AP courses." They further assert that "the claim that taking AP courses boosts a student's chances of college admission needs some qualification: it depends on the college" (5)

Such questions about AP's benefits are succinctly echoed in a 2023 commentary published by the Brookings Institute (Kolluri et al.), in which economics professor Stephanie Owen posits the following, emphasizing the difference between course completion and exam results, and also the disparities between privileged versus disadvantaged students in AP success-based discussions:

> Although students who take AP courses or exams tend to have better outcomes than those who don't, knowing the "effect" of AP requires more careful analysis. The types of students and schools who participate in AP tend to be higher achieving to begin with, so it would be naïve to conclude from simple comparisons that AP causes students to do better in college. The best causal evidence suggests that AP *can* benefit students... however, the positive effects of AP are largely tied to taking and doing well on the associated exams. Simply taking AP courses without taking and passing the exams seems to have no effect on outcomes... and many who take the exam do not receive a passing score. The disparities between course- and exam-taking are particularly pronounced for the most disadvantaged students.

Among the researchers who have done analyses of how (and whether) AP works in high schools, how it is sold to students and parents, and where its shortcomings lie, is Dr. Annie Abrams, whose insightful 2023 book *Shortchanged: How Advanced Placement Cheats Students* stems from her perspective as a teacher of AP English courses in a private high school (Bronx Science). Abrams declares that the College Board is "closing in on ownership of a national curriculum that not only holds high schools, but also universities, to the company's academic standards and its philosophy of education" (6). She further contends that

> the Advanced Placement program's spread may sound like a step forward in terms of educational justice, but it represents a hoarding of power and wealth and the destruction of some of the "cultural values" *Brown v. Board of Education* sought to protect. As wealthy private schools and top-ranked colleges stop participating, public school students' success in the program relies on conformity to the increasingly rigid expectations of a powerful centralized authority. The College Board's approach to education is undemocratic. (16)

Indeed, the College Board's philosophy and centralized control is clear in its sole authority over the outcomes of AP courses and the metrics used to measure whether students have achieved them. As I noted earlier, the statistics regarding AP coursework and exam results show clear discrepancies between the equalizing message of AP and the demographic results of its exams, which result in a bifurcated enrollment in Gen Ed courses on campuses. And of course, AP does not measure how well students have mastered *an actual college course* offered by a particular institution, nor does it measure how well a student understands the teachings of said course in the context of their overall degree, or a larger program of General Education. It only measures whether the student met the standards as set forth by the exam. In this way, the College Board's philosophy of education is easily divisible from specific pedagogical practices and their associated assessments on actual college and university campuses.

Abrams's contentions about the nature and import of AP in high schools today is grounded in her historical analysis of how AP has morphed into something that takes up only the most elite aspects promoted by its postwar founders. Abrams carefully charts the advent of AP in the context of the Redbook's and Harvard's aggressive attempts to build a more informed and educated democracy as a prophylactic against communism and other dangers facing postwar America. Abrams illustrates how AP was designed to streamline requirements for top students—especially wealthy white males—and positions it within discussions of the Kenyon Report and of higher education as key to a lasting democracy between WWII and the mid-1960s. As she notes, the AP program was summarily (and ironically) rejected by many on Harvard's own campus; for example, a faculty member in 1961 commented in *The Crimson* that "Liberal education should not be viewed as a prison term with one-fourth off for good behavior" (qtd. on 71).

Despite these significant obstacles in regarding AP as equivalent to an equalizing college course experience, and despite the risks to student well-being that the hypercompetitive nature of AP poses, the College Board's rhetorical authority still has a clear hold over American high school students and families. This results in a blind trust of AP's promises of an edge over one's peers, even as such rhetoric of competition is devoid of any local context(s) or considerations posed in external, critical studies of the curriculum.

One example of this rhetoric is in a one-page, downloadable flyer by the College Board called "Benefits of Taking the AP Exam," with the tagline "AP can benefit your teen in many ways" (https://apcentral.collegeboard.org/media/pdf/benefits-of-taking-ap-exams.pdf). In this four-color, easily digestible and printable document directed at parents, the three bulleted tags in all-capital letters are STAND OUT, SAVE TIME, and SAVE MONEY, as follows:

> **STAND OUT:** Taking an AP course and exam is a great way to stand out to colleges. All AP Exam scores show colleges your teen is serious about their education, willing to take on a challenge, and has completed college-level work.
>
> **SAVE TIME:** By earning advanced placement your teen may be able to skip introductory college courses, freeing up time in their schedule to pursue a double major, study abroad, or take part in an internship or other special program.
>
> **SAVE MONEY:** AP credits can help lower college costs. Some students even graduate college early because of the credits they earn in high school through AP.

At the top of this flyer is a photo inset of a student, "Melissa," who is quoted as saying, "The great thing about taking an AP exam is that I was able to earn *15 college credit hours* which is equivalent to an entire semester." Melissa is noted as being an "AP Alum" now enrolled at Columbia University, whose most recent acceptance rate (for the class of 2028) was 3.85 percent (Hamilton and Spurr, "Columbia Admits 2,319 Students"). Below Melissa's photo is the assurance that "Regardless of your teen's score, preparing for and taking an AP Exam sharpens the skills they need to transition from high school to college." This flyer also provides a link to free AP resources and encourages parents to have their teens watch the "Daily Practice Sessions" provided by AP, in order to prepare for the various year-end exams across subjects.

There is much to analyze in this deceptively simple document. Clearly it hits on the three "pain points" for parents and students: costs, time, and admissions anxiety. But by featuring Melissa, and communicating that she "saved" an *entire semester* of college, the message also works with a sophisticated integration of purposes. As a private, elite university located in one of the most expensive cities in the United States, Columbia University's 2024–2025 total cost of attendance—the figure used by institutions to communicate full costs, and which includes tuition and fees, estimated housing and food costs, and other related expenses—is $93,417, comparable to the cost of attendance noted for the University of Pennsylvania in chapter 1. A back-of-the-napkin calculation of one semester of Melissa's total costs thus would be $46,708. Since she has a semester's worth of AP credits, she could knock off that figure from her total bill for her degree, by graduating one semester early. However, the flyer also lets parents know that this extra savings of time can be *repurposed* to a double major, study abroad, or an internship. So, as the message's logic goes, you can shave off a semester of *college* with AP credits. But really, you can shave off a semester of *General Education* with AP credits, to be used for something else implicitly more important to your teen's education, especially if you don't need to save money. If we recall my brief discussion of Penn student choices in enrollments over time, we can see parallels here between course choices and overarching economic rationales *against* Gen Ed.

Perhaps the shrewdest choice made in this flyer, however, is to include a student who was admitted to Columbia, as a representative sample of implicit success for all test-takers. Here the clear message is, AP can help you get into colleges where statistically speaking, virtually no one does. For the class of 2028 (Fall 2024), Columbia admitted 2,310 of 60,248 applicants, which was actually slightly *less* than its acceptance rate over the previous year by 0.05 percent—a figure that may seem meaningless to many readers, but in practice means fewer real students in an already ridiculously small pool of admission offers. In June 2024, *US News and World Report* ranked Columbia #12 on its list of best national universities; each of the top 12 on this list is an elite private university, with Princeton University currently being ranked #1.

I don't know Melissa, but I am going to hypothesize that it wasn't only or primarily her AP credits that helped her to "stand out" to Columbia, given its venerable reputation. Making Melissa the literal poster person for AP credit showcases a student whose college admissions results represent only the tiniest fraction of high school graduates nationwide, with the implicit message that it was AP that got her there. Such messaging is a dog whistle to parents who want their students to attend elite universities, whether or not they have the funds to send them there. History also foretells here: In 1959, when General Education programs were being put in place by colleges and universities nationwide as an equalizing measure for higher education, social critic Vance Packard termed people who relentlessly sought better conditions for themselves and their families in a competitive arena of American material culture "strivers," a term that Jennifer Morton, cited in chapter 2, also employs when discussing first-generation college students and their conflicting ethical paradigms regarding upward mobility.[29] Economic conditions in the US today make virtually everyone a striver, especially in pursuit of the perceived maximal benefits of an elite college education. And the College Board knows it.

Ironically, perhaps, Columbia is one of several elite private institutions that does *not* accept AP for exemption of all or even most Gen Ed subjects. While it does provide exemption for certain languages in the AP program (French,

German, Latin, and Spanish), students who receive a score of "5" on their English Language or Literature exams instead receive something Columbia calls "advanced credit" with "no exemption." The same is the case for AP exam credit for both History and Physics.[30] Indeed, the more elite the university (and the more specialized and integrated its core curriculum is, including coursework that crosses disciplinary boundaries and thus is more difficult to match to subject-specific exam credits), the less likely that it will accept AP credits for exemption of specific Gen Ed requirements. Instead, these institutions (including Harvard) accept such credits as Columbia has—for placement into a more advanced version of a course subject, echoing David Jolliffe's declaration from earlier in this chapter.

So, while Melissa may have earned a semester's worth of credit at Columbia, it almost certainly wasn't toward introductory courses in these subjects noted above.[31] What this might also tell us about how elite versus non-elite institutions view AP as an industry providing *equivalent* courses to their own is something that should be keenly noted by students and parents. The message such universities as Columbia are sending to AP is, our curriculum is better than yours, and it has the power, as a private institution, to declare this. Many other (public) colleges and universities do not. This does not make the declaration less true.

Melissa is also framed as an "AP Alum." Of course, to be an alum of an institution means to have graduated from it. Melissa didn't "graduate" from anything, as AP is not an institution. Or is it? Insofar as AP has its own curriculum, it also has its own levels of recognition for students, depending upon how many AP exams they take, and with what resulting scores. Such is yet another layer of AP's rhetoric of exemption—a set of awards scaled to how many courses a student can bypass via AP exam scores. The College Board calls these "AP Scholar" awards, which as far as I have been able to tell, have zero bearing on college admission decisions, even as the AP website claims that "The AP Scholar Awards are academic distinctions that students may cite among their credentials on applications, résumés, and so on."[32] Still, they are a savvy rhetorical tool that highlights collective achievements in AP *exams*, and encourages students to take more exams (and achieve higher scores) as well.

The AP Scholar program is outlined at https://apstudents.collegeboard.org/awards-recognitions/ap-scholar-award, and includes three levels—AP Scholar, AP Scholar with Honor, and AP Scholar with Distinction, plus the AP Scholar International Diploma.[33] Readers may hear an echo in this structure of levels of recognition at high school or college graduations—that is, honors, high honors;

cum laude, magna cum laude. To qualify for AP Scholar, a student must receive scores of 3 or higher on three AP exams; for Scholar with Honors, scores of 3 or higher on four exams *plus* an average of 3.25 across all test scores; and for Distinction, a score of 3 or higher on five exams, plus an average of 3.5 across all test scores. Each of these Scholar designations results in a printable certificate that students can receive by logging into their profile in the College Board's AP system website.[34]

These damaging and pervasive rhetorics of competition—which I submit also motivated the student whom I profiled in my personal story of Gen Ed at Illinois—are not entirely divisible from other rhetorics of AP, as I discuss below. Rather, they form the baseline for arguments supporting AP's links to student academic success, and by extension, student career success, all of which are dependent upon a college degree completed in a "timely" manner.

AP in College: The Rhetoric of Remediation

Though I have framed the rhetoric of AP thus far as one that fends off its many detractors, Advanced Placement also has its advocates, particularly in circles where public schools are anathema and where conservative politics aiming to separate schooling from governmental or other oversight prevail—as they do in the current presidential administration. Four years before Annie Abrams's critical study of AP was published, there was Chester E. Finn Jr. and Andrew E. Scanlan's book *Learning in the Fast Lane: The Past, Present, and Future of Advanced Placement* (2019), which unapologetically promotes the AP curricula as a great, elite product that struggles against various social and political conditions but still perseveres. The authors hail from the Thomas B. Fordham Institute, which promotes conservative ideologies about education, including school choice, and claims to forward "ambitious standards in all academic subjects, strong assessments of student learning, aligned and well-implemented curricula, and common-sense accountability for schools and children across the achievement spectrum; and high-quality charter schools and other proven models of educational choice, particularly for the children and families that need them most" (https://fordhaminstitute.org/about).

Finn and Scanlan characterize AP as a brave and sturdy soldier on the higher education landscape struggling to provide high-quality curricular opportunities for worthy students. Here is an extended example of their own rhetoric regarding AP, from their book's introduction:

> Delivering on AP's promise also grows palpably harder as the program expands and diversifies... [including] fending off critics who would rather devote all available resources to low achievers and struggling learners; retaining the loyalty of upscale parents who fear that their kids' experience (and advantage) may be dimmed by the inclusion of "those other" students; dealing with blowback from AP's democratization as some exclusive private schools and colleges begin to shun it; and contending with a surge of rival offerings (notably "dual enrollment" programs) that seem to promise easier access to surer college credit. (3)

The authors go on to frame the questions that structure their book, which will examine these battles in the form of an AP "biography—the clear-eyed and friendly kind" (5):

> How is the College Board handling such dilemmas?... As AP enlarges its footprint and extends its mission, how well is it preserving the features that made it worth expanding in the first place, particularly its unapologetic rigor, its commitment to liberal education, and its stealthy furnishing of quality education choices? How acute is the tension between accelerating proven high achievers and assisting a diverse population of kids to get a leg up on college? How effective is AP, actually, as in those roles today, as it evolves from a low-profile elite option to a big-time reform strategy for policy and philanthropy? (3)

With props to the authors for making their political positions crystal clear from the outset, as with the messaging from AP itself, there is much to unpack here—about social class, remediation, and the purposes of college. We can start with how the passage calls out "low achievers and struggling learners" in contrast to the students for whom AP was designed (children of "upscale" parents). It is true that AP was originally intended for higher-achieving students—and since has been widened to include anyone and everyone who wants to take the courses. This of course is a decision that increases the profit margins of the College Board and helps them sell their courses and tests to as many students as possible, as noted earlier. The authors here are opposed to such "democratization," however, not because those "other" students might struggle in AP or be promised college credits that they cannot get; instead, they are opposed because they want AP to continue to serve "high achievers" as opposed to a "diverse population of kids." This rhetoric is (not-so-veiled) code, in socioeconomic terms, for not just wealthy versus poor students, but also for white students versus students of color.

Further, the authors' championing of AP's "unapologetic rigor" and its roots in liberal education is worth noting, as the authors would seem to be arguing that AP has been dumbed down to serve a wider population who cannot handle, or does not deserve, its intended rigors. Again, I do not disagree that the AP *exams* are one instance of compromise of rigor—as I will detail later—as are perhaps some of the courses, though it is hard to define "rigor" in this case. Many AP courses—for example, APUSH, as Annie Abrams also notes—are filled with massive amounts of information to memorize and somehow sort and interpret in one or two semesters' time. My daughter found this "rigorous" from a pacing perspective that exhausted her physically and mentally, a common response from students taking AP curricula.[35] Regardless, the speed and content coverage in AP and its examinations is based on current efficiency principles on the part of AP, not because it has been proven that a wider population of AP students cannot *handle* more rigorous assessments than those offered.

Ultimately, as champions of AP, Finn and Scanalan frame diversity and democratization of educational experiences as the *enemy* of liberal education—to which I take obvious and serious exception, but which I need to acknowledge as being part of the wider rhetorical problem with Gen Ed in the United States. This positioning makes liberal education an endeavor for some but not all, and presents AP as an elite and "stealthy" educational product for, plainly, elite (white, upper-class) students who attend "exclusive private schools and colleges"—a group of institutions that the authors fear will abandon AP if it becomes too much for "those other" students. Such flies directly in the face of the principles of the architects of General Education, aka liberal education, curricula—also white men, also privileged, yet invested in equitable means for educating all students, even if we include the AP program as part and parcel of early Gen Ed–related initiatives.

Finn and Scanlan's positioning illustrates long-standing issues in what Jack Schneider terms the "tug of war" regarding Advanced Placement's status. Schneider summarizes what was then the problem, AP courses as a *credential*, observing that "as more college and university applicants submitted transcripts filled with AP courses, the credential value of AP was weakened. . . . The result has been that while many schools in underserved communities are still playing catch-up, many of the US's 'best' high schools are dropping AP entirely" (814). Schneider reports that "In 1969, only 14% of high schools had students taking AP exams, and over half of the schools that had students taking the exams had fewer than 10 doing so" (820). Indeed, in 1986—when I was a senior in high school taking AP Literature and Composition, one of only two AP courses offered at my Midwestern high school—there were 7,201 schools and 231,000 students participating in AP. That number would "explode," in Schneider's terms, by 40 percent between 1990 and 2000 (821; 822).[36]

Schneider surmises that "The College Board's attempt to tighten restrictions on what can and cannot be labelled AP may be effective in maintaining the standard of the AP curriculum. That alone, however, may not be enough to control damage to the AP brand. . . . Nor will it address the fact that, as it has expanded, AP has lost its exclusivity" (824). Schneider concludes that given these various issues as well as AP outcomes for various groups, "Advanced Placement, like many other promising school reforms in the US designed to address inequities in education, has failed to level the playing field" but still remains an attractive option for students from lower-income families or low-resource high schools who need any kind of advantage for college admissions (828). Such a problem is where rhetorics of remediation take full hold, on the part of AP supporters and anxiety-fueled students and parents.

AP and its supporters promote a rhetoric of *remediation* by claiming that students who get credit for AP courses and thereby bypass General Education requirements are *on track* as college students, as they avoid the "repetitive" work that General Education provides. In contrast, the students who lack such credits and take those Gen Ed courses—are by definition *remedial*, as they are repeating work they already did in high school. This would include, incidentally, a very *wide* range of students—from those who truly are doing preparatory work in college, to students who did not take AP courses but who are otherwise fully prepared for college-level work, to any student who took an AP course or courses in high school but did not get college credit via the AP exam. Given the rates of AP credit earned by students of color, the group being exempted from General Education coursework and thus being labeled "on track" is majority white (and Asian), leaving the majority of the populace enrolled in Gen Ed courses to be everyone else—including first-generation and low-income students. Or in Finn and Scanlan's terms, "those other" students.[37]

Such rhetoric of remediation may be also reinforced by universities themselves, in their messaging about Gen Ed requirements. For example, the University of North Carolina system's page on AP credit both affirms their adherence to the "3 or better" rule for AP credit discussed earlier in this chapter, and the value of AP more generally, in its role in "promot[ing] student success in higher education":

Under this policy, students who earned a score of "three" or higher on their AP exams will receive credit from all 16 universities within the System.... By establishing a uniform threshold for credit on AP exams, this policy gives more students access to college-level coursework even before they've graduated from high school. Because the State of North Carolina funds these exams, students essentially earn free credits towards a bachelor's degree for every AP exam score of "three" or higher. With this policy in place, students acquire credits faster, graduate on time, and enter into the workforce sooner. (University of North Carolina System, "Understanding")

Embedded in this statement are three assumptions. First, college should be completed as quickly as possible so that students can start their postgraduate careers. Second, that *without* AP credits, students will not graduate "on time." And third, that the acquisition of credits is a timed race, not a scaffolded learning process—and that AP helps students go "faster" to win it.

The University of Wisconsin, Madison, has a similar statement on their Office of the Registrar page, wherein they specifically name General Education as well:

The University of Wisconsin–Madison grants advanced credit for the successful completion of college-level course work while in high school and for high achievement on Advanced Placement (AP), GCE Advanced Level (A-Level), Cambridge Pre-U, International Baccalaureate (IB), and College-Level Examination Program (CLEP) exams. Credits earned may be awarded toward general education requirements, degree requirements, or elective credit. The purpose of awarding advanced credit is to recognize advanced high-quality work, to preclude the duplication of courses, and to provide increased flexibility for students who wish to complete two majors, earn a certificate, or graduate early. (https://registrar.wisc.edu/credit-by-exam/)

Such messaging about AP's value is even more directly addressed to students on the website for the Minnesota Office of Higher Education, whose section on Advanced Placement explains why AP courses are a "good deal," with certain points emphasized (in bold below as in the original text) and additional FAQs, all framed for an audience that is wholly unfamiliar with AP as a curricular concept. The concept of "doing better" implies a lesser need for introductory (or remedial) coursework; the additional points about saving time and money are self-explanatory:

- The course work is college-level. **You may do better in college classes later because you'll know what to expect.**

- You take college-level courses in your high school. **This gives you a taste of college-level courses within your high school walls. Check if your high school offers AP courses** [link].
- Students have the potential to earn both high school and college credit **if they receive a qualifying score on the AP exam. This can save you time and money when you actually get to college.** (https://www.ohe.state.mn.us/mPg.cfm?pageID=327)[38]

These various institutional rhetorics are unsurprising given the level to which colleges and universities are deeply invested in time-to-degree statistics in relation to their national reputation, and given that these are three public universities who enroll a significant number of in-state students who may also be attending college locally in order to save money, as discussed in chapter 2. The percentage of undergraduate students who graduate from four-year institutions in six years—the current metric for "on-time" graduation in the United States—is carefully monitored at the institutional, state, and federal levels. Universities who exceed the national average (the last reported number for which is 62.2 percent, with women continuing to graduate from college at slightly higher and faster rates than men)[39] tend to openly celebrate such achievements. In contrast, institutions who fall below it are regarded as troubled, or even failing.

Universities also have invested in improving their completion metrics by other, more subtle means, including explicit sponsorship of AP teacher training designed to improve applicant profiles among students from state "feeder" high schools. Such has been a quiet practice for at least three decades. For example, archives at the University of Georgia show that in 1985, additional funds were requested to hold an Advanced Placement summer institute for high school teachers from across the state in order to train them in the teaching of AP courses across various college subjects. This request came from the UGA Director of Special Programs at the time, Gene Michaels, to then Vice Provost for Academic Affairs Virginia Trotter, framed as a benefit to the institution. Among the benefits articulated were recruitment of the "best and brightest students in the state," who would be taught by high school AP teachers—a group that therefore "have a favorable experience" with UGA. Since Oglethorpe University, a private college in Atlanta, Georgia, had a strong AP program for teachers already, promoted by a "slick brochure," the letter makes clear that UGA should follow suit and build on the inaugural program it had offered the previous year under more financially constrained circumstances.

Other documents in this archival file indicate that AP exams in Georgia were up 15 percent in 1985 over 1984, and that, given further projected growth across the southern region in AP test-takers, additional sites for AP teacher training were sorely needed. This would include "maintaining quality control" as the number of test-takers increased.[40] This document also shows practices in comparative states in the region, including Florida, whose public school systems received "additional state and (1.3 F.T.E.) for all students who score 3–5 on AP exams," which further illustrates my points above regarding the importance of AP to local high schools. Such growth of AP in Georgia continued in subsequent decades. A 2017 news release from the Governor's Office of Student Achievement, State of Georgia, noted that between 2012 and 2016, the number of Georgia test-takers increased from 68,259 to 84,697, with a very slight increase in the number of scores of 3 (54.6 percent to 56.4 percent) over this four-year period.[41]

This UGA institute also continues to this day, offered by the Center for Continuing Education and endorsed—as noted on the registration website, by the College Board.[42] In 1988, the University of Georgia won an Advanced Placement Program Award from the College Board, yet another recognition among a suite of such prizes described above, given to colleges and universities who have "a strong AP credit policy and statement of encouragement for secondary schools to implement AP courses and special recognition for those institutions sponsoring AP Summer Institutes for AP teachers to receive curriculum training."[43] This is one of many AP summer programs offered in person as well as online throughout the country, sometimes by geographical region and sometimes by specific institutions (for example, the aforementioned University of Wisconsin, Madison).[44]

The partnership forged between colleges and universities and the College Board therefore explicitly supports training of more qualified AP teachers, which in turn will result in greater uptake of AP programming at high schools, which in turn will produce more qualified applicants to said colleges and universities—and perhaps, implicitly, steer those AP teachers toward promoting the college or university where they trained to their own best students, come college admissions season, thereby increasing the enrollments and achievements of many in-state students, aligning with goals for this population outlined in chapter 2. Such completes a perfectly designed admissions circle that includes students of perceived superior ability and excludes remediation of less prepared students, that is, those who would not place out of General Education courses via AP exams.

There are contrasting views of such institutional metrics, however, in light of the "completion agenda" that abounds in higher education—present in the very name of Complete College America, and its local instantiations, such as Complete College Georgia (CCG), which has a broad and ambitious mission overtly tied to reducing or eliminating remediation in all postsecondary settings. As academics and other readers know, *remediation* is a dirty word in higher education, chiefly set upon writing and mathematics courses often populated by lower income students, students of color, and other marginalized students—including English language learners (ELL students) in institutions where separately designed courses do not exist for them. CCG's aggressive mission and action plan observes that "both of the two-year colleges in the USG provide remediation to 59% of entering students, and 14 state colleges provide remediation to 48% of entering students" (Complete College Georgia, "Completion by Performance"). CCG argues that "current methods of remedial education must be changed to meet college completion goals," as only 24 percent of students receiving remedial education in the USG's Bachelor of Arts and Sciences degree programs complete a degree within six years.

In response to these statistics, the CCG site states that Georgia created a "Transforming Remediation Work Group" that provided the following recommendations: "Define college readiness and take appropriate actions in K–12 to ensure that graduates are college-ready; Change assessment and placement policies and practices for students applying to college to clarify what constitutes readiness for success in the first year of college; Develop alternative pathways for students who are significantly behind; [and] Restructure traditional remediation using customized pedagogical approaches" (Complete College Georgia, "Completion by Performance"). Each of these measures seems to correctly point toward student support in areas where extra help is needed. However, none address the more holistic education of the student once they are admitted to college—only the restructuring of "traditional remediation" in order to prepare them for higher-level subjects. In rhetoric and writing studies, we would see the "stretch" model begun at Arizona State University to be one such restructuring; in mathematics, this method is labeled as co-curricular instruction.

How these programs scaffold to subsequent courses *or* fit into goals for General Education are not covered by CCG, which itself has a singular mission: more college graduates, in a shorter period of time, and the elimination of remediation. Part of this mission also includes a plan "to shorten the time to certificates and degrees through three areas of work: (1) expansion of articulation and transfer agreements (see appendix under 'Articulation Agreement'), (2) construction of a student-centered transfer portal, and (3) expansion of

Prior Learning Assessment [PLA]" (Complete College Georgia, "Completion by Performance"). Therefore, CCG is not just about improving instruction in remedial areas; it is also about shortening time to degree overall, including via credit for lifelong learning. As part of this plan, a stated goal is also to "increase by 20 percent the number of credits that students receive through PLA including CLEP, AP, IB, portfolios, exemption exams, military experiences, and business credentials." Increasing AP credits = less time spent in college = faster time to degree. We only need to fill in the blanks to leap from this equation to another: General Education = remediation.

Such emphasis on the completion agenda is exactly what regional accrediting agencies, the ones that certify institutions for ongoing operations and receipt of federal funding, have cautioned against, however. One such agency, the Higher Learning Commission (HLC), included a section of their 2019 publication *Defining Student Success Data Recommendations* that asks, "What are the implications of the completion agenda to the current conversation on student success?" It answers, in sum:

> The current conversation around student success as completion has privileged certain types of learners and behavioral norms for what a "good student" does. This leads to institutional responses that are at times helpful, and at others, unhelpful to the goal of increased completion and success. Current completion metrics do not capture the work unfolding within institutions of higher learning to support learners, focusing instead on the institution as the metric of success—meaning a student is only deemed successful upon completion from a particular institution, not from the various educational experiences with which they engaged along the way to successfully achieve goals from the system of postsecondary education as a whole. (6)

The stereotypical idea of a "good student" in American higher education includes many things—a strong work ethic, good grades, even (erroneously) good character. It often excludes students enrolled in remedial courses, or students who need additional academic or other support. The HLC's study further notes that "What is needed is an understanding of the students of today, models to support their growth and development, along with institutional responses that align with institutional missions as well as the students served" (6). They ultimately ask, "To what extent is the success-focus driven by institutional success rather than student success" (7)?

The importance of the time-to-degree metric for various stakeholders in higher education makes the rhetoric of AP all the more powerful, especially for students and families who cannot afford to attend well-resourced colleges and universities where they might receive well-funded, additional learning support and quality advising that will help them finish their degree "on time." This is particularly critical for low-income students receiving Pell grants, as those are limited to twelve semesters or six years of study, and other institutional aid packages designed to meet the resulting gap between the Pell and tuition and fees often are for shorter periods.[45]

When we layer this condition onto the general trend of more elite institutions *not* taking AP credit (or taking it only for select courses), it's clear that the dichotomy of success versus failure is also couched in the dichotomy of standard versus remediation, with those students possessing AP credits occupying the "standard" category in their progress toward a degree. AP also has had an explicit hand in defining K–12 college readiness through its "Excelerator" program, which in 2012 claimed "a suite of focus areas designed to determine the level of contribution certain programs bring to a district's college readiness infrastructure. Current focus areas include the Advanced Placement Program®, middle school and elementary school."[46] A 2017 summary also published by the College Board noted that "there are clearly articulated expectations regarding the benefits of AP and its curriculum framework that are communicated as early as middle school in order to foster a college ready culture in schools and with students and families."[47]

This means the concept of pre-college credit for General Education exemption, as well as for shortening time to degree and thus being "successful," is seeded by the College Board in the minds of students (and their families) *as early as the sixth grade*. As AP's rhetoric of competition and remediation trickles down into still younger student populations, the program is particularly reliant upon these early rhetorics of efficiency that advance its exam products to future generations.

As I will now examine, these efficiency rhetorics include awarding more "passing" scores across AP exam subjects, which allows for the widest uptake of credits possible.

AP (Exams) in Practice: The Rhetoric of Efficiency

In addition to promoting rhetorics of competition and remediation, AP also is significantly fueled by a rhetoric of *efficiency*. One could in fact argue that the other two rhetorics could not exist without this third one, as to be competitive is to use one's resources wisely and in a nonwasteful manner, just as to be remedial is to be repetitive, slow, and unable to do things right "the first time." But the rhetoric of efficiency not only undergirds the motivations of students and families, and governmental agencies; it also, and importantly, drives the measurement of students themselves via AP examinations and the conditions set forth for scoring them.

A primary site for examining AP's emphasis on rhetorics of efficiency, therefore, is in the annual AP readings, which currently take place both online and in person, populated by thousands of high school and college teachers of writing paid $30 per hour to score exams using a rubric set by the College Board and under the strict guidance of College Board officials.[48] Below are data from interviews I held with two AP Language and Composition exam readers from 2024, one of whom scored online from their home in the southeastern United States, and another who scored in person, in a convention center in Cincinnati, Ohio. Each are college teachers of writing. I have assigned them aliases—Dan and Julie, respectively—to allow them to speak freely about the conditions of the scoring sessions and the rhetoric guiding them.

Dan read AP exams for the first time in 2024. Julie read AP exams in person in 2024, as she had also done in 2019. In between these years, Julie also participated in two online scoring sessions from her home, in the initial years of the COVID-19 pandemic when scoring first went online for all exam areas.[49] Both Dan and Julie scored question 2 (Rhetorical Analysis) for the AP Language and Composition exam—the other two questions focusing on "Synthesis" and "Making an Argument." These "free response" questions constitute 55 percent of the total exam score, with multiple choice responses constituting 45 percent. Dan and Julie both read handwritten exam responses that were scanned electronically into a database by AP. Dan used his home computer, while Julie used a desktop computer at her table at the reading site.

I do not claim that all AP exams are scored in the manner or with the same rhetorics that my interview subjects describe below; I do not have data from other AP readers in other subjects such that I can make that claim. I also would point out that different AP exams are going to be very different in scope, by design; an exam on AP Calculus, for example, would be unlikely to have much wiggle room with right or wrong answers, or extended essays (though the extent to which points are given for "showing your work" may allow for leniency here).[50] Given the focus of this book on not just the rhetorics of General Education past and present but also how they affect postsecondary writing instruction as part and parcel of Gen Ed, however, my focus on the AP Lang scoring process is, I believe, an apt illustration of AP's efficiency rhetorics in action.

"Can You See It as a 3?"

I have only scored AP exams once myself, in May 2000, at the end of my first year as a new assistant professor. I read for the AP Language and Composition exam, though I do not remember which of the three essay questions to which I was assigned. I had also done other paid work for the College Board while in graduate school—scoring GMAT (Graduate Management Admission Test) exams on-site in New Jersey and via computer in Evanston, IL, and TWE (Test of Written English) exams on-site outside Oakland, CA. So when I was selected to read for AP, I was already well versed in the structures, strategies, and expectations of large-scale scoring. I had also worked as a writing placement coordinator as a PhD student and assistant director of composition, and at the time of scoring for AP, was serving as codirector of the writing program at my university, like many other college faculty also reading AP exams with me.

In 2000, AP reading was a week-long endeavor (Sunday to Saturday) in early June, with five hundred or so other teachers in a hotel in Daytona Beach, Florida, one of several AP reading centers across the country. The reading was a reasonably collegial endeavor that paid $1,200 plus all travel expenses, with all meals provided on-site—good money back then for a week's work outside the academic year. We read from 8:00 a.m. to 4:30 or 5:00 p.m. each day, with an hour break for lunch and one fifteen-minute break in the morning and in the afternoon. We were able to talk quietly with the seven other faculty readers at our table plus our table leader, who answered questions, provided periodic norming, and generally offered reading support. As a parting gift, we each got a T-shirt that said, "Life's a Beach, and Then You Read," branded with the AP logo, and a sturdy gym bag that my husband still uses as a carry-on for airplane travel (never let it be said that the College Board does not provide quality swag, per its own promotional rhetorics).

I came away from that week's experience both impressed and amazed at the efficiency of the overall process, and also dismayed at that same efficiency, including how little time it allowed for the kind of thought and care that writing teachers normally put into assessing student work. I scored hundreds of exams per day, a figure not uncommon for the more experienced readers working alongside me. We were held together by a strict, but holistic, rubric for the exam's total score on a scale of 1–9; exams that were awarded total scores of 4 and 5 were "borderline" in terms of quality and competency. I never knew how the math of totality worked in AP behind the scenes to achieve these 1–9 scores, however, we were each scoring student responses for just one question, on a scale of 0–4—neatly making a division between "upper" and "lower" half scores, a common assessment rubric, or paradigm.

Any AP reader from this time period—and likely ones subsequent to it—will recall the famous mantra of "Can you see it as a 3?" This question was asked in our periodic norming sessions in response to so-called "borderline" responses that teetered between competent (3) and not competent (2), with the open acknowledgment that a 3 was the threshold for college credit. The question was also repeated when a reader would ask a table leader about a particular essay that they found problematic. The framing of this question—which effectively asks, *how can you reframe your own assessment standards to fit the idea of this response being "competent" and thus worthy of college credit?*—is quite different from *do you think, in your professional opinion, that this essay is competent (3) or not (2)?* In assessment parlance, we would call this "reading supportively." In the context of AP scoring, it was a bit more forceful than that.

On the two ends of the scale where competency was more or less clear, a score of 0 would be given to any answer that was "non-responsive." An example of a 0 that stands out from my reading experiences was a student test-taker who drew a picture of a flower accompanied by the words "I'm sorry." Other students receiving a zero might have written on different topics altogether from the prompt, or simply complained about taking the test, or about AP, or about something else entirely—a phenomenon Dan and Julie both acknowledged continued in 2024, with Dan fascinated by the affective engagement some of these students would demonstrate to reach out to their exam readers. These "0" responses—which were and still are fairly rare—contrasted with occasionally insightful and engaging, and equally rare, mature responses to the prompt that easily garnered the highest response of "5" on the rubric, at the top end of scoring. Readers could score these fast—as they were "no-brainer" quality responses.

Yet the vast majority of the essay responses fell in between these poles, with some responses being very canned, or nonspecific in their examples and argument, or slightly to moderately immature. In my year scoring AP, many of these responses were given a 3—by me, and by others—which was deemed better than falling into the notion of "everything's a 4," a trap that commonly accompanies reader fatigue about halfway through the week's scoring. A 3 is at least *defensible*, as it is a mark of competency, but not of high quality, as noted earlier in this chapter, with AP's assessment of it being a grade of B- to C. These responses, and their resulting scores hanging around the vast middle of the scale, struck me as entirely predictable, however, given the typical range of seventeen- to eighteen-year-old students' writing abilities, especially in a timed, high-stress setting such as the AP exam.[51]

My own observations about student response quality, efficiency principles in scoring, and assessment practices of AP overall in 2000 were grossly magnified in my interviews with Dan and Julie in 2024. Both commented on a severely efficiency-minded scoring process; a curtailed community engagement amongst readers; a deepened concern for the lack of professional development and edification in the reading process; and a mixed range of student responses that in their cases revealed an extreme "teach to the test" emphasis rewarded in the scoring itself.

In my semistructured interviews, I asked Dan and Julie to comment on (1) how the AP officials at the reading messaged information and instructions to readers; (2) how messaging affected scoring, and how scoring was done; (3) the conditions of scoring, including hours, pay, and other structures; (4) the community of readers, or lack thereof, during the scoring; and (5) anything else that they felt would be important for readers of this book to know. Their responses were strikingly similar, even though they do not know each other, did not score together, and have different academic training that led them to their work as writing teachers (Dan has a PhD in rhetoric and composition, whereas Julie has a PhD in American literature).

The only real difference between their responses was that Dan's were still characterized by some bewilderment at what he had just participated in. Julie's responses were contrastingly informed by how her reading experience had changed from past in-person reading, and from more recent online reading experiences for the worse. I'll focus first on their observations regarding messaging and scoring, as those are most directly related to my arguments regarding AP's efficiency rhetorics, and then briefly discuss their observations about community and working conditions—which are also quite important to efficiency rhetorics, as speed and accuracy in scoring is dependent upon a workforce that wastes little time on community.

Reading the Exams: Alone, Together

Both Dan and Julie commented on the limited communication that they had with their table leader during the reading process, which negatively impacted their experience and their knowledge of where and how they might improve in their work. When I asked Dan about any communications he had with the Chief Reader, he commented, "I have never heard that term [Chief Reader] before." His only directives came from his table leader, whom he described as a retired high school teacher who spoke with his fellow readers at their (virtual) table twice during the week, via Zoom.[52] Julie, who scored in person, reported easier access to her table leader, and two visits from the Chief Reader: once on the first day to provide an overview of the scoring process and to go over rules for reading, and again on the third day, to let readers know that they were running behind in scoring (due to online readers at home scoring "too slow"), and so the in-person readers would need to start thirty minutes earlier and stay thirty minutes later in the day as a result (but would be paid for doing so).

Both Dan and Julie said conversation with other readers was minimal to nonexistent during scoring; Julie had the ability to talk with other readers on lunch hours and breaks, and in the evenings at the reading site. Dan had no such opportunities, as he was scoring from home. Julie commented that readers were upset about various messaging related to *pacing*; the AP officials had told them that if they read between 15 and 45 essays per hour, they were on target. Fewer than 15 was too slow, and more than 45 was too fast (as Julie commented this range was problematic, as "once readers at home figured out that they would be paid the same for reading 15 essays as reading 44, why should they go faster?"). Both online and in-person readers were warned of their pace periodically throughout the reading, through the computerized scoring interface. Readers were also given "stars," which appeared on the side of their reading screens, based on how well their scores compared with the second (or first) reader of an exam. Readers would receive the most stars for matching the other person's score exactly, and the least by being discrepant (more than one number away from the other reader's score—i.e., a 2 versus their 4).

Julie reported that many readers complained that these were demoralizing metrics, with many threatening to quit (and that one was dismissed before the reading's end, for either speed or inaccuracy). However, such exchanges between readers in the online setting were few and far between, because the Zoom messaging function was set to be operational only between the table leader and the individual reader, not between readers. Dan thus reported that he would see his star ratings go up and down in a sidebar while he was reading from home, but he never knew how to improve them, nor did AP officials give any specific feedback on his scores (though Julie and I agreed that a rating indicating discrepancy for someone who had been giving lots of 2 scores would probably cause them to just raise them to 3 scores for subsequent essays read).

At no point did Dan or Julie remember the table leader, Chief Reader, or any other AP official providing specific support on speed or perceived accuracy. Neither reported going over responses as a table, as would have been common in my AP reading session in 2000 and also in Julie's prior experience reading in-person in 2019. Instead, readers were left to interpret these metrics individually, on their own, even as many readers—according to Julie—had to "recalibrate several times" throughout the week in order to pass AP standards and keep reading.

Scoring the Exams: "Does it have any kind of thesis?"

In addition to being monitored for pace and accuracy, Dan and Julie reported that readers were strongly encouraged to give points "wherever possible" on all sections of the Rhetorical Analysis essay. In particular, they both commented that even though the scoring rubric for question 2 states that a thesis receiving one point "responds to the prompt with a defensible thesis that analyzes the writer's rhetorical choices" ("AP English Language Scoring Rubric Free Response Question 1–3"), readers were encouraged to give credit for a thesis statement if there was anything even *resembling* one—including a declarative statement such as "the author uses rhetorical devices," which do not promise or lead to an argument-based essay, but instead just reflect a statement of fact. This is because the score for the thesis section of the Q2 essay is either zero points (no thesis) or one point (thesis present). The quality of the thesis is not further evaluated. Dan and Julie also report a strong message from the table leaders to give points "as much as possible" across all three areas of the scoring—thesis, evidence and commentary, and sophistication.

However, whereas readers are encouraged to give one point rather than zero points for a thesis, they are discouraged from giving one point (versus zero) in the scoring category for "sophistication." As Julie reports, AP officials wanted "90 percent of test-takers to get one point for a thesis, but only 10 percent of test-takers to receive one point for sophistication." Indeed, the AP rubric's comments in the sophistication section state that "This point should be awarded only if the sophistication of thought or complex understanding is part of the student's argument, not merely a phrase or reference." This leaves the majority of the response's points coming for the evidence and commentary section, with a score range therein of 0–4. Julie and Dan also noted that scoring was accompanied by instructions that, mathematically speaking, a response will have far less chance of receiving a 3 or higher if it does not get that one point for the thesis statement.

Given the importance writing teachers place on crafting a strong thesis—as the foothold for the argument to follow—this AP scoring emphasis is, to put it mildly, against best practices. By emphasizing this aspect of the scoring and de-emphasizing points for sophistication, AP is also virtually guaranteeing an appropriately shaped bell curve of scores, with 5 being the least frequent, or the smallest number of scores on the curve. Further, Julie reported that an essay could be scored 0-2-0 across the three categories, but *not* 0-3-0. In other words, an essay had to be determined as possessing a legitimate thesis in order to get a score of 3 or higher.

Dan commented that he was told the "factual accuracy" of the thesis didn't matter, and the essay did not have to prove that the writer actually *understood* the principles of rhetorical analysis, despite it being the focus of this question. He also commented that midway through the week of scoring, AP officials sent out a PowerPoint detailing the results of the previous year's tests, as well as the percentage of colleges and universities in the United States who accept a score of 3 or higher for college credit. Dan did not know why this PowerPoint was shared, as it was distributed without comment through the ONE (scoring interface) portal. He assumed that it was to reinforce the importance of scoring essays at a level of 3 or higher, wherever possible.[53]

Community and Working Conditions: "Like working in telemarketing as a teen."

As noted above, Dan and Julie reported little opportunity for readers to interact with one another, especially in online scoring. Both also commented on the resulting lack of professional community amongst readers, and how this affected reader morale. Julie reported that the high school teachers in her in-person session far outnumbered the college teachers; she further reported that these high school teachers clearly held their students to high standards and seemed disappointed that the exam did not appropriately measure or reward the execution of those standards in the exam responses. Julie feels the exam itself "does a disservice" to the hard work of high school AP teachers and their commitment to student success. She further noted that her 2024 reading experience gave her far less opportunity to talk with the teachers and other college instructors about their experience. These observations echo much of Annie Abrams's arguments, above, regarding the quality of AP versus the motivations and expertise of high school teachers in their own classrooms.

Dan reported almost no opportunity for community, leading to his own disappointment that the AP reading experience did not live up to its professional development promises, and his comment that the experience was instead similar to his time "working telemarketing as a teen." He even noted that in comparison with the paid meals for in-person readers, online readers are given a total $35 Uber Eats credit for the week's scoring, which we agreed encouraged both isolation of experience, and maximal efficiency (i.e., don't leave your house for food, or stop to cook—just take a quick break to answer the door) that often characterizes such telework across industries. The purported social community and networking that Dan had heard about as part of the positive "lore" from other AP readers past was altogether absent. This was a problem for Dan, as he had signed up to be an AP reader in part because his home institution was reconsidering AP cut (minimum for credit) scores, and he wanted to therefore learn more about the overall process and meet other teachers like himself. He did not achieve either of these goals.

AP's Economies of Scale

Dan's perception that he was assured of having positive experiences as an AP reader is probably correct, as publicity for the AP reading experience frames it as a wholly beneficial one for potential participants, versus the efficiency-minded and somewhat isolating and demoralizing experience that it actually is in practice. In a flyer soliciting new AP readers that I received in June 2018, when participating in an AP "VIP" session for college and university stakeholders, the reading experience is touted as one that "gives teachers a chance to exchange ideas with faculty, teachers, and AP Development committee members; [e]stablish friendships within a worldwide network of faculty members; and [b]ecome familiar with AP scoring standards, which provide valuable knowledge for scoring your own students' essays." The flyer further observes that "Readers have described the experience as an intensive collegial exchange and one of the best professional development opportunities available."

This VIP session that I attended, spread over three days at an AP reading site in Salt Lake City, Utah, reinforced much of the three rhetorics that I spotlight above, and the principles of AP's mission that Dan and Julie reflected on during their interviews. The session was led by three AP representatives from the Higher Education Outreach division and one representative from the Professional Learning division. In addition to the aforementioned flyer soliciting AP readers, my fellow VIP participants and I—a group of seventeen college faculty and administrators leading undergraduate education, such as university registrars, associate deans, curricular directors, and testing coordinators—were provided with a folder packed with various documents promoting the value of AP. These included a glossy publication called "AP Student Success at the College Level," labeled "key research," as well as a personalized set of AP scoring data keyed to one's home institution.

Inside and on the back of the folder were student testimonials (again, with profile photos, like in the AP flyer featuring student Melissa). These testimonials seemed more rhetorically keyed to our administrator audience. For example, student Tyler says, "Your support of AP credit and placement allowed me to see a part of the world I had always dreamed of seeing and discover where my true passions lie." Student Roshini stated that "AP gave me an openness, work ethic, and focus that I've carried through to rigorous college courses." And student Lexi stated, "Because of all of my AP credits, I was able to dive straight into my major within my first year"—the latter likely aimed at showing good progress toward time-to-degree. I, on the other hand, read this testimonial and lamented Lexi's rush into specialized coursework, knowing that a significant number of students change their majors anyway before they graduate.[54] Tyler's statement must implicitly refer to using his otherwise Gen Ed requirement space to do study abroad or some other "part of the world," implicitly also more valuable than taking Gen Ed courses, and Roshini's statement implies that AP makes students into *good* students, as a positive cause-and-effect—echoing other rhetorics of completion and efficiency, above. Note that Tyler also uses the term "credit and *placement*," correspondent to administrators' awareness that the latter rather than the former is of greater benefit to their institutions' enrollment bottom line(s).

Lexi's testimony seemed to also key to the "AP Student Success" glossy publication in our folders, which stated that "students who took AP exams were more likely to have declared a major than non-AP students" (5), again showing that such students were efficiency-minded themselves. This same brief noted that students who earned higher scores on AP exams (3, 4, or 5) had "a higher likelihood of graduating in four years" compared with those who didn't receive those scores (College Board, "AP Student Success" 7). This, of course, correlates to the two groups' number of earned credits—but again, is a metric that focuses on college completion. Comparatively, the publication stated that "underrepresented students who earned a score of 3 or higher on at least one AP exam had a *higher probability* of graduating from college in five years or less" than students of the same ethnicity or socioeconomic status who did not take AP (8; emphasis added).

Our VIP folder also included an introduction to the (then) new AP Computer Science Principles exam, a handout on the "Rigor of AP, with a Focus on Academic Skills" offered by the AP Capstone course (which we were told was offered at about one thousand high schools so far and was partially modeled on the IB curriculum), and a separate preview booklet for the newly revised AP US Government exam. Our tour of the Salt Lake City site further included a "behind the scenes" look at some of the operations, including a preview of the (amazing) portfolio work submitted by AP Studio Art students. I recall that peek into students' work as being touted as one illustration of the "quality" of AP courses and students. Yet I believe these portfolios instead illustrated other researchers' observations noted above: that many students succeed in AP because of who they *already are*, not because AP *turns them into* high achievers (or artists).

Finally, we VIP participants were also given a sheet of AP "Reading Facts" to anchor our experience on the visit; this provided a year's data set we might compare to the earlier stats from 2013 to 2023 that I reported in the start of this chapter. The fact sheet claimed that in 2018 there were a total 5.2 million exams taken, by students across 22,500 schools, who numbered 2.8 million test-takers examining in thirty-eight subjects. This fact sheet also emphasized the scale of the business commitment by AP, as "reading logistics" included twenty-nine hotels for reader scoring and lodging, forty-five vendor commitments to support reading sites, 55,000 meals and breaks served, and 225 tours and visitors hosted. This work was done across four reading sites in Salt Lake City, Tampa, Kansas City, and Cincinnati, with approximately 14,500 readers working in person and approximately 2,800 readers working online (College Board, "AP Reading Facts").

My handwritten notes from the visit also indicate that AP officials at this meeting told us that 40 percent of all high school students in the United States take one or more AP course, but only 40 percent of these students get college credit by achieving a score of 3 or higher. Readers might recall that this participation figure was even lower in 2023. My notes also indicate that we were told that while 73 percent of seniors in rural areas have access to AP courses, in 2015, only 23 percent of these students actually took one. Our not-so-veiled job following this visit, as VIPs? To take this information back to our campuses and encourage more uptake of AP exams at our colleges, and with our feeder high schools, to keep improving these numbers. We were also to report on the vast research that AP officials do to improve courses, exams, and students' experiences. I left feeling skeptical that this was a job I wanted to accept.

Such a massive operation as AP certainly cannot function without tightly controlled efficiency measures. Sometimes these measures fail, of course, as when AP exams are lost in transit, or exam score reporting goes awry, or profit-growing measures end up violating students' rights to privacy.[55] But these economies of scale that undergird AP are anathema to those of us who teach writing and administer writing programs, and who celebrate the scaffolded, human-centered messiness of learning across all high school and college subjects, and vice versa. Real professional development is appropriately complex, as is student learning; both involve dialogue, scaffolded opportunities, reflection, and review. Sometimes students change majors. Sometimes Gen Ed courses lead to new areas students did not know they would love. Sometimes college isn't a linear process from start to finish. Sometimes systems break down, because such is to be human and experience failure. In the AP machinery, there is no room for these considerations. All that matters is the exam.

I am also reminded here of rhetoric and writing studies scholars who study the relationships, boundaries, and affordances between college and high school curricula and research. For example, Amy Lueck, in her 2020 *A Shared History*, elegantly articulates the dangers of the "commodification of writing":

> We can't hold the front line at the boundaries of the college. Not only is that boundary historically and intellectually unstable, it keeps out as many allies as insurgents. Protecting the sanctity of our own discipline and insisting on the separateness of institutions and their pedagogical values serves as a means (however inadvertent) of marginalizing the work of K–12 teachers ... [and] serves to devalue writing insofar as, from the point of distance across this divide, we cannot properly defend *all* writing from accountability assessment, timed testing, and other policies and practices that contradict our disciplinary knowledge. (182)

In Dan's and Julie's descriptions of the 2024 AP Language and Composition scoring sessions, above, we see these commodification dangers at work, despite the College Board's assurances that AP exam reading is a valuable professional opportunity that incorporates both high school and college teachers' expertise in its design. In Dan's and Julie's readings, there was no room—or time—for encouraging or assessing elements of development, trial and error, growth, or failure in students' responses, or for sharing best practices in addressing these. In the overall rhetorics of AP, such recursive messiness gets in the way of clear-cut goals in selling an educational product: the courses and the tests.

Assessing student learning is also complex—and for formative assessments, time-consuming and developmental in nature. AP exam scoring is a summative assessment by contrast. Such formative work *can* be done responsibly, when it is called for in the learning occasion. But for Dan and Julie, AP scoring was not that. Ruled by various levels of efficiency, the community of professional development *and* assessment was absent. Such is the result when we replace an entire General Education curriculum, meant to equalize and liberate students, with a business model for credit allocation that is divisible, stackable, and saleable to anxious, stressed-out students and their usually well-meaning parents, who just want their children to get ahead in (and get done with) college.

Across the AP experience, disaggregation of the learning experience from codified learning assessments rules the day. Though rhetoric and writing studies, as one of many disciplines in the university, is far in its pedagogies from the mechanized, efficiency-based rhetorics of AP, it is still in danger of further divorcing itself from the larger mission of General Education as it turns inward, rather than outward, and fails to strongly voice the importance of first-year writing within Gen Ed and on college campuses. My next chapter argues that we take seriously the dangers of another pre-college program, dual enrollment, in the fight for General Education. I ask: Who are the rhetorics of writing studies actually liberating on the twenty-first-century higher education landscape—and at what larger costs to its role in maintaining the integrity of General Education as a whole?

4
Liberatory Mythologies

Dual Enrollment / Dual Credit and the Rhetoric of Writing Studies

> While we might well wish to expand the imaginative horizons of our students and help them formulate both more ambitious and far-reaching goals for their own intellectual development, and also more complex ways of understanding their own situatedness within the culture, we cannot ignore the work we are paid to do: educating people who come to us, at whatever level of sophistication, in the fields of our specialization. More directly, we cannot educate students to our own purposes, ignoring their own.
> —Marjorie Roemer, Lucille Schultz, and Russell Durst, "Reframing the Great Debate on First-Year Writing," 1999

Now that I've told the tales of Gen Ed's origins and rhetorical histories, the rhetorics of state policies and politics shaping local Gen Ed curricula, and the efficiency rhetorics of pre-college testing programs affecting how students, parents, and the public view Gen Ed, in this chapter I'll turn to two last sites of rhetoric that are key factors in reclaiming General Education as a liberating enterprise in the United States: dual enrollment / dual credit (DE/DC) programs, and the field of writing studies itself, specifically the field's relationship with and advocacy for the first-year writing course as taught on college campuses. My argument in this chapter is not against my own field, nor is it for radical transformation of field practices. My aim, instead, is twofold:

for readers outside writing studies to learn more about DE/DC and how its uptake or lack thereof in Gen Ed disciplines affects their students' lives, and for readers inside writing studies to learn about ways that our field might better advocate for the course at the center of our field's history.

It's my further hope that *both* of these readerships will also appreciate my argument that DE/DC is, in many cases, doing measurable uplift work to first-year writing taught on college campuses, at virtually no cost to students or their families. DE/DC also has demonstrated local crossover benefits between high schools and colleges that indicate more potential on the horizon for additional such growth. As Tyler Branson has persuasively argued, there is a value in some local "liminal" classroom spaces that DE writing occupies, wherein students can "practice college writing" ("College Composition at Midwest High" 192). Burdick and Greer have comparatively observed that informal mentoring relationships between high school and college teachers provide the best results in DE pedagogical transfer, as well as the impetus for more and better collaborations between high school and college faculty (101–102), an argument echoed by Joseph Jones (53). In these and other scholars' work, it's clear that DE/DC is both a contested demarcation between K–12 and college pedagogies, and also a possible site for beneficially blurring those boundaries with input from faculty on both "sides."

The observations above would indicate to me that faculty who teach writing and administer writing programs on college campuses need to both recognize the affordances of DE/DC when it is *working* in local settings, and simultaneously step up and take ownership over their campus pedagogies, lest they cease to exist in a short number of years. My argument is rooted in the belief that all pedagogies are local, but also that we no more universalize college writing instruction at the high school level than we can eliminate successful high school DE/DC programs that are important to local communities. And that we in Writing Studies cannot continue to operate by ignoring this difficult pedagogical divide in the hopes that everything will just work out for both high schools and colleges in the end. That's not how higher education policy has *ever* worked, as I believe this book has thus far demonstrated.

Below, I first argue for the unique position of writing instruction in Gen Ed and in the public's view of literacy, then move to an examination of how DE/DC works nationally and also locally, in one state known for higher education controversies. I conclude with an argument for writing studies to increase its advocacy efforts in this area, possibly by emulating other humanities fields such as philosophy, that have more visibly and effectively staked their claim in Gen Ed principles. But to situate all of the above, let's first discuss the cultural position of first-year writing (aka "college" writing, aka composition, aka expository writing . . . and many other names, as was discussed in chapter 2). We might also call this next section, "Why I don't tell fellow passengers on my flight that I am a writing professor."

Big Bands and Grammar Drills: First-Year Writing in the Public Consciousness

First-year writing occupies a significant position in the American cultural imaginary, both as a Gen Ed requirement and as a freestanding course with an identity all its own. In Gen Ed, it is a course (or course sequence) that "everyone" takes, often against their will, and not without various attempts to bypass it—enabled by mechanisms such as AP, as discussed in chapter 3. Its exemption is also enabled by other on- and off-campus testing that allows students to demonstrate "proficiency," as if writing were a universal, quantifiable skill that could ever be mastered. First-year writing holds a more fraught position than almost all other subjects in Gen Ed, as the act of writing itself—in personal, academic, and professional settings—is something that people profess to simultaneously know everything and nothing about. Writing is both a school subject *and* a means of communication over which the American general public feels fierce ownership. Such is part and parcel of America's love-hate relationship with literacy as a marker of enculturation and as a lexical harbinger of social class.

These feelings about writing instruction, including opinions about the gatekeeping function it possesses in colleges and universities (often as a prerequisite to other higher-level courses across the curriculum) and its lingering value in a person's life and career, were succinctly framed by Sharon Crowley in 1998, in *Composition in the University*:

> Freshman English is a sentimental favorite in America, like big bands and Colin Powell. If you don't believe me, talk to your colleagues and neighbors about the introductory course they took as undergraduates. Some will depict it as an endless drill in grammar and mechanics but will assure you nonetheless that knowledge of those arcane arts contributed to their survival in college. Others will recall their course as a comfortable seminar taught by a tweedy professor who introduced them to the Great Texts of Western culture. In either case, people will remember their experience fondly, if not positively. Freshman English is a lot like "hell night" in fraternity initiations:

people do it because it was done to them, everybody sentimentalizes it by forgetting its more painful aspects, and nobody notices its potentially deleterious effects until somebody complains or gets hurt. But it inevitably creeps back into place and is thriving again. (228)

Crowley's critical characterization, the tenets of which I believe remain unchanged some twenty-eight years later, draws upon cultural mythologies about both college and literacy acquisition that many Americans share and which drive public discourse about writing requirements themselves. We might map these back onto our metaphorical Gen Ed menu of foods, from chapter 1. First-Year Writing is the vegetable that you have to eat before you can have dessert. It is the bland soup your grandma makes, about which your parents whisper, *just get through it and be nice and you can have some mac and cheese later*. Like other rites of passage and oft-standard milestones in a person's life (e.g., receiving annual vaccinations as a baby, learning to read as a young child, passing your driver's license exam as a teenager, and paying income taxes for the first time as an adult), even if difficult at the time they happen, first-year writing *must* happen to each of us per agreed-upon metrics for the overall social good. It is thus part of all college graduates' collective memories, which wax and wane depending upon a person's social and intellectual positionalities at the time when such memories are recalled.

But such memories are of an *instructional experience*—or to continue the food metaphor, one particularly tedious family dinner—that students are not likely to connect logically or intellectually to others in their college curricula, something increasingly the case in the years since Crowley made her observations above. Nor is the writing course's required status one that students and families easily accept as necessary, given financial and social pressures discussed previously in this book to "take care" of Gen Ed requirements, including first-year writing, before entering college. Further, students are unlikely to see their writing course experience as discipline-specific, as one might a history or biology or sociology course. At best, writing is viewed by students as an "English" or "grammar" class that extends (or duplicates) work done in high school—even if the content and purpose is quite different—further reinforced by the ENGL or ENG or similar course rubrics that exist in many university course catalogs yet fail to capture current pedagogies or disciplinary formations.

As was true when Crowley's book was published and also in the decades before and after it, writing (like introductory math) was and is perceived as a *skill* for most students who take a first-year writing course. Writing, for these students and most of the public, is not a subject and also not a discipline—just as Gen Ed is a graduation requirement, not an articulated *program*. With sufficiently high SAT or ACT subscores in English, or on the ACT English essay, students on many campuses also may bypass the writing requirement. Such is a credit option only afforded otherwise to the other (perceived) core skill-based course in Gen Ed, mathematics. Such intake assessments complicate and differentiate first-year writing's identity among other subject-specific requirements within Gen Ed, and also make it more susceptible to arguments for exemption, since "skills" themselves are easily framed as remedial—whereas knowledge of US history, concepts in biology, or theories of sociology are far less so. Such is further evident in national studies measuring high-school-to-college remediation that focus solely on writing and math as "basic" skills in student learning, and no other subjects in the curriculum.[1]

The discipline of writing studies has long since espoused liberatory and myriad goals for itself but, I argue, has moved away in the last several years from its advocacy for its first-year writing course, and therefore, for General Education. Writing studies at present also fails to employ and align with public-facing promotional efforts present in other fields that skillfully educate the public on the capacious goals of a liberal education. Such lack of advocacy and alignment is particularly critical, if not ironic, given similar liberatory rhetorics coming from competing actors, such as AP and DE/DC, that promise to help marginalized students move through Gen Ed in settings outside the traditional college classroom and subsequently earn undergraduate degrees more rapidly and at higher numbers.

These discoursal moments with public-facing approaches fall largely under what I term "community relations"—in other words, the way we do or do not talk about the structure and benefits of first-year writing to students and parents and with the general public. They are primarily reflected today in the discipline's policy and research statements on organization websites, which are readily accessible by interlocutors inside and outside academia. Across these present and absent rhetorical formations regarding the first-year course, writing studies is not doing enough to strongly voice its importance and use value against other available pre-college credit mechanisms for Gen Ed, as discussed throughout this book, that imminently threaten the course's longer-term existence on college campuses. The mechanism that I profile and dissect for these purposes is DE/DC, offered in high schools nationwide.

I further challenge faculty and administrators who teach and lead writing programs to consider who writing studies' seemingly isolationist efforts ultimately benefit, and who they harm. Have our efforts to become a fully-fledged discipline whose identity eclipses the first-year course—or in some cases, divorce ourselves from it altogether—overlooked the commonalities and values we share with other disciplines within the Gen Ed curriculum? In gaining disciplinary status, and with it increased legitimacy as scholars and researchers, has writing studies sacrificed some of its unity present earlier in our history? If so, what should we do now, as we struggle to not just thrive but *exist* in an American higher education system that has first-year writing curricula teetering on the edge of obsolescence, and with them a significant part of the discipline that holds primary standing within Gen Ed curricula as a whole?

Becoming a Discipline: The Exclusionary Consequences of Inclusion

Behind the collective memories and perceptions of writing instruction amongst public and academic stakeholders lie multiple mythologies about the core benefits and outcomes of the first-year writing course itself. Such mythologies have accumulated over the sixty-plus years in which writing studies, née composition studies, has been a discipline—the exact start date depending upon where one marks its beginnings. Options include the year 1950, at the start of CCCC, as discussed in chapter 1; the year 1963, as Stephen North contended; the year 1966, at the Dartmouth Conference; or "around [the year] 1971," a marker that Crowley uses in *Composition in the University*.[2] As scholars and teachers in writing studies have attempted to address these benefits and outcomes in kind, and also simultaneously deepen writing studies' research mission and disciplinary identity, they have trained their focus on numerous theoretical paradigms that would signal its relevance amongst other disciplines in academia.

Since rejecting, in the early 1970s, so-called current-traditional rhetoric codified at many (but not all) US colleges and universities, writing studies has deployed numerous frameworks for its teaching and research. These have been designed to keep its work reflective of other emerging intellectual trends in academe, and also respondent to critical social issues. These frameworks include (in alphabetical order): anti-racist pedagogies, cognitive theory, community and service learning, critical pedagogy, cultural studies, developmental studies, disability studies, ethnography, expressivism, feminist studies, first-generation studies, genre theory, labor-based grading, LGTBQIA+ studies, literacy studies, multicultural rhetorics (including African American, Latinx, Asian American, and Native American rhetorics; and associated movements such as SRTOL and AAVE), machine learning (including [mis]uses of AI), multimodal rhetorics (including sonic rhetorics), portfolio assessment, process theory, second-language studies, social justice, sociolinguistics, teaching for transfer and transfer theory, translingualism, transnationalism, working class studies, writing about writing, writing across the curriculum, and writing in the disciplines.

Each of these frameworks have surfaced as more or less dominant over the last fifty years, with some rising and then receding from view across passing generations, as would be the case in other disciplines as well. Unlike other disciplines, however, such waves emphasizing various frameworks may be witnessed as correspondent to advents in the material conditions of teaching and learning (including online instruction) and accompanying shifts in working conditions overall in higher education, since writing studies is particularly attuned to such conditions and also beholden to them, given the massive scale of the first-year course as a requirement, and the various areas of the curriculum in which writing is a component (especially in WAC and WID pedagogies). First-year writing is also a course, given its small class size, that uniquely relies on contingent labor, including graduate student workers, as instructors of record (versus the "teaching assistant," section leader, or grader function that such workers fill in other academic fields that offer introductory courses at scale).

In the approaches and frameworks listed above, many instances of disciplinary boundary crossings are apparent—not just within the humanities but also the social sciences and, most recently, computational sciences. Such boundary crossing has led writing studies to declare itself an interdisciplinary field not easily classified within traditional field-based boundaries. Hence the emergence of independent writing departments and schools separate from English departments, of doctoral programs with variously labeled permutations (rhetoric and composition, composition studies, writing studies, technical communication, etc.), and of specialized sites of writing research and pedagogy across campuses. The discipline's breadth has also resulted in a proliferation of scholars who present and publish their work in venues outside of the confines of the liberal arts. At the same time, myriad examinations by writing studies scholars over the last twenty years regarding disciplinary identities have evidenced viewpoints into the growing pains as well as the emerging questions that accompany such growth.[3]

As part of this growth, we witness a concomitant stretching and pooling of writing studies' research- and teaching-related identities under larger umbrellas that signal to a wider audience of academics a distinct research mission clearly separate from its oft-located parentage of English studies.[4] Such is evident, for example, in CIP (Classification of Instructional Program) codes from the National Center for Educational Statistics, the purpose of which is to "support the accurate tracking and reporting of fields of study and program completions activity."[5] Most academic fields pay close attention to how they are classified by CIP codes, as such can impact grant applications and other funding based on program growth. Revised CIP codes for writing studies were for this and other reasons put into place in 2010, following the work of a committee of senior scholars led by Louise Wetherbee Phelps of Syracuse University.[6]

The new CIP parent code created was 23.13, Rhetoric and Composition / Writing Studies, with new subcodes carrying the parent "23" designation for Writing, General; Creative Writing; Professional, Technical, Business, and Scientific Writing; Rhetoric and Composition; and Rhetoric and Composition, Other. Prior to 2010, the correspondent CIP codes were English Composition (23.04), Speech and Rhetorical Studies (23.10), and Technical and Business Writing (23.14), with Creative Writing possessing its own freestanding code (23.05). Yet the "23" designation is still classified by the NCES as "English Language and Literature/Letters," which does not accurately represent writing studies' disciplinarity. Such is a keen reminder that field perceptions, despite best efforts, still differ from public and other academics' perceptions of what writing studies is, and as part of this, what the first-year writing course is and can be.[7]

As writing studies has endeavored over the past several decades to engage with the research methods of other disciplines across the university, and in the process, has shaped itself into a discipline in its own right, internal processes to establish this identity have largely resulted in inward examinations of its purpose and mission, and pedagogies, exclusive of first-year writing. This is perhaps because as writing studies grows, many (but not all) of its scholars and teachers seek to distance themselves from the first-year course, given its fraught historical identity, its labor models, and its propensity to be labeled remedial, as noted elsewhere this book. Complicating the identity of first-year writing further is that the people teaching it are not necessarily credentialed in the field per se—including graduate students from English literature and creative writing (and other humanities fields), and both part- and full-time contingent and tenure-track faculty who teach the course but who have degrees in other fields.[8] In sum, writing studies wants to be *more* than first-year writing, an argument with which I am sympathetic as a scholar, but not necessary in agreement with as an advocate for Gen Ed.

The resulting isolation of first-year writing—whether intentional or not—from other Gen Ed core subjects makes it a disciplinary orphan, less connected to its parentage than we might see in other fields with introductory courses.⁹ This separation from many research pursuits also means the course is less likely to be part of key conversations about General Education reform happening outside writing studies itself. Disciplinary histories that emerged around the start of the twenty-first century, also coinciding with the fifty-year mark of the first CCCC meeting—for example, Connors; Crowley; Roemer et al.;[10] and Goggin—positioned the rise of writing studies, and with it first-year writing, in the liberatory context of post–World War II educational reforms, as had Berlin before these. But the ways in which writing studies theorists today consider whether and why the course should change are rarely, if ever, in such explicit historical conversation with Gen Ed principles.

In fact, first-year writing is not the only site for potential student liberation through active learning and critical reflection, but also, its core liberatory pedagogical mission *can* inform and amplify similar efforts elsewhere—nascent or otherwise—within Gen Ed. As both field leadership and faculty on the ground tinker again and again (and again) with the delivery and import of first-year writing courses, sometimes without clear regard for rising external competitors who would supplant such courses altogether, we lose the opportunity to strengthen the importance of writing and literacy in postsecondary education through such broader alignments. Faculty in writing studies often have their backs turned to other attempts at progressive amendments to curricula that could quite literally determine the future of our discipline. It's time we turn around and see our liberatory efforts as not discipline-specific but *movement-specific*, with the movement being General Education.

In order to illustrate my argument on a local level, with a phenomenon that is emblematic of how first-year writing (and other Gen Ed subjects) are endangered by the ongoing absence of full-throated advocacy measures, I now move to a discussion of competing messaging about first-year writing on and off campus, in a bellwether state that I also profiled in chapter 2, and which comes up again repeatedly in discussions of higher education reform: Texas.

Freeway Flyers on the Rhetoric Highway: OnRamps and the University of Texas System

A phenomenon on an epic scale that poses a threat to the viability of General Education curricula on college campuses is dual enrollment and dual credit (DE/DC). DE/DC is the biggest—and also the most legitimate, in pedagogical terms—anti–Gen Ed operation today. This is because, in most cases, DE/DC relocates college Gen Ed courses wholesale to high school campuses, wherein students may receive credit for both high school *and* college requirements at the same time. DE/DC is anti–Gen Ed not due to its content, therefore, but due to how its very structure systematically breaks apart the scaffolded learning of Gen Ed programs into discrete, stand-alone courses somehow *both* high school–appropriate and college-appropriate in their content and delivery, functioning as divisible units of pre-college credit. As Amy Lueck has noted, "the focus on 'standards' for defining college-level writing is inadequate insofar as it perpetuates notions of writing as acontextual, institutional types as stable, and education as equivalent to credentialing for future opportunities, to the neglect of students' complex present experiences, needs, and desires" (175). DE/DC, like AP, teaches students that the boundaries between high school and college are so porous as to be meaningless, which negates the mission and benefits of General Education itself.

DE/DC poses a serious threat to college campus writing programs, because, as noted above, first-year writing courses are most likely to be framed by the public as skill-based and as remedial—making them ripe for curricula that showcase writing instruction's overlapping, logical use value across high school and college. DE/DC is also a threat because writing studies as a field has mounted no recent significant challenge to DE/DC in the form of public-facing arguments that might help change the minds of students and parents. Unlike AP, DE/DC courses operate as incoming transfer credits based not on timed-test exam scores earned after the course experience, but on complete courses that strive to mirror specific local postsecondary pedagogies by design, thereby capitalizing on writing studies research by carrying it into high school classrooms.[11] DE/DC courses are also tuition-free or tuition-subsidized; widely available across all fifty states; and increasingly backed by extensive professional development for participating teachers, in order to bring their pedagogy and curricula in line with state educational standards, as, ideally, disciplinary best practices. In a very real sense, DE/DC is a national site of *relocation* for first-year writing itself.

This structure and logic underlying DE/DC is all good news for the students enrolled in its courses. It carries a stronger likelihood of a quality learning experience than was the case in similar programs offered thirty or more years ago, when DE/DC was first emerging across state K–16 systems.[12] It is further good news for the DE/DC teachers, who are professionally supported and often in dialogue with faculty at local colleges and universities regarding course design and outcomes, and who may see DE/DC as the opportunity to teach a more advanced course than their regular teaching assignment would typically allow. And it is good news for the high schools, who can add to their state's quality metrics, discussed in chapter 3, by declaring students are taking more "college level programming" beyond just AP, via robust enrollments in DE/DC that are memorialized in state articulation agreements with local colleges and universities.

Yet it is bad news, in turn, for writing studies as a discipline, and for the long-term viability of first-year writing on college campuses, as a fundamentally important piece of an integrated and scaffolded General Education program rooted in inclusion and opportunity, and productive guided discourse between and among intellectually and socially developing adults across various subjects.[13] The better and more readily available imbedded DE/DC programs, the less students see the logic of paying tuition to take these "same" writing courses on a college campus, versus in the convenience of their own high school, from teachers they already know, while satisfying their high school graduation requirements concurrently. The first-year course exists for students as a free-floating skills requirement that just simply needs to be *done*; why not do it in the comfort of your own high school classroom?[14]

This student-centered logic and its uptake is reflected in the massive scale of DE/DC offered nationwide at the time of this writing. According to statistics offered by the National Alliance of Concurrent Enrollment Partnerships, 34 percent of all US high school students, or one in three, take college courses in high school (a dramatic increase from the 10 percent, or one in ten, who did so in 2010), with 80 percent of those students taking said courses at their local high school. Overall, 88.98 percent of US high schools participate in DE/DC agreements and structures—the highest being in Georgia, which boasts a 100 percent participation rate (https://www.nacep.org/resource-center/nacep-fast-facts/). And English 1102, or the second of the two first-year writing courses in the USG, is the most frequently enrolled course within Georgia's DE/DC programs.

When we combine these rates of uptake with other exemption mechanisms for first-year writing (and other Gen Ed courses) as discussed in this book, it's easy to see how the long-standing enterprise of first-year writing taught on college campuses, to what college admissions offices call FTF or "first-time freshmen," is very much in danger, and with it the structural, intellectual, and—yes—economic foundations of a discipline that offers widespread benefit and impacts across the curriculum.

Even though I have been quite critical of the various macroeconomic-based arguments for the reduction or elimination of General Education nationwide thus far, the microeconomics of first-year writing curricula are particularly keen for readers to remember nonetheless, especially when we consider writing studies colleagues working in two-year colleges, and also four-year regional universities, who may have majority teaching loads in introductory writing courses, and who also do important research into its students and practices.[15] While statewide transfer agreements theoretically have a positive impact on two-year college enrollments, they also mean a wider and arguably less appropriate population of students entering these courses—versus the original mission and target population of two-year colleges, discussed in part in chapter 3. Many students today, including those from families above the middle class, enroll part-time or full-time at two-year colleges simply to get "cheaper" college course credit for transfer, or to partake in courses that may also be erroneously perceived as less rigorous than those offered on a four-year campus. At the same time, exemption methods and DE/DC courses taught in high schools potentially negatively benefit two-year college enrollments by stripping faculty of the core pedagogical work they do as trained professionals in the discipline in their own local writing classrooms.[16]

This rapid growth across both course offerings and student participation in DE/DC as relevant to first-year writing is no better illustrated than in Texas. As noted earlier in this book, Texas has an extensive system of both common core and common course numbering across its many postsecondary institutions, designed to enable seamless transfer and maximal efficiency in the delivery of General Education, which help to meet state metrics for access and also allow for financial benefits for Texas postsecondary operations as a whole. Texas is also home to a massive dual enrollment system called OnRamps, created in 2011 and implemented in the 2012–2013 academic year specifically for the UT flagship system only. According to its public-facing website housed by UT–Austin, OnRamps "prepares students and teachers for success in the classroom and beyond" and further purports that its mission is to "build partnerships across K12 and higher education to raise the bar on dynamic experiences that advance student success while lowering barriers to access and opportunity" (https://onramps.utexas.edu/).

OnRamps operates via cooperation with all nine of the UT campuses with undergraduate programs, but is designed by faculty at the flagship campus at UT–Austin, "for high school students to engage in authentic college experiences and for their teachers to deepen their content knowledge and impact in the classroom" (https://onramps.utexas.edu/what-we-offer/distance-ed/districts/). As such, OnRamps possesses by design some of the centralized values of the flagship that Texas politically prioritizes. Such values are also present in other state systems where R1 universities dictate policy or processes that must be followed on non-flagship system campuses where students, mission, and resources may dramatically differ yet fail to be recognized as pertinent to courses regarded as "equal" across the system as a whole.

OnRamps courses are offered across two settings, with differing modalities: in-person on high school campuses, taught by high school teachers, or via distance learning, by a "University faculty member and appointed academic course staff." This is different than some other DE/DC programs around the country that also allow (or require) high school students to physically attend class on the college's campus. For the online version, "OnRamps students complete assignments, engage with scientific software, and network with other students, among other things, through the same learning management system (Canvas) that is used by undergraduates at UT Austin" (Giani et al., "OnRamps" 2), a directive that again invokes the practices of the flagship. In this critically important way, OnRamps is effectively a hybrid of other DE/DC programs nationwide, with the college-located course option being taught online only—making it broadly available to students who otherwise have no local teacher or course on the ground, or who have other personal or educational reasons for needing to participate in what used to be called distance education. These online students thus do not even get the on-campus enrollment benefits, such as a window into campus life, that other DE/DC students in other states might comparatively experience.

The OnRamps programming is further keyed to metrics in the State of Texas Education Agency's *Accountability Manual*, which states that students who "complete an OnRamps dual enrollment course [can] qualify for at least three hours of university or college credit in any subject area from the OnRamps program."[17] Given this broad charge and state directive, OnRamps operates on a massive scale. In the 2022–2023 academic year, it enrolled 41,791 unique students across Texas, with 93 percent of those students earning college credit. Those who do not receive credit, per an eligibility assessment made at the mid-term grade, may remain in the course to receive high school credit only. Students receiving credit for both high school and college from OnRamps are given separate course grades for their high school and college transcripts, and retain the option of not "claiming" OnRamps credit for admissions or transfer (Giani et al., "OnRamps" 2). Nearly half (42 percent) of OnRamps students in 2022–2023 were first-generation students; of the total enrolled, 52 percent of students identified as Hispanic, and 8 percent as Black.

These demographics allow OnRamps to advertise itself as a program designed to promote equity and access in higher education, in ways that traditional campus-based college writing demographics—dependent on both external exemption measures such as AP, SAT, and ACT, and also institutional placement measures—may not. Consider this paradigm: Whereas college writing courses enroll whomever is *left* after all exemption credits and first-year course placements are determined (or exhausted) on a given campus, with resulting populations often containing more underrepresented and marginalized students than not, OnRamps *targets* these same students in order to provide them with a means of taking first-year writing course *before* entering that arguably disproportionately enrolled space and being thereafter regarded by peers and even the institution itself as "remedial" students. That is powerful rhetoric based on reality.

Such a system also specifically affects students who might otherwise place into basic writing—still a course that nationwide enrolls many underserved students and students of color, and which may not always recognize alternate language models as accepted academic discourse.[18] If students successfully complete an OnRamps course (or any DE/DC course) for first-year writing credit, they will not take a placement test when they get to campus. Whether the course accurately measured and reflected their abilities in relation to said local placement exam cannot be determined, since the DE/DC course negated the placement occasion altogether. This should give my writing studies colleagues some pause. Does placement matter still, and if so, who are we placing in writing courses after all these presorting mechanisms are complete?

In sum, OnRamps allows these students to *get ahead*, in rhetorical terms, rather than be regarded as *falling behind* in the college setting, as Gen Ed courses are so often cast in the public sphere as causing. While this rhetorical framing is only possible due to the ubiquity of exemption mechanisms that presort students into the haves and have-nots of General Education before college begins, it is a powerful message nonetheless. One might go so far as to argue that as AP exemption credit rises, so, too, must DE/DC programming, for purposes of social justice. What is left out of this conversation so far, from expert voices in writing studies, is an argument for the place, purpose, and future of the traditional first-year writing course that all these student populations are striving to *not take* on our college campuses, and how it can respond to issues of equity and purpose, if not financial cost (which unfortunately is out of our local faculty control).

OnRamps employs myriad student support services for disadvantaged students, which also allow it to stand apart from other, more problematic DE/DC programs nationwide, and at the same time be less susceptible to the equity gap found in many such programs (B. Schneider 36). Policy briefs published in 2018 and 2023 by the Education Research Center at UT–Austin further assert that for OnRamps students in the 2015–2017 cohorts, the percentage of OnRamps credit eligible students not attending postsecondary education was "less than half the rate of non-OnRamps students (17.9% vs. 43.6%)" (Giani et al., "Policy Brief"). In addition, "OnRamps participants were also nearly twice as likely to attend a four-year college compared to non-OnRamps students (52.3% vs. 29.9%), and roughly two-thirds of OnRamps credit eligible students attended a four-year college (66.9%)" (Giani et al., "Policy Brief" 3).

However, *where* those OnRamps students went to college was less straightforward, according to the 2018 brief:

> Although UT Austin was the most popular institution, the vast majority of OnRamps students who attended colleges enrolled in institutions apart from UT Austin. Second, although enrollment in out-of-state institutions was the fifth highest when all three cohorts (2015–17) were combined, more OnRamps students enrolled out-of-state than in any other postsecondary institution for the 2015 and 2016 cohorts for which out-of-state enrollment data was available. (Giani et al., "Policy Brief" 4)

These data would seem to point to mixed results for the program's goals, which are to improve and streamline experiences for in-state students, in particular Black and Hispanic and low-income students who want to attend UT institutions, and also to keep those students *in-state* for college (a goal of all articulation agreements, but especially DE/DC). This is an important consideration, since according to the 2018 policy report, participation in DE/DC programs in Texas has increased by "roughly 650% since 2000" (qtd. in Giani et al., "Policy Brief" 8), in part due to a state requirement, stated in Texas Education Code §28.009, in which "students may earn the equivalent of at least 12 semester credit hours of college credit in high schools" (8). This means students can bring in *a full semester's equivalent* of Gen Ed credit to UT institutions as first-year enrollees, bypassing four to five subjects across the curriculum in the process, including first-year writing.

Comparatively, the 2023 policy brief (written by the same lead author of the 2018 brief) found that OnRamps students "accumulate significantly more SCH (Student Credit Hours) compared to non-OnRamps students, and this relationship grows over time" (Giani et al., "OnRamps"). The report also found that in relation to minority populations, "OnRamps credit was associated with a near-doubling (89% increase) in Black students' likelihood of earning a bachelor's degree" and also increased likelihood for women students versus men students, with the overall student population's likelihood "of earning a bachelor's degree increasing for each OnRamps course they take." The report further questioned whether students enrolled in OnRamps may already be academically inclined to succeed, but concluded that since OnRamps is open to all high school students—much as AP operates—the population as a whole does not fall under this classification by student preparation. Given its lack of placement requirements, OnRamps is thus actually *more* open than first-year writing courses on college campuses that use ability testing.

As a program designed to cover as much of the General Education curriculum as possible, OnRamps currently encompasses sixteen college-equivalent courses across four areas of the curriculum: Science, Mathematics, Technology, and the Humanities—the latter of which includes the equivalent to Rhetoric 306, the first-year writing required course within the UT system.[19] The "rhetorical pedagogy" employed in the OnRamps course, entitled "Introduction to Rhetoric: Reading, Writing and Research: Reading and Writing the Rhetoric of American Identities," and which carries a prerequisite of High School English I and II—or the freshman and sophomore level required English courses in all Texas state high schools as part of the K–12 TEKS (Texas English Knowledge and Skills) paradigm—is described this way:

> Many of the assignments in the OnRamps Rhetoric courses include substantive revision or peer review components designed to promote lifetime habits of critical thinking, analytical reading, substantive revision, research, and reflection to prepare students for future leadership roles and civic participation. Rhetorical Pedagogy features writing feedback, peer review, research, inquiry-driven discussion and paper conferences. These activities are designed to accelerate critical thinking skills, metacognitive skills, communication skills, and ultimately, to prepare students for participation in civic life. ("Pedagogy")

The course's "big ideas" are further classified as the following: "Rhetorical Situations"; "Giving and Receiving Feedback"; "Drafting and Revising"; "Leadership Communication"; "Formulating a Research Question"; "Conducting Research"; "Evaluating Sources"; and "Analyzing Arguments" (https://onramps .utexas.edu/what-we-offer/distance-ed/rhe/). It's clear from the tenets of this Rhetoric 306–equivalent course that the collective best practices and ongoing pedagogical values of writing studies are known to program architects and are carefully reflected in course design, as in on-the-ground Rhetoric 306 courses on UT campuses.

To add to its appeal and public-facing discourse, the name of OnRamps itself vividly invokes rhetorics of speed and efficiency, correspondent to the public's valuation of same. It begs students to imagine a freeway system of colleges and universities whereby those entering via the prescribed routes (OnRamps) are traveling at a speed that allows them safe and effortless entrance. When one "travels" via OnRamps, they are theoretically *better* prepared to be on that freeway of higher education in Texas—and with a reduced burden (metaphorically speaking) of tolls to pay along the way, in the form of tuition-bearing General Education courses. This kind of rhetorical framing certainly supports and is supported by other such framings of AP, and also common course numbering. DE/DC, as exemplified by OnRamps, is part of a larger ecosystem of agents working independently but with shared ideologies regarding the negative or nonexistent value of on-campus General Education curricula, with first-year writing courses one of the easiest targets of them all.

With growing and powerful local DE/DC programming such as this, employed in a huge university system that annually enrolls more than 256,000 total students,[20] how does the field of writing studies comparatively communicate the current value of its first-year course and its role within the discipline's larger mission, and with what level of historical and institutional memory? Such are the questions guiding my analysis, below, of public messaging by the Conference on College Composition and Communication (CCCC) and its lacking attention to the dire state of first-year writing on college campuses and, by extension, General Education curricula as a whole.

Conveying Policy, Past and Present: The Rhetoric of Writing Studies

For readers who are unfamiliar, the CCCC is a large member organization, numbering three to four thousand, focused on college-level teaching and research in writing studies. It formed, as discussed in chapter 1, as a subgroup of the National Council of Teachers of English in 1950. Across its more recent history, a conflict between the teaching and research areas of its membership and the public-facing identity of writing studies as a discipline has been readily apparent. In her 2018 CCCC Chair's Address, Carolyn Calhoon-Dillahunt highlighted the national trends in pre-college credit mechanisms that have long since forecasted the demise of first-year writing, addressing James Berlin's observance in *Rhetoric and Reality* (1987) that "[earlier] predictions of the demise of the freshman writing course [have] proved to be inaccurate" (qtd. on 278). As Calhoon-Dillahunt, who also serves as faculty at a two-year college and as a past officer in TYCA (the Two-Year College Association), reflects, "I can't help but wonder, in the current political and economic climate, if [these] warnings were not erroneous, but premature" (278). She later in her address argues that such trends

> put first-year writing—and the students and programs (including graduate programs!) that such courses support—at risk. As a discipline, we bear some responsibility for its endangerment. Despite the significant space that first-year writing occupies in our discipline, our scholarship fails to account for the "teaching majority," or the spaces in which they work. (281)

She goes on to cite Holly Hassel and Joanne Baird Giordano's "Occupy Writing Studies" (2013), highlighting their observation that "a majority of postsecondary writing instructors will not spend their careers teaching upper-division courses, training graduate students, or researching narrowly focused issues in rhetoric and composition" (281). Calhoon-Dillahunt concludes that these representational conflicts, as well as the labor model that staffs first-year writing courses—which, as noted earlier, includes many teachers who are not members of the discipline—create circumstances whereby it is "easy to farm out the task [of teaching writing] to overworked high school English teachers or literature graduate students and enable competency exams to substitute for teaching and learning" (282). She forcefully further argues that "First-year writing is the space where we can best exercise our power through disciplinarity" (282).

Such assertions in Calhoon-Dillahunt's address regarding disciplinarity and the marginalized status of first-year writing partially echo Lil Brannon's earlier (2015) commentary on the growth of writing studies as a discipline, specifically her observations that, despite her and others leaning toward the "abolitionist" position on the first-year writing *requirement*,

> the 1980s generation wasn't asking *not* to teach writing, or *not* to run writing programs, or *not* to continue practical research in the teaching of writing. Yet that appears to be one of the unintended consequences. In effect, we've changed more toward English than they have changed toward us, and the result has been that we are more like the humanities disciplines—marked by preoccupations with research activities too esoteric to be valued by people outside the academy, activities that have been partly responsible for marginalizing the humanities both inside and outside the university. It may be time

for an examination of conscience and to ask ourselves... have we made the teaching of writing, particularly first-year writing, any better? (518)[21]

Brannon's questioning of whether the discipline is actively seeking to improve first-year writing, as well as her observation of writing studies' desire for a strong research profile befitting of other academic fields, are germane to the position of the first-year writing course within larger discussions of pedagogy in General Education programs. Brannon here makes a critical observation as well regarding English departments—whom writing studies has sought to be separated from, sometimes as memorialized in famous utterances[22]—and the mission of writing studies, which in her view has resulted in a structural divorce hampered by a theoretical kinship that does not benefit the longevity of the field.

The CCCC Chair's Addresses, as a genre, are a key opportunity for the discipline's leadership to articulate goals for the future and challenges that may impede its progress. Yet the audience for these addresses—both in print and in person—are other members of the discipline itself (plus the occasional visitor, reporter, or passerby, for the in-person talks, or other academic researchers who might find *CCC*, where chairs' addresses are printed each February, in an online search). The more public-facing work that the CCCC—and by extension or parentage, the NCTE—does to promote writing studies as a discipline, through current position statements and other published policy documents, would seem to belie the notion that first-year writing has the power that Calhoon-Dillahunt asserts it should, or the centrality to the field's mission that Brannon similarly asserted, *or* the value of first-year writing instruction that some, but not all, previous and subsequent CCCC chairs extoled in their own addresses.[23]

Certainly scholars in writing studies have also individually addressed issues related to DE/DC and its drawbacks across the last two decades, in part through landmark collections on the topic (Hansen and Farris; Denecker and Moreland, *Dual Enrollment*). Other writing studies scholars have made strong arguments about first-year writing per se in relation to various national conversations about higher education and the public good, including the centrality of the course as a site of research that integrates with the role of writing across disciplines and within higher education as an enterprise. These include empirical studies of first-year writing versus AP course outcomes in the work of college sophomores (Hansen et al.); the relationship between writing assessment and accountability metrics in higher education (Adler-Kassner and Harrington);

the connections between "habits of mind" and the liberal tradition as reflected in the CWPA *Frameworks* document (Johnson); and the value of seeing writing studies professionals as interlocutors in faculty development conversations (Artze-Vega et al.).

I do not therefore argue that *no one* in writing studies over the last decade has cared about first-year writing, nor that there does not exist good and important research happening on the local level that will positively impact first-year writing on individual campuses, and in the field. I also recognize that the NCTE has separately engaged in advocacy for writing teachers, particularly at the K–12 level. As Tyler Branson has extensively documented, the NCTE has engaged in what he calls "careful policy critiques" effecting K–12 teaching and learning, including concurrent enrollment (*Policy Regimes* 6). Branson provides an intricate dissection of specific national policies on DE/DC and the local enactments of these policies in high schools, as well as the relationship of these policies to NCTE's work. I comparatively spotlight here the lacking rhetoric of CCCC as the parent organization for the discipline, and of the measure of the discipline's *public*-facing work, as writing studies grows and regularly expands its mission and definition. I thus define "discipline" here not as the conglomeration of all K–16 teachers of *English* writ large, as represented by the NCTE, but the specific college-level discipline of writing studies that is represented by the CCCC. My concerns are how we as a discipline *talk* about who we are, and what we do, specifically in relation to first-year writing and General Education.

As a starting case in point, the CCCC Strategic Governance Mission Statement, adopted in 2012 and posted on the publicly accessible front page of the CCCC website, reads as follows:

> By 2022, CCCC will be a clear, trusted public voice for the teaching and learning of writing, composition, rhetoric, and literacy in all higher education contexts. We will advocate for a broad definition of *writing* (including composition, digital production, and diverse language practices) that emphasizes its value as a human activity that empowers individuals and communities to shape their worlds. We will be the leading voice in public discussions about what it means to be an effective writer and to deliver quality writing instruction. We will provide conditions under which teachers and scholars can discuss, build, and practice sustainable, relevant, and ethical models of teaching and learning. We will encourage and support a wide and vibrant range of scholarship at the leading edge of knowledge about writing, composition, rhetoric, and literacy. To support this work, CCCC will enhance participation by members who represent a diversity of races,

cultures, languages, identities, institutions, and institutional roles. (https://cccc.ncte.org/cccc-about/)

These laudable goals, crafted in 2012 and not since updated, promise some good work: to be a voice in "all higher education contexts"—which would include, to my mind, the national context of both pre-college credit mechanisms *and* Gen Ed reform—and to lead conversations on effective writing and writing instruction. But when we examine the current policies of CCCC—which currently number a staggering *thirty-nine* separate positions covering a vast range of topics, specifically "Statements on Teaching and Learning in Postsecondary Language and Literacy Classrooms"; "Statements on Social and Linguistic Justice and Anti-Racist Policies"; "Professional Standards and Resources: Research"; "Professional Standards and Resources: Teaching"; "Professional Standards and Resources: Working Conditions"; and "Statements on Current Issues"—advocacy for first-year writing against Gen Ed's detractors and within its structures is less visible (https://cccc.ncte.org/cccc/resources/positions).[24]

I believe that a more openly aggressive use of arguments of value is possible in order to reach beyond our own ears and eyes and into the spaces where parents and students, and other members of the general public, are otherwise persuaded against the worth of first-year writing. Again, this goes to the question of whom the practices of writing studies ultimately benefit when applied outside of the field's boundaries themselves, and how we convey the importance of first-year writing within our disciplinary mission(s).[25]

Comparing the discipline's evolving position on DE/DC provides for a case in point. In 2011, the CCCC charged a task force on Dual Credit and Concurrent Enrollment in Composition; for full disclosure, I was a member of this task force, during my term as a member of the CCCC Executive Committee from 2008 to 2011. The ensuing November 2012 policy document approved by CCCC and its parent organization, the National Council of Teachers of English, and titled "Statement on Dual Credit / Concurrent Enrollment Composition: Policy and Best Practices" in great part reflected the expertise of Christine Farris, (since retired) writing studies faculty at Indiana University and an early field expert on DE/DC and coeditor of the aforementioned 2010 collection *College Credit for Writing in High School: The 'Taking Care of' Business*. At the time of the first policy's implementation, DE/DC was not new but was gaining traction in states like Indiana, where measures created by state legislatures were already in place to streamline Gen Ed coursework through, for example, standard AP credit policies across the state university system.

This 2012 policy was drafted and approved around the same time that a wave of other public advocacy efforts were underway in writing studies, including the Council of Writing Program Administrators' *Framework for Success in Postsecondary Writing* (2011), endorsed by NCTE and by the National Writing Project and released as part of a major joint press event, organized by the late Kent Williamson, at the 2011 CCCC annual convention in Atlanta, GA. Four years prior to this statement's adoption, Linda Adler-Kassner published *The Activist WPA* (2008)—and thereafter, as then president of the CWPA, led the drafting of the *Frameworks* document noted above. The year after the first DE/DC policy statement was adopted, in 2013, NCTE also published a research brief entitled "First Year-Writing: What Good Does It Do?" This brief, which outlined the four benefits of the first-year writing course—"Fostering Engagement and Retention," "Enhancing Rhetorical Knowledge," "Developing Metacognition," and "Increasing Responsibility"—also declares the following, which zeroes in on the appropriateness of DE/DC in relation to the stated goals and benefits of first-year writing:

> Allowing college credit for writing courses completed while in high school will not help students to fully develop capacities for engagement, persistence, collaboration, reflection, metacognition, flexibility, and ownership that will help them to grow as writers and learners. . . . Decisions regarding college writing course requirements and student placement should acknowledge that writing development occurs over time and reflects students' emotional, social, and cognitive maturity. Writing competence—for students of all ages—is continually developing and depends on exposure to many diverse experiences requiring writing, revision, problem solving, and creative thinking. (3)

This 2013 policy statement is a strong voicing of the first-year writing course's benefits as they occur on college campuses; it also bears vestiges of the metacognitive effects and values of General Education, though does not explicitly hail Gen Ed in its argument. Of particular interest is the idea of *ownership*, which is implied to be impossible in the high school setting, given its attendant conditions as part of compulsory education enrolled by minor students. The policy also calls attention to student developmental stages regarding maturity—a problem also with DE/DC courses that may include students as young as fourteen years old.

This policy, however, is no longer archived on the NCTE website, which only includes policy briefs from the year 2021 forward, nor is it archived on the

CCCC website, either. So, a person would have to know that said policy existed, and then google it for discovery, or accidentally find it while doing internet research.[26] It is not, thus, easily discoverable by the general public. Neither is this 2013 policy statement included in the list of "position statements" within the "resources" tab on the NCTE website (https://ncte.org/resources/position-statements/all/#CCCC/2486), as such statements are only archived back to the year 2015. This may be because NCTE and CCCC no longer include among their officers an archivist, who would ostensibly be in charge of this work, or because it is focusing on more current statements as reflective of the current organizational membership and leadership.

The 2012 CCCC policy statement on DE/DC that the 2013 NCTE policy statement ostensibly builds on in its argument was supplanted by an updated statement, authored by a new task force, seven years later in November 2019, titled "Joint Position on Dual Enrollment in Composition," the full text of which is publicly available on the CCCC website at https://cccc.ncte.org/cccc/resources/positions/dualenrollment.[27] The 2019 statement is noted to be "the collective position of the Conference on College Composition and Communication (CCCC), the Two-Year College English Association (TYCA), the Council of Writing Program Administrators (CWPA), and the College Section of the National Council of Teachers of English (NCTE)," thus incorporating a partnership across field organizations not present in 2012 efforts. Examining the further differences between the two policies illustrates rhetorical shifts in the organization's messaging on DE/DC across a seven-year period that also witnessed significant growth in such DE/DC programming nationwide.[28]

The original 2012 statement is a relatively concise document that provides citations of numerous current field resources on dual credit and dual enrollment, and divides its primary areas of concerns into (1) the composition course itself; (2) the preparation and support of teachers and administrators; (3) students; and (4) assessment. After stating its endorsement of National Alliance of Concurrent Enrollment Partnerships (NACEP) accreditation processes for DE/DC courses, the policy statement calls for further "discipline-specific guidelines and high school/college English alliances at the local and state levels" to ensure quality of instruction and student experience. In its summary recommendations, as outlined in the statement's third paragraph, the policy declares that

> decisions to recognize course equivalency and/or to develop DC/CE composition must include re-examination of our assumptions and practices with regard to the on-campus version of composition: the rationale for its requirement, issues of transfer and exemption, curriculum design, instructor

preparation and support, and assessment. Clearly, we want to protect the integrity of our profession and the quality of our programs. At the same time, we need to offer the CCCC membership guidelines and resources specific to DC/CE to deal with the challenges they face in their teaching and administrative practices. Only with such a statement of guidelines does it seem feasible for CCCC to support dual credit / concurrent enrollment composition. Across the high school / college divide, we want to keep front and center the needs of student writers at all points in their development and protect the rights of teachers and writing program administrators.

The 2019 statement comparatively includes the same four areas of focus above, as well as an updated list of resources on DE/DC. However, its opening statement of intent preceding these areas of the report is far less declarative in tone, as it states:

> The Conference on College Composition and Communication (CCCC) recognizes the increasingly large number of students earning college credit for first-year composition (FYC) while still in high school. Research suggests the value in Dual Enrollment (DE) programs; it also suggests some challenges and inconsistencies across them. Thus, this position statement attempts to address both the value and the challenges, to help ensure students' success within these programs, and also to bridge high school and college writing contexts more cohesively, in particular for those instructors teaching in DE programs.

The opening goes on to further outline the policy statement's general intentions:

> This joint statement, representing the collective position of the Conference on College Composition and Communication (CCCC), the Two-Year College English Association (TYCA), the Council of Writing Program Administrators (CWPA), and the College Section of the National Council of Teachers of English (NCTE), aims to (1) Outline collective curricular outcomes for FYC and provide recommendations for DE instructor preparation and support; (2) Recommend guidelines for student readiness, including habits of mind and academic experiences (i.e., with reading, writing, and critical analysis) (3) Provide direction on assessment, including placement of students, assessment of instructors, assessment of students, and programmatic assessment. (CCCC, "Joint Position Statement")

This opening of the 2019 policy statement is followed by a brief "background" section not in the original 2012 statement, which notes that "within the last decade, DE programs have proliferated in an educational landscape driven mainly by these four areas: (1) the college- and career-readiness initiatives; (2) the increasing costs of college tuition; (3) the nationwide education budget cuts; and (4) a subsequent drive to shorten students' time to degree," all of which were also in place in 2012 to one degree or another, though not noted here as such. It goes on to comment that, after realizing "points of consensus" in DE position statements created over the last decade by various stakeholders, "our joint statement is aimed at all teachers, students, program advisors, and administrators involved in DE programs and seeks to move us toward a shared understanding of the ways FYC can be successfully and meaningfully delivered to high school students."

It is reasonable to see the 2012 CCCC policy statement on DE/DC, as well as the subsequent broader 2013 NCTE policy statement, as a declaration of the importance of the on-the-ground college course in relation to other formations found in DE/DC, as well as a call for increased field attention to promoting the value of first-year writing. Such was appropriate for the organization and its priorities at the time, and was backed by strong research that examined DE/DC programming and its effects. In contrast, the 2019 statement reads as a concession of current national socioeconomic conditions that require cooperation and collaboration with sites of DE/DC instruction in first-year writing, absent the strong tone of advocacy for what traditional (college campus–based) courses may offer students, their families, and the public. It is collaborative in tone, certainly an important stance for CCCC's work as an organization overall. Yet that spirit of collaboration, I would argue, in turn concedes defeat of the design and delivery of the first-year course as it was originally intended, on college campuses.

One might also note the explicit call in the 2012 statement to defend the first-year writing course, terming it "the on-campus version of composition" as well as the open call for a formation of "the rationale for its requirement"—an important directive, given the usual absence of such rationale within disciplinary discourse, as noted earlier in this chapter. The 2012 statement also invokes the "integrity of our profession," signaling some concerns that so-called farming-out of first-year writing to other sites of instruction and control could dilute this integrity, at least in part. Each of these 2012 policy framings suggests *advocacy* for the original delivery mechanism of the course on college and university campuses (and later, online versions also offered for degree-seeking college students studying on these same campuses).

This call for advocacy, and rhetorical framings of first-year writing's use value, is missing from the 2019 document. I have no insight into or information about the committee's discussions when writing the 2019 policy statement, nor do I intend to cast aspersions here on the process by which this document was constructed, or the people who surely worked very long, and hard, as unpaid volunteers, to write it. Further, I understand well the difficulty of creating such policies and meeting the needs of multiple stakeholders, on a schedule that corresponds to rapidly changing conditions for teaching and learning faced by writing studies as well as other disciplines. Still, the resulting CCCC policy that has now stood for six years running bears little resemblance ideologically to the 2012 version, even if it is ostensibly addressing the same subject, from the same vantage point, and is addressed to the same audience, and even though DE/DC has only grown exponentially since 2012, as noted above.

A second examination of writing studies' public-facing work and agreed-upon advocacy measures may be undertaken with one of the most recent CCCC policies, on the "Postsecondary Teaching of Writing" (November 2023). This policy is framed by several extended arguments about what constitutes "sound writing instruction" across various learning contexts and within various institutional conditions for such. However, it makes no mention of any of the pre-college credit mechanisms discussed in this book, nor of General Education as a concept. The closest it comes to addressing such external pressures on teaching and learning in the writing course, including first-year writing, is in the policy's fourth paragraph from the end, which reads, in full:

> With confidence in higher education down sharply in recent years across the nation, the need for strategic, public-facing research that documents the important work we do as literacy educators is urgent. Our call for replicable, aggregable, and data-supported research . . . is especially urgent today when the value of higher education is no longer regarded as self-evident by many Americans (Blake; Brenan; Tough). To move this important work forward, we invite our colleagues to become teacher-scholar-activist-organizers. The exigency for such work is compelling. (CCCC, "Principles")

What I find most striking about this paragraph (which also cites numerous field scholars by year of their past works) is its invitation to members to "become teacher-scholar-activist-organizers," when the CCCC as a whole—as represented publicly—is doing little of this work currently, at least regarding first-year writing. Citing the scholars that it does in this statement is important—as it brings their work to the forefront for those who may not realize that it exists. But to do so in the absence of *any mention* of the external threats to writing in colleges and universities and especially first-year writing as the core of Gen Ed, is puzzling, especially given other points within the principles of "sound writing instruction." These principles variously include that writing is relational, can only be assessed with locally constructed measures, and "unsettles language and ideas about writing that standardize and exclude," the latter focusing mainly on language and literacy standards that marginalize certain groups, including remediation. But, I would argue, it is highly applicable to the oft-divisive and even segregated results of General Education's credit mechanisms, past and present, and its impending demise as a whole. But what is *really* striking about the policy is its conclusion, which reads, in full:

> We encourage language arts teachers to create conditions for learning to thrive (Love; Rose). Doing so, we must acknowledge—and address—structural/institutional barriers to college writing. Who are we limiting access to? Who do we consistently leave out? When we cultivate learning with the needed support systems and conditions, we generate change and new possibilities, hope and opportunity, and student success. We also strengthen our democracy and our collective ability toward "a more perfect union."
>
> We are in a moment of mass misinformation designed to use language to divide rather than unite us and to further increase rather than rebalance the power differential between rich and poor. As such, it is incumbent on language arts teachers across institutional boundaries to provide learners and the nation with critical thinkers, discerning minds, and considerate citizens who can continue pursuing the light, the *sueños* that brings so many to America and keeps our nation strong, free, and truly equal.

Aside from framing the members of CCCC as "language arts teachers," which would seem to confuse both the pedagogical level of the membership and the audience for this statement (as such a term would make more sense for the NCTE, itself chiefly K–12 teachers), this conclusion is quite noteworthy as an example of how an expanded mission that aims to be exceptionally inclusive results in a (possibly inadvertent) exclusion of the core course that undergirds many members' lives and work. Invoking the language of democracy and yet not tying it explicitly to General Education is a glaring missed opportunity for advocacy. Further, noting differentials between "rich and poor," as well as "a more perfect union," and also using a Spanish term (which roughly translates to "dreams") to hail the NCTE 2022 conference theme ("¡Sueños! Pursuing the Light!"), which signals inclusivity of members' diverse identities, creates an explicit opportunity to declare the importance of on-campus writing programs as core to these democratic principles for *all*, articulated also in the General Education movement.

I want to state unequivocally that the work of CCCC is vast, and that the organization itself has undergone many changes, and also restructuring of its various representational bodies, in order that it might reflect our changing higher education landscape and its inhabitants. Chief among these changes is a greater explicit attention to diversity, equity, inclusion; anti-racism; and social justice, especially for use within recommended pedagogical frameworks. These are all commendable and needed changes for a rapidly evolving field. However, as an organization that represents writing studies writ large, and thus has the singular *public opportunity* to not only defend General Education writing courses but also participate in the movement's potential revival, it openly falls short.

As I close this chapter, I want to turn briefly to how another field in the humanities that also offers introductory courses publicly promotes itself and, by extension, also makes visible the work it does with students entering and discovering the broader values of its field: philosophy.

Keeping Up with the (Disciplinary) Joneses: Advocacy Models Beyond Writing Studies

Much of the scholarship on General Education reform is written for and by those in the fields of educational policy and higher education assessment and design, and arguably fails to circulate beyond these professionally oriented audiences. Writing studies has the same uphill battle in disseminating its own policies, certainly, especially as a field that most all of the public doesn't actually recognize *as* a field. However, this lack of recognition and uptake outside writing studies' own boundaries is doomed to be part of a continuing vicious circle so long as writing studies does not try—or try *harder*—to make its disciplinary case within wider Gen Ed conversations, many of which *do* make it to the ears of the public when part of national news stories on higher education.

The field of philosophy is a fellow humanities discipline also beleaguered in its own right by the pressure of economically minded forces seeking to reinscribe the purpose and import of higher education. In philosophy's public-facing work, I argue there exists a potential model for writing studies, of how to communicate a discipline's value to the public, as well as how to engage prospective students in core courses that could later lead to full participation in a related major or minor field of study. Below, I walk through that engagement as an example of what writing studies could also do to shift its rhetoric toward more publicly engaged discourse that champions its first-year course and its disciplinary reach and use value.

I knew very little about philosophy until I served as the interim chair of its department at the University of Illinois–Urbana Champaign during the academic year 2021–2022. This appointment stemmed from circumstances I have written about elsewhere (Ritter, "Importance"); it also gave me the opportunity to gain a wider worldview on the humanities as a whole. What I *did* know going into the job was that philosophy is a discipline that many consider dense, even obtuse, and which does not have a reputation for being particularly public-facing or friendly to scholars outside of its confines. It might thus surprise readers here—as it did me—to learn that the American Philosophical Association (hereafter APA) takes this reputation and its associated challenges seriously and has responded with an array of promotional materials that both encourage the public to engage with the discipline, and also point to the influence of philosophy's work in the larger milieu of higher education.

Unlike writing studies, philosophy has no universally required course in the Gen Ed curriculum, but many students do take introduction to philosophy, introduction to logic, or introduction to ethics courses taught by philosophy faculty for General Education credit. Philosophy also has many subfields, some of which (philosophy of math, philosophy of science, and computational philosophy) also provide it with a presence in Gen Ed requirements for quantitative methods, alongside other options in mathematics and statistics. Also unlike writing studies, there is no AP Philosophy course offered by the College Board (yet), nor are there DE/DC programs offering philosophy courses in the high schools (that I know of). So while one might argue that philosophy's stake in the battle against pre-college credit mechanisms is not comparable to that of writing studies, I would also observe that philosophy *still* has had the wherewithal nonetheless to mount a compelling, vocal case to public audiences for its place both within General Education curricula specifically, and higher education broadly. As readers may recall from my discussion of Penn's most popular undergraduate courses over the last sixty-plus years, Philosophy was the *one* humanities field whose enrollments had stayed relatively stable.[29]

As relevant to the writing studies conversation, philosophy also shares a strong and obvious history with rhetoric, due to its origins as part of the trivium. We can see vestiges of this relationship in current journals such as *Philosophy and Rhetoric*, for example, and in scholars' shared interests in ancient and medieval texts and authors whose work may be claimed by both fields.[30] I recall the building where I did all my undergraduate work at the University of Iowa was the English-Philosophy Building, or EPB for short, signaling to students and faculty some kind of geographic, cross-disciplinary affinity (though never did I take a philosophy course as an undergraduate; I was too terrified). Regardless of how one shapes its origins in relation to the work of writing studies, or to other disciplines, philosophy is nonetheless both a sister field in the present-day humanities paradigm within liberal arts colleges, and also a field in grave danger of elimination within those same colleges. Such news of the philosophy major's discontinuation is regularly circulated both inside and outside the field's channels, as part of ongoing coverage of the projected demise of the liberal arts more broadly.[31]

Further, because philosophy as a field has been historically overwhelmingly white and male, making it a site of study that has felt hostile to women and persons of color, the APA website, which is brightly designed and easily navigable at https://www.apaonline.org/, includes a separate section on institutions which have received censure from the APA for exclusionary practices of one kind or another. It also contains a significant trove of resources related to diversity, equity, and inclusion, including the MAPS (minorities and philosophy) graduate organization, whose tagline is "Map for the Gap," and whose landing page, as of this writing, links to a massive fundraising campaign (https://www.mapforthegap.com/).[32] The field's stated principles regarding DEI, as well as other best practices for departments and curricular programs, are laid out in an APA departmental handbook provided as a PDF on the site, printed copies of which I distributed to all philosophy faculty and referenced throughout my year as interim chair. Such inclusion-based values are ones that philosophy shares with writing studies.

The main APA website demonstrates notable public relations savvy with its three vertical banners on the landing page, which link to recent activity on the organization's Facebook page, its X (formerly Twitter) feed, and its blog—each of which, at the time of this writing, had activity no more than ten days old and as new as four hours prior. The landing page also has links to announcements, information about upcoming field events, recent field scholarship, and careers (notable is the link to what is called "PhilJobs," a searchable database at http://philjobs.org/, not unlike the *MLA Job List* in that it lists all faculty openings in philosophy throughout the year).

But what makes philosophy a most interesting discipline to analyze against writing studies in my discussion of Gen Ed values in this book is its particular section on the landing page termed "Advocacy," which includes a link to the APA "Public Philosophy Committee," whose last fifteen years of annual reports are hyperlinked, and whose general charge is to "to find and create opportunities to demonstrate the personal value and social usefulness of philosophy."

Their activities include "establish[ing] ties to national and local media" and "organiz[ing] and support[ing] programs that demonstrate the personal value and social usefulness of philosophy, such as suitable lecture series, and radio and television appearances by philosophers" (https://www.apaonline.org/group/public). This page also includes a link to all APA policies, including the "Statement on the Role of Philosophy Departments in Higher Education" (https://www.apaonline.org/page/role_of_phil). Elsewhere on the site is the "Department Advocacy Toolkit," for chairs and deans (https://www.apaonline.org/page/deptadvocacytoolkit).

I want to briefly unpack this policy statement and toolkit as key examples of how philosophy might serve as a model for what writing studies could be doing, comparatively, to communicate with the public. The APA has, in my opinion, masterfully developed responses to questions about philosophy's relevance to students and their families today, and to the general public. Even better, their public-facing work shows how they *anticipated* certain issues relevant to the public in the design of their materials, and also the reactions of skeptical philosophy faculty who may not believe in the need for such wider engagement. Theirs is a straightforward, accessible approach that does not shy away from self-promotion, but neither speaks in terms of or about conditions that are outside the general public's frame of reference, or outside the values that philosophers themselves hold as teachers and scholars.

The APA Advocacy Toolkit, created in 2018, is described as one "intended to provide strategies that may be useful to programs that are at risk, programs hoping to insulate themselves against future risk, and programs aiming to strengthen and/or expand." The site further notes that ideas in the Toolkit "have been selected from across different types of institutions and departments. It is up to the faculty members within a department to decide which ideas will be most effective [locally]" (https://www.apaonline.org/page/deptadvocacytoolkit). The Toolkit is accompanied by several downloadable flyers advertising philosophy, including the "Why Study Philosophy?" general flyer, and also other flyers profiling various celebrities and cultural figures who hold either an undergraduate or graduate degree in philosophy. These each include a quote from the celebrity themselves as well as a photo and are print-ready to display or distribute to students (when I was a chair, the most popular celebrity among these was Rashida Jones, whom students recognized from *The Office*).

The Toolkit is a downloadable PDF designed as a guidebook, with very brief, one- to three-page, chapters on topics, in alphabetical order, such as

"Admissions," "Advertising," "Data," "Development," "Interdisciplinarity," "Marketing," "Merchandise," "Programming," "Recruiting," "Social Media," and "Undergraduate Community Support," among many others, each with hyperlinks to external resources where one can read and learn more. This is, truly, a soup-to-nuts guide to building, sustaining, and promoting a program and department, including a clear eye toward many of the areas in which academics as a group resist participation as part of their job duties (e.g., fundraising, publicity, and marketing).

Two sections of special interest in the Toolkit that relate directly to General Education are in the "core curriculum" and "values" chapters. For "core curriculum," the guidebook provides a primer, explaining that "colleges and universities often have foundational or core requirements. Introductory courses in philosophy, ethics, and logic traditionally have been included in those General Education requirements at many institutions." The chapter then includes these specific suggestions:

- Ensure that such courses continue to serve the goals and objectives of the core curriculum.
- Ensure that such courses provide students with an opportunity or invitation for further study in philosophy by introducing the variety of topics and methodologies in the discipline.
- Ensure that such courses champion the relevance of philosophy to a wide array of career paths by connecting philosophical topics or methods to real-world practices (e.g., the study of democracy for civic engagement, the study of objectivity for social scientific practices, the study of values for interpersonal relationships, etc.). (14)

Taking this instruction on General Education a step further, this section of the Toolkit also notes:

> Both the APA Committee on the Teaching of Philosophy and the American Association of Philosophy Professors (AAPT) can assist departments in developing both new individual courses and new courses of study for the major and minor. The APA/AAPT Teaching Hub routinely offers faculty development sessions that focus on general education issues at the three APA divisional meetings. And the journals *Teaching Philosophy* and *AAPT Studies in Pedagogy* publish articles on the ways in which philosophy departments can contribute to general education.

Similarly, the section on "values," which is the last chapter of the Toolkit, exhorts faculty and department chairs to communicate the value of philosophy at every opportunity. Lecture introductions, study halls, department social events, and every course the department offers are opportunities to speak to not only the willing audience of existing majors, but also new students and other faculty who may attend. Communicating the value of philosophy to your own majors may seem futile, but remember that they represent the department in large and small ways in their courses and social encounters. They need to hear ... about the value of philosophy frequently so that they repeat it often. (55)

What is especially interesting about this last appeal is its focus on spreading the good word of philosophy, as it were, through the voices of *students* in the major—a zone approach, in football terms, to both offense and defense. It also exhibits an awareness of the importance of repeated messaging across contexts—including to those audiences *inside* the field, who will then learn (implicitly) to transmit them and disseminate core values of the field to others.

The Toolkit overall demonstrates both the organized simplicity of a multiprong plan for survival—necessary, given the fragility of philosophy at budget-conscious state institutions often dependent upon the choices of politicians—and the cool-headed instructions for the newly initiated on how to launch this plan on their own campuses. Philosophy as a discipline has taken the initial important step of reinterpreting its mission and purpose for the higher education landscape—deliberately looking inward as well as outward in its future plans. To say it plain, this takes a lot of guts—and a lot of work outside many faculty's own comfort zones. Faculty in writing studies, in my own experience at least, are no exception here.

This positionality, and guts, is clear in the second document of note, the "Statement on the Role of Philosophy in Higher Education." This document is interesting to compare with statements from the CCCC, above, as it not only discusses the ways in which philosophy courses, including those at the introductory level should be taught, but also makes clear how the discipline's work fits into other academic and public spaces, and into the national (and international) conditions for higher education.[33] Though this statement has not been revised since 2008, it somehow still feels more current than CCCC statements drafted ten to fifteen years later. This statement is divided into six sections: "Fundamental Contributions to Education"; "Contributions to an Institution's Core Curriculum"; "Relations to Other Areas of Intellectual Inquiry"; "Contributions Beyond the Curriculum"; "Service, Major, and Graduate Programs in Philosophy"; and "Measures of Programmatic Success."

It's important to note here that the APA as an organization has *more* publicly available policies, statements, and reports than CCCC overall. (The APA's policies number seven; plus thirty statements, of which the 2008 statement is one; and fourteen reports, plus ten years [2014–2024] of letters and statements from the board of officers.) However, many of these are on very minute or hyperspecific issues (for example, a statement on interviewing in hotel rooms, or on department rankings—a particularly sensitive topic in the field—as well as a policy on revoking prizes and awards) and as such really run the gamut of both outlining disciplinary-specific operations on the national-international and local levels, and providing ideological and value-based statements about the work that the field actually does. This plethora of documents and policies makes the 2008 statement even more impressive, given that it attempts in many ways to encapsulate many of these field values and practices into a digestible, public-facing utterance.

Yet it is its organizational audience awareness that is most important to my argument here, as it takes as a given that the discipline *must* provide a rationale for itself within higher education, and that it must also outline its various complementary *rather than competing* missions. In fact, the preamble to the statement's six areas makes such purposes clear:

> Higher education in America frequently undergoes reassessment, external and internal, formal and informal. Colleges and universities review their programs; the officials who determine the budgets scrutinize costs and benefits; students and potential students compare institutions for quality and relevance to their degree goals. This intensive reassessment can be due to changing demographics, rising costs, and in many institutions, a growing concern by students with the likelihood that their courses will help them to find rewarding employment. Internal reassessment can be a sign of responsible self-analysis.... Occasions like these provide an opportunity for philosophers and philosophy programs to state or restate the case for their centrality and indispensability to their institutions' mission. We believe that this statement can be helpful in making that case. We also believe that this statement can be of use to admissions offices, deans' offices, and development offices, in furtherance of the tasks of student recruitment and donor development.

At its close comes the enveloping assertion that "far from being an academic luxury, philosophy should play a central part in any well balanced college or university curricula." Within the second area of focus, "Contributions to an Institution's Core Curriculum," the statement notes that philosophy provides instruction in logical reasoning, values, and global issues, within the latter category reminding readers that "philosophers have made and continue to make significant contributions to ongoing debates on a number of issues that go beyond national boundaries, such as environmental pollution, global climate change, and the status of global ecosystems; global trade and national exploitation; human rights . . . and the repatriation of cultural objects." And under the third area of focus, "Relation to Other Areas of Intellectual Inquiry," it argues that

> in exploring concepts and methods of inquiry used by other disciplines, in taking up questions that disciplines generate about their own subject matter, and in examining the questions that are fundamental to any area of inquiry concerned with producing knowledge about the world and making value claims about that knowledge, philosophy fulfills a unique and important role as a meta-discipline. It provides a kind of understanding of the other disciplines, particularly of their presuppositions, standards of evidence, and modes of explanation, that other fields of study neither attempt nor are able to provide.

One might see this last assertion as a challenge to other fields to frame their work as both widely applicable and *useful* across academia and in the greater public good. But for my purposes, I also submit that writing studies *itself* could have written such a declaration, focused on how such work happens in the first-year course and is scaffolded thereafter in subsequent writing courses across the curriculum and within the disciplines. Again, to be clear, I am *not* saying that writing studies should engage in a turf war with philosophy on these issues; frankly, I think it would lose. What I want to do here is bring awareness of how other disciplines *can and do* lay claim to their value in General Education, in higher education, and in the ongoing maintenance and growth of a functioning democracy.

The case that I hope to have persuasively made in this chapter is twofold: first, that writing studies needs to present a stronger and more publicly voiced stance regarding its first-year course in the face of extremely viable options such as DE/DC, and second, that such public advocacy should be generously framed and accessible to a wider range of readerships—including those from the field itself—perhaps as modeled off disciplinary work in philosophy (and other fields, such as history, which via the AHA does similar excellent public-facing work that I did not have space to outline in this chapter). An uptake of my call from field leaders and those working on the ground in writing programs who can help to shape and influence the work of such leaders would be a significant step both toward bringing writing studies into the hopeful revival of the General Education movement, and toward reframing the rhetoric of writing studies as relevant to its long-standing core liberatory mission.

As I discuss in my conclusion, which closes my story of Gen Ed with some current rhetorics of higher education and my own personal reflections on these, we need all hands on deck in order to provide cogent, informed responses to members of the public as to why Gen Ed's on-campus structures and underlying educational values still matter to our democracy today.

CONCLUSION

Will the Circle Be Unbroken?

The Challenges of the Paper Ceiling

As I conclude my story of Gen Ed, I invite you to look back with me at the responses to it that I sampled at the start of this book. These responses—of not knowing, not understanding, or worst of all, not *caring* about Gen Ed—are of course representative of the deeply entrenched problem that forms the foundation of all other problems that I have discussed, in the tales of government and politics and corporate alliances with educators and those being educated that make up each of my chapters. I ask you now, how might we reconcile academic and nonacademic apathy about Gen Ed in ways that allow us to revive the Gen Ed movement across all subjects, including first-year writing, while also recognizing forces working against higher education that make Gen Ed not only logical but also urgently necessary?

First, we would need to agree, as a citizenry, on the actual purpose of college. Right now, there is a clear division between those who see college as an innate good that edifies a person, educates them about the wider world, and prepares them to be part of a functioning democracy, and those who see it as simply an (expensive) means to a better personal economic end. Further, the idea of being an informed citizen is at odds with how that citizenry is actually represented and regarded within Gen Ed as a whole. For example, in 2023, Colleen Wynn and Elizabeth Ziff highlighted work done at the time by the American

Association of University Professors (AAUP) denouncing fifty-seven bills across twenty-three states that targeted what faculty can teach. They observed that "not all bills target general education courses, specifically, [but] many target its content, such as readings on race, gender, and sexuality." Such work served as a primer for more widespread state legislative acts discussed elsewhere in this book and happening in 2026, in response to and in agreement with President Trump's own political agenda.

For example, there is the "General Education Act" put forward by the Ethics and Public Policy Center, the James G. Martin Center for Academic Renewal, and the National Association of Scholars. On its surface, this act looks to be a call for the restoration of the core values of Gen Ed—and in many ways, it is, given its statement that "distribution requirements, at best, have replaced preparation to be a free citizen with pre-professional preparation in the social sciences or the sciences. Public universities' first duty to the citizens who fund them is to educate their children to assume their role as citizens. So too is public universities' duty to their students." It also calls for a separate school of Gen Ed on public university campuses, which, again, seems like a step in the right direction for making Gen Ed prominent and agentic within college curricula.

But the proposal also emphasizes, among other things, "Western" values and the "greatest books of Western Civilization," which we know to be exclusionary toward many populations whose works and teachings are also part of a well-rounded Gen Ed curriculum. And the National Association of Scholars, like the Hoover Institution, purports to be bipartisan but is widely recognized as a conservative organization that, for example, lobbies against multiculturalism and DEI work, acting as what some consider a right-wing think tank. Their call is thus not entirely in the spirit of Gen Ed in the twenty-first century. Instead, it is one that perhaps is appealing in some very basic aspects, yet would stand to limit students' exposure to truly diverse subject matter that is important to their civic understanding and to their own positioning as American citizens in a democracy.[1]

Complicating these politically fueled versions of General Education that both embrace its postwar values *and* aim to conscribe Gen Ed of the present and future by severely tailoring its interpretations to *only* viewpoints held by conservatives, there is an equally strong force affecting Gen Ed's futures. That is the rejection of the belief that college is a credential that must be completed in order to get a job and acquire a standard of living as good or better than the previous generation. Those holding this viewpoint are often—but not always—the nonacademic public. This latter group sees college as too expensive, too laborious in its requirements and layered institutional structures, and not site-specific; their concept of "college" is one that can be done anywhere and in any time frame. College is not correspondent to a person's developmental growth, per this belief system, and so it need not happen on a physical campus. This movement is what we may see, in principle, as an apolitical force, though given the current overlap between conservative values and non–college educated citizens, it has the power to become rapidly politicized over the coming years of the current presidential administration.

Given the forces noted above, in rhetorical terms, until and unless we come to some measure of stasis on this defining question of what college is, and what it is *for*—and, indeed, what Gen Ed *means* within that valuation of college—we cannot hope to have a strong and successful General Education movement afoot in the United States. This is the problem I want to wrestle with in this conclusion, with an eye toward future possibilities, and hope. In doing so, I encourage readers who agree with my desire to revive the General Education movement and all that it stands for, to keenly observe and have responses to the opposing view of not just General Education—but also of college itself—as a divisible set of requirements scattered across the landscape of state and corporate interests in efficiency measures. Whether the current controlling image of Gen Ed is an assembly line, or a "stackable" set of products, or a platform for returning to values that exclude millions of students' lived experiences, Gen Ed champions out there need to understand how much of the public sees higher education more broadly, if they want to formulate persuasive responses in kind that push us forward toward reviving the Gen Ed movement for our current times.

Do We (Really) Want to Be Educated Anyway?
American Views of Higher Education

A November 2023 poll published in *The Chronicle of Higher Education* (*CHE*) asked a random sampling of 1,025 adults the question "how well do colleges educate students?" Note the phrasing here, which was not "how well does *college* [as a collective] educate students" but instead how well *colleges*—the actual institutions themselves—do that work. The survey responses were: 41 percent "good," 31 percent "very good," 14 percent "not so good," 9 percent "excellent," and 5 percent "poor" (https://www.chronicle.com/article/where-the-public-sees-value-in-higher-ed?sra=true). These poll results seem relatively encouraging—though it's impossible to tell how "good" versus "very good" was defined, for example, or what these people felt would be the needed changes to college operations that would move the needle in their assessment from one level to the next one higher.

Another poll, conducted by *CHE* itself in September 2023, provides a little more of such specific data. In it, 80 percent of college graduates said their degrees were "worth it," with those carrying no student loan debt and with incomes over $100,000 more likely to answer in the affirmative. Similarly, 78 percent of all respondents would encourage a close friend or family member to get a four-year degree, a number that increased to 85 percent for those with such a degree. Particularly interesting written responses to this question about the worth of college included those that went beyond the scope of instructional experiences and into life skills and habits of mind, and which also easily map onto the goals of General Education:

> "Bachelor's degrees are almost mandatory for higher-paying jobs," one said. "College also exposes you to people different from where you grew up," said another. "It helps you figure out who you are and who you want to be." Preparation for work and life was a common theme: "Achieving a bachelor's degree demonstrates the ability to set and achieve goals," a respondent wrote, "to persevere toward goals, to manage your time productively, to work with teams and to face and overcome problems." (Kelderman et al.)

The other main measurements taken in this *CHE* poll were, first, how a four-year degree versus several alternatives—trade school, other professional or technical training, work apprenticeship, military service, and union membership—is beneficial. The strongest support for college in the affirmative was over trade school (37 percent), and the lowest, over union membership (20 percent), with most responses (40–49 percent across other categories) judging that college and any of the above alternatives are "about the same" for a "successful livelihood." The second and final measurement was whether college as an endeavor provides benefits to various groups of society. The poll indicated that 46 percent felt that college benefited those who graduated from it, with only 13 percent feeling that it benefited those who started but did not complete a college degree. Comparatively, 40 percent saw college as benefiting the local community, 39 percent the state as a whole, and 40 percent society overall.[2]

For the relatively small percentage who did not see how *some* college might benefit citizens, there is work to be done to better promote *any* measure of higher education as something providing lifelong benefits. The differences over the value of a degree as correlative to income are also notable, and relate to other issues of social class. In considering the "some college" realm, we might look to the uptick in so-called lifelong learning that emerged in the US immediately prior to the COVID-19 outbreak. Such was in response to the enrollment cliff to come in or around 2025, and also the rise of interest in postgraduate adult education in the US. So long as colleges and universities are investing in—and profiting from—such extended educational endeavors, the rest of us in higher education, including writing studies, might study those rhetorics as applicable to General Education, which is often (but not always) enrolled by traditional-age students (i.e., those ages eighteen to twenty-four).

The results of the September 2023 *CHE* poll are further similar to those conducted in a Gallup polling, reported in July of that same year, which show that only 17 percent of those Americans surveyed have a "great deal" of confidence in higher education, versus 28 percent in 2015, with stark differences in confidence levels between Republicans (19 percent) versus Democrats (59 percent) and measurable differences between those surveyed who have earned a postgraduate degree (50 percent) and those who have not (39 percent) (Brenan, "Americans' Confidence"). And as my fellow academics know, some of those confidence levels have to do with curricular choices—which lead to responses and proposals designed to repair what conservatives see as higher education's positions and stances, such as those from the National Association of Scholars, noted above.

Here, it's not hard to see the influence of American political platforms on the view of higher education. Hopefully when President Trump completes his term in office, we will also still have a Department of Education, despite calls for its elimination within Trump's "Agenda47," and despite the president's adherence thus far to the specifics of the principles regarding education and the public good in the Project 2025 document that he disavowed during his presidential campaign.[3] Republican pundits also point to an increasing Democratic emphasis on aspects of higher education that would seemingly have little to do with the "fundamentals"—including increased DEI measures in college and university operations that have, subsequently, been stricken down or dismantled by state legislatures, primarily in "red" states, including one profiled earlier in this book, Florida. In late January 2025, the University of North Carolina system—highlighted in chapter 3 regarding AP credit and Gen Ed policies—officially eliminated all Gen Ed courses and requirements across the sixteen UNC campuses related to diversity, equity, and inclusion, effectively canceling hundreds of courses in progress for the spring 2025 semester and leaving the problem of making up those lost credits to students and the faculty teaching them.[4]

All of this means that readers who want to help revive the General Education movement have a few things to consider in how they rhetorically frame their appeals. First, among these is that the Gen Ed movement itself has both liberal and conservative bells that ring within it, as illustrated above. Conservatives hear words such as "democracy" and "freedom" and think: back to basics, majority-led values, and homogenous approaches to education and citizenship. Liberals hear those same terms and think: equity, access, multicultural values and marginalized voices, and diverse approaches to education and citizenship. If Gen Ed advocates can get past the historical origins of the Harvard plan—namely its all-white, all-male, elite-college-only authorship profiled earlier in this book—there is much within it that can help advance the causes of liberal education today, in both senses of the term. At the same time, the values that the plan upholds are likely to be shared by those same political actors nostalgic for more homogenous (read: white, conservative) days in American life, and who also seek to reduce Gen Ed to a package of sellable goods. This is why rhetoric and representation are so very important. Gen Ed needs to be a whistle that *all* dogs, figuratively speaking, can hear.

A window into the conflict between liberal education's values and the political ideologies that form cultural battlegrounds for pundits of higher education, especially regarding the privileged classes, is Rob Henderson's concept of "luxury beliefs." Henderson articulated this concept in a multimodal opinion piece (a five-and-a-half-minute video accompanied by a voice-over by Henderson) in *The New York Times* in July 2024 (Henderson et al.).[5] Henderson's analysis targets "ideas held by privileged people that make them look good, but actually harm the marginalized," and that might be considered "virtue signaling with consequences," when enacted on elite college campuses.

Henderson focuses on several current hot-button issues, including defunding the police, legalizing drugs, and eliminating the SAT for college admissions, each of which he claims harms, not helps, marginalized and poor students. As a former low-income child raised by a drug-addicted single parent, he claims personal legitimacy in this debate. To Henderson, there are three "golden rules" undergirding the actors holding such beliefs: "Play the Victim," "Protest Without Penalty," and "Push the Less Privileged Down." In illustrating each of these rules, Henderson highlights the social status of student and faculty protestors in contrast to those who are actually affected by the issues under protest—both on the campuses themselves (e.g., custodians and groundskeepers who clean up after the protestors) and globally (e.g., the tent encampments of spring 2024 centered on the Israel-Palestine conflict). Henderson contrasts these current protests with those held during the 1960s Civil Rights Movement, which in his view lacked the insincere motives he sees held by today's protestors. Henderson concludes by calling for today's protestors to focus attention on "everyone but themselves" and accept the sometimes serious consequences of social action, including expulsion from college.

As historian Jonathan Zimmerman has succinctly outlined in his study *The Amateur Hour* (2020), college campuses starting in the 1960s began to be associated not only with civil unrest but also a population that, due to expansions in higher education related to access and equity and the youth movement against the Vietnam War, were viewed as less suitable for college than previous generations and less understanding of the social norms of higher education. The rise of the "mass class," that is, the lecture course (169), and the proliferation of teaching assistants aiding it, correspondent to the shifting emphasis on research over teaching at large universities, further exacerbated the distance between faculty and students, which slowly grew following the expansion of the American university post–World War II. So, while Henderson's argument highlights the baseline division between ultraliberal educational outcomes and the common societal good that further fuels anti–Gen Ed and related efficiency movements today, it is not an argument unique to the twenty-first century, but rather a new version of older concerns.[6]

None of Henderson's critique is about General Education, or even the structure of higher education itself. Unfortunately, I can't think of a major student movement in my lifetime that focused on demands for a revival of Gen Ed values, or for equity-based measures in Gen Ed curricula. This is even though, certainly, we have all witnessed student protests over the years regarding college admissions practices, organized (i.e., union) labor movements, administrative budget cuts, and other issues relevant to students' lives. Still, I believe a concept such as luxury beliefs is worth highlighting here, as it exemplifies how divided Americans are about the purpose and value of a college education, especially an *elite* college education, and how such division becomes mass-media subject matter digestible in both small and large rhetorical utterances.

Further, whether you subscribe to the beliefs that Henderson pans in his analysis, which have sometimes simmered to a boil over the last several decades, it's evident that higher education increasingly is viewed as a site for conflict between the haves and have-nots in America, and rightly so. We know that intergenerational wealth determines a number of future opportunities for people, and that students who have parents with college degrees are more likely to attend and graduate from college themselves (Carnevale and Rose; Haveman and Wilson). We know that college and university faculty are more likely to have attended elite institutions for their graduate work, and that the more elite the institution, the more likely it is to hire faculty with an equally elite educational background (Wapman et al.). And we know that one's birth class, despite the various affordances of American culture and a free and fair democracy, is nearly impossible to traverse without one or more significant intervening factors. Beyond these wider truths in American culture, we also know that children's conditions for learning and for healthy social development, as well as career goal attainment, are heavily influenced by their family's socioeconomic level.[7]

As David Labaree summarized in *Someone Has to Fail*, "the American language of educational goals arises from the core tensions within a liberal democracy" that struggles to meet its collective needs of, first, "*democratic equality*, which sees education as a mechanism for producing capable citizens"; second, "*social efficiency*, which sees education as a mechanism for developing productive workers"; and third, "*social mobility*, which sees education as a way for individuals to reinforce or improve their social positions" (16). Ironically, and as I have attempted to illustrate throughout this book, General Education—if freed from the constraints put upon it by efficiency measures of pre-college credit exemption mechanisms, dual enrollment and dual credit competitors, and statewide efforts to reduce Gen Ed offerings to interchangeable widgets that presume to create mobility amongst students—could help to *bridge* our existing educational divide toward the first overarching goal of democratic equality. Instead, it has so far fallen victim to rhetorical frameworks that demonize its value within the same three areas of collective need that Labaree lists above.

In terms of political battles, we might think of General Education as the metaphorical child caught in America's twenty-first-century ideological divorce. It is a child of whom neither parent (federal and state government and higher education) proclaims to want primary custody, yet one that each will also weaponize in public settings to get what it wants. The challenge I offer here is to rescue this unwanted (and misunderstood) child and, in the process, make both sides see the care and feeding of General Education more clearly, and the opportunity that General Education provides to unite rather than divide us. Such clarity of purpose is difficult, however, when students are face-to-face with another phenomenon of twenty-first-century progress that has significant uptake: the so-called Paper Ceiling Movement.

The Paper Ceiling and the Politics of Credentialing

In telling the stories of Gen Ed that highlight its rhetorical constructions from the postwar era to today, I cannot overlook the way that rhetorics of higher education are informed by opposing forces that exercise their supremacy within the American workforce itself. While most college students are taught that a degree is the only path to a "good" job, such a directive is simply circulating lore, lacking research-based citations in individual conversations to back it up, and importantly, missing a definition for "good." The website for the nonprofit organization Opportunity@Work, however, is one source providing such research, as part of its argument for expanding pathways to those so-called good jobs in American culture. Its website centers on "The Paper Ceiling," whose term of course skillfully plays on the so-called glass ceiling, which is a term for the limits to qualified women's advancement into management and executive leadership positions across various white-collar professions.

Opportunity@Work describes the paper ceiling as "the invisible barrier that comes at every turn for workers without a bachelor's degree." It heads up a movement called "Tear the Paper Ceiling," which is backed by the belief that

> the paper ceiling is not a force of nature beyond our control. It is the sum of institutional and individual choices that prioritized hiring shortcuts over real skills. Now, a movement has begun. Workers and companies uniting to create a new and more equitable future of work in which skills matter more than what's on paper. A future that is back in balance, when both STARs and employers can thrive again. A future that starts by working together to tear the paper ceiling and see the STARs beyond it. (Opportunity@Work, "Paper Ceiling")

Here, STARs stands for those individuals who are skilled through alternative routes, such as the military, on-the-job experience, or—as relevant to General Education—community college, or partial completion of a two- or four-year degree. The highlighting of "skills" that are not "on paper" in part hails the structures of adult competency-based education, discussed earlier in this book, wherein students receive college credit for work experiences. But Opportunity@Work goes beyond advocacy for this measure alone, further highlighting professional inequities for racial and socioeconomic groups that encompass STARs, who are 61 percent of Black workers, 55 percent of Latinx workers, 50 percent of white workers, 66 percent of rural Americans, and 61 percent of veterans (https://www.tearthepaperceiling.org/about-stars). Such individuals, the organization notes, earn less on average than in 1976, and are victim to a wage gap that has doubled since 1994.

At the core of the paper ceiling concept is a critique of core elitist values in American culture: that the only way into the upper economic rungs of our society is with a four-year degree, which many citizens do not (or cannot) earn. This criticism also runs throughout other phenomena discussed in this book, in particular dual enrollment in the form of early college, which allows students to emerge from high school with a two-year college degree also in hand. Four-year college has long been arguably characterized publicly as the dream for *all* Americans, across generations, ensuing social movements, and shifting demographics, with two-year college seen as the home for have-nots who are also seeking a technical certificate in a limited-income field of work, or who lack the academic record, finances, or both to be admitted to a four-year campus. General Education itself exists at the nexus of two- and four-year degrees, making it a fruitful and also vexing site for equity-minded educational policy tug-of-war.

These implicit elitist frameworks further sustain the notion that individuals with useful skills and the desire to work are significantly shut out of the higher strata of job opportunities in the country, and at the same time potentially diminishes the use value of such pursuits beyond specific career preparation. On its site, which is replete with statistical research, graphics, and images to support its argument and claims, Opportunity@Work notes the growing scarcity of jobs for workers who lack the four-year degree, as "between 2012 and 2019, 69% of new jobs created were in occupations which require a bachelor's degree or higher for entry. This left only 31% of new jobs available to the 50% of the workforce who are STARs" (Opportunity@Work, "Paper Ceiling").

We might logically assume that the paper ceiling discussion—which rightly calls out the overvaluing of a college degree in sectors where such credentials may not be necessary—is primarily led and backed by organizations without a stake in the economics of higher education. Oddly enough, that is not the case. The College Board—whose AP program I analyzed in chapter 3—is in fact a "partner" with Opportunity@Work (and its collaborator in publicity, the Ad Council), as are numerous businesses and foundations across the country, ranging from high-dollar-value tech corporations such as Google and IBM, to retail behemoth Walmart. An online release by the College Board on September 21, 2022, proclaimed that it was

> investing in BigFuture® to help more students connect to educational opportunities that lead to good careers. BigFuture is a free, comprehensive set of digital resources that helps all students take the right first step after high

school. Today's high school students deserve to enter a workforce that recognizes their talent, even if they don't pursue a 4-year degree. (College Board, "Tear the Paper Ceiling Partnership")

If you are thinking, the College Board has finally found a way to corner the *entire* post-high-school college and careers market, you are right. The "BigFuture" resources available on a separate site linked to and maintained by the College Board (https://bigfuture.collegeboard.org/) include the tagline, "Your Future, Your Way: Plan for College and Career." The site includes three student-centered, interactive tools: the "career quiz," the "college quiz," and the "scholarship quiz." When one clicks on the tab "About BigFuture," this summary appears (formatted below as on the site itself):

> When everyone's future looks different and there are so many options to choose from—it's getting started that matters.
> That's where we come in. BigFuture is a free online planning guide that helps all students take the right first step after high school.
> You can check out careers you're interested in. You can find colleges based on what's important to you. You can discover ways to pay for college.
> When you're ready to get started, BigFuture offers the information you need to make the right decision for you. Because when life feels uncertain, your future doesn't have to.
> Let's begin exploring. Your future, your way.
> (https://bigfuture.collegeboard.org/about-us)

It's hard to know where to start unpacking the logic of the College Board's alignment with the Tear the Paper Ceiling movement, but I'll take a stab thusly: By creating both resources that purport to help students obtain pre-college credit *and* resources that point students toward careers that do not require a college degree, the College Board can theoretically capitalize on both such audiences as consumers of its profitable testing options. Want to undertake a career that requires some college, but not a full four-year degree? Get some AP credit; enroll in a community college with that credit, reducing your time-to-degree; and then finish. Or not. Want to get credit for prior college work as an adult student seeking to re-enter the workforce with additional credentials? Take the CLEP exams, and use them toward a two-year (or four-year) degree, which you may finish. Or not. Whether a student *completes a degree* matters not in the credit equation. All that matters, as I have argued previously in this book, are those tests. And the viability of the tests in gaining credits that would ostensibly improve a student's college or work plans helps build a loyal customer base for the College Board's products and solidifies the reputation of the College Board in national classroom-to-workforce conversations.

Also important to note here is the explicit rhetoric of personal choice directed at students in the BigFuture directives (including its name, which portends, of course, great things). As I discussed in chapter 1 and reminded readers elsewhere in this book, the choices that students make are at the heart of Gen Ed's successes and also its challenges and failures. But this rhetoric that *panders* to student choice sidesteps issues of societal pressures or specific workplace requirements that students cannot control, and seems to elide very real family circumstances that may dictate student choices above all. BigFutures is all about *you*, the student, as is so much of the rhetoric used by the College Board. This contrasts with the aggregate advocacy by Opportunity@Work, which itself is very much in the context of specific socioeconomic conditions that to an extent lie *outside* an individual's control, until we change the way we think about credentials and the workforce.

Regardless of which actor is most loudly heard in the anti–paper ceiling movement, it's clear that students have concerns about how a college education will impact their future such that Gen Ed, as a liberating endeavor, barely registers for them. I thus conclude here by turning briefly to models of reform that Gen Ed advocates might consider, and that skeptics might also, simultaneously, embrace.

Bigger Pictures and Possible Futures: The NSSE and Curricular Configurations

To close this book with a little less doom and gloom than I have otherwise offered, I want to examine recent results from the National Survey of Student Engagement (NSSE), which is taken annually by students completing their first year at a four-year college or university, and also by students finishing their fourth or senior year at the same institution. The NSSE is usually administered by college offices of institutional assessment, who are also responsible for analyzing national results in relation to those of their own campus.

The NSSE charts student responses to indirect measurements of their own learning across several modules, as a kind of pre- and post-test of what they have gained through college. These include a module on civic engagement, which includes questions like how much the student's institution emphasizes free speech and expression, voting in local, state, or campus elections, or being an "informed and active citizen." The module also measures students' self-assessments of their ability to, for example, contribute to a community's well-being or helping others resolve disagreements. As such, this section of the NSSE probably bears the closest kinship with the core values of General Education, that is, building an informed democracy that understands how local and global conditions affect the experiences of others, both distant and close in kin.

The 2023 NSSE results in the civic engagement module are noteworthy in attempting to answer the question of whether General Education is serving its original, core purposes, if we assume that (1) some students' perceptions were formed, at least in part, through Gen Ed curricula; (2) such perceptions are reinforced throughout later college experiences; and (3) are thus aggregations of a complete college education also informed by social phenomena that carry forward to graduation.

Measured on a Likert scale of 1 (poor or very little) to 5 (excellent or very much), 61 percent of first-year and 67 percent of fourth-year students in 2023 felt they were very good to excellent at helping others solve disagreements; 64 percent of first-year and 72 percent of fourth-year students felt they were very good to excellent at leading a group welcoming of different backgrounds; and 65 percent of first-year and 72 percent of fourth-year students felt they were very good to excellent at contributing to a community of well-being.

Similarly, 57 percent of first-year and 65 percent of fourth-year students felt their institution emphasized quite a bit to very much the importance of being an informed and active citizen; 66 percent of first-year and 63 percent of fourth-year felt their institution emphasized quite a bit to very much free speech and expression; and 58 percent of first-year and 68 percent of fourth-year students felt their institution emphasized quite a bit to very much voting in local, state, or national elections.[8]

Observable from the above statistics is a notable increase across all categories from freshman to senior years except the emphasis on free speech and expression. The latter could be due to events during a particular year (with 2023 graduates entering college before COVID-19 and graduating during its latter waves that required campus shutdowns and social distancing, for example) or due to a national shift in youth viewpoint regarding freedom of speech on campuses overall. The statistics also do not control for students who may have started their college career at one school and completed the NSSE survey later at another; in other words, some of these fourth-year students could have transferred from an institution that had more open and ready encouragement toward free speech than does their current institution.

But what I want to most emphasize in providing these NSSE statistics is the *hope* that college is, in fact, *changing* students' perceptions of what it means to participate in a civic democracy—with General Education as a foundational part. A more extensive analysis of these metrics would chart NSSE responses over a ten- to twenty-year period to see if the concurrent demise of General Education enrollments and curricula may be correlated to such responses, though such would not provide proof of causation. It is alongside these current figures—which I think signal promise for ongoing development of civic understanding amongst college students—that I want to profile one university that I think is getting Gen Ed's founding ideals and purposes right.

Pennsylvania State University includes twenty so-called commonwealth campuses besides its main flagship campus at University Park, and thus is among those giant state systems controlled by a research-focused flagship under discussion in chapter 2.[9] I had the opportunity to visit Penn State back in 2016, meet with its Gen Ed stakeholders, and learn more about its approach to this curriculum. Penn State's Gen Ed program is notable for being one of the most prominently voiced programs across the many other large public universities I have examined in my research for this book. While Gen Ed may be executed through many rhetorical frameworks and with many local strategies across small and large, and public and private, colleges and universities, it is the flagship campuses that often receive the most national attention and are also the most attuned to their *research* mission over their teaching mission, by virtue of selectivity and, thus, institutional design.

In the late 2010s, Penn State decided to overhaul its General Education program, as many other universities have also done in the last two to three decades. During this time, it created an Office of General Education, led by a faculty member whose title is Assistant Dean for General Education. Nowhere on the Penn State Gen Ed site is there mention of career competencies, workforce development, or check-box requirements that otherwise characterize much public messaging about General Education. Instead, Penn State declares the purpose of its General Education program to be to "enable students to acquire skills, knowledge, and experiences for living in interconnected contexts so they can contribute to making life better for others, themselves, and the world" (https://gened.psu.edu/about-our-office).

The site does include a link to a "General Education Planning Tool" for students, but it also explicitly notes therein that such a tool is designed "to increase the value of your education, and so you can be more effective and deliberate in your choices" (https://genedplan.psu.edu/). The structure of the

Gen Ed program itself requires program courses to demonstrate two to four of the following "key objectives": "Effective Communication," "Key Literacies," "Critical and Analytical Thinking," "Integrative Thinking," "Creative Thinking," "Global Learning," and "Social Responsibility and Ethical Reasoning"—each of which both harken back to principles in the postwar General Education movement, and also to the AAC&U VALUE rubrics. Courses themselves fall under either "Foundations" (writing and speaking and quantification) or one of five "Domains" (arts, humanities, health and wellness, natural sciences, and social and behavioral sciences). Finally, the program also requires so-called Integrative Studies courses, which combine the work of two knowledge domains in interdisciplinary and synthetic study (https://gened.psu.edu/faculty-staff/about-general-education/learning-objectives-and-foundation-and-domain-criteria).

The PSU Gen Ed website guides faculty through these areas, and also provides resources for assessment, advising, and grant opportunities, including PSU's "Faculty Scholars" in Gen Ed, who are selected competitively from across the campuses and serve three-year terms, with supplemental pay (https://gened.psu.edu/faculty-staff/general-education-faculty-scholars). The website also has resources for students, and links to Senate reports and other news about General Education on campus overall. The purpose of this book is not to compare or contrast specific Gen Ed programs, nor is it to campaign for a particular shape or structure for programs themselves; there are many, many other books on liberal education reform and structures that do this important taxonomical work. Nonetheless, I see Penn State's program as the closest we might come to both providing a comprehensive, broad-coverage model of General Education and also backing that with articulated cross-disciplinary values and acknowledgment of how various areas of the university can come together through Gen Ed to create new paths of meaning for students and faculty alike.[10]

The kind of program mounted by Penn State is a *lot* of work, but to my mind, it's worth doing if we want to save Gen Ed from disappearing altogether. In *Unmaking the Public University*, Christopher Newfield outlines the idea, imagined by the emeritus president of the University of Wisconsin system, of "de facto privatization," in which public university systems will be divided into "specialist" regional universities that focus strictly on workforce preparation, and "creative" universities, which continue an in-depth, highly interdisciplinary research mission. This latter group contains the flagship research universities, for example Penn State University Park, or in my state, the University of Georgia (192–193).[11] Newfield connects this divide-and-conquer structuring of public higher education to the "end of the majoritarian vision of quality for all," in that it erroneously reseparates creativity and the masses in order to save money in the short term. It revitalizes a class system that belonged to the assembly-line approach to labor management that the knowledge economy had supposedly made obsolete, while damaging both social justice and effectiveness. When forced to participate in this return of social and economic leadership to a small elite through the downgrading of mass higher education, the public university sides with the backward current of contemporary history [that] undermine[s] general development and its broad public constituency in one misguided move. (193)

Aligned with Newfield's arguments for rebuilding funding for public higher education and reinvesting in the public good is Chris Gallagher, who conveys his vision for so-called integrative learning as a solution in *College Made Whole* (2019). Gallagher reviews the growth of higher education for the masses, including the impulses of the General Education movement, concluding that "higher education provides individual advancement in ways that simultaneously provide social advancement" (45) even as students often experience learning as "fragmented, disjointed ... less than a sum of its parts" (48)—something Gen Ed detractors obviously capitalize upon in offering various pre-credit mechanisms outlined in this book.

Gallagher's solution includes a return to the "depth and breadth" model advocated in the Redbook, both within General Education requirements and the major, wherein "depth means learning how to be an expert [and] breadth means learning how to be a *non*-expert," which helps students recognize the limits of their own perspectives and expertise while also valuing that of others (61). Key to such work, for Gallagher, is adherence to the following principles: (1) designing "coherent curricula" that "promote holistic educational experiences"; (2) prioritizing integrative learning in all courses and curricula; (3) "motivat[ing] and reward[ing]" faculty in learning about integrative work, and for collaboration; and (4) incorporating integrative learning into assessment (66–67).

I would submit that the Penn State model incorporates each of these principles and priorities, and in the original spirit with which I believe Gen Ed was intended. Now it's up to Gen Ed advocates to bring these principles and priorities to the table in other settings, including organizational policy work and public advocacy, in order to set them against other efficiency-minded, cost-cutting, time-saving measures that will, in due time, make it far less easy to say that we do, in fact, teach and learn in a truly free society.

Coda: The Circle

I will close this book with a personal story, because the process of becoming educated is always personal in the choices it requires us to make, as noted earlier, as are the consequences of those choices.

I grew up in a working-class, suburban, Midwestern family, raised from the age of seven by a divorced mother and factory worker who had herself grown up on a farm surrounded by early-twentieth-century country and bluegrass music. I always knew I was *supposed* to go to college, even though neither of my parents had done so, but beyond that, I never much thought about why or how. My family probably thought I would go into a career in music, since as a young child I learned to play the violin and developed something near to perfect pitch in the process. I also often found myself actively listening to my mother absentmindedly playing her banjo on evenings when the power went out (frequently) or when there was nothing good to watch on television (semifrequently), and we had run out of board games to play or summer storms to watch out for. Ultimately, I decided I wanted to be a writer, because I had learned in high school that music was hypercompetitive and that I lacked the stomach to endure that kind of pain. This led to me going to college for journalism (which I ditched for English) and then graduate school for English and creative writing. Thereafter, I became a faculty member, a scholar, and also an administrator, all of which was a path that I could never have imagined in my youth.

Not yet knowing where those next decades would end up taking me, however, I knew that I loved to sing. And so, as my mother played the banjo on those nights with nothing else to do, one song I still recall above many others was "Will the Circle Be Unbroken," technically a Christian gospel hymn but nonetheless one in my mother's repertoire alongside songs like the Carter Sisters' "Keep on the Sunny Side." My mother was also musically inclined, and a product of her antisocial parents' informal relationship with religion. They were "country" people who feared God, but also rejected churchgoing as a means of demonstrating that fear in a public way.

My mother, in turn, passed this fitful hybrid belief system onto me. And so, such generically religious hymns were part of my happenstance upbringing, and entertainment, in the socially and economically turbulent 1970s, when there was not much else in the world to keep up our spirits—a feeling that some citizens, including myself, feel again in 2026. The 1970s were a time, however, when education was seen as an inarguable good, and also a time when I assumed things would *have* to get better—perhaps after I became an adult, perhaps after college, perhaps at some vanishing point in the future. And so, I absorbed the memorable refrain of the modern version of the song, which my mother would play and to which I would sing along: *will the circle be unbroken / by and by lord by and by / there's a better / home a-waiting / in the sky lord / in the sky.*

By recalling this song, and the feeling it brought of possible light after a lot of darkness through a renewed unification of souls and purposes, I do not mean to convey that General Education is my religion, though there are certainly worse things to which a person might devote themselves. But I do mean to make a connection between the hopefulness of that song—which of course is really about the promise of meeting your loved ones in heaven after death, for those who believe in such eschatological conditions—and my own hopefulness that somehow, those of us working in academia can someday witness a (happy) reunion with General Education, despite the bleak political times in which we live. In my lifetime, if not before the rapidly approaching end of my academic career, my rational mind tells me that General Education will cease to exist in college and universities. But that is not what the hopeful child inside me wants to believe.

Instead, in writing this book, I believe it is still possible to keep the circle of higher education—as it was imagined nearly seven decades ago at the birth of the postwar Gen Ed movement—unbroken. And in doing so, we simultaneously take the other circles of racial and social marginalization, of corporate greed, of public university system machineries, and of efficiency mechanisms that cross many groups inside and outside higher education, and break those instead. We then can realize and reanimate the goals of liberal education as relevant to all our lives, our educational paths, and our careers in the twenty-first century, in the process rescuing the dignity and integrity of higher education as a whole.

Notes

Introduction: The Story of General Education

1. For more information, see https://usprogram.gatesfoundation.org/news-and-insights/articles/student-perceptions-of-american-higher-education.
2. For more information, see https://research.collegeboard.org/media/pdf/student-parent-attitudes-college-admissions.pdf.
3. See, for example, popular press articles that in early 2025 attempted to chart Trump's often mercurial but also single-minded views of education as a public good, including Oladipo; Fore; as well as Pandey on Trump and the "educational divide" in politics.
4. Black high school students, particularly Black males, are the population least likely to complete a calculus course, which impacts their ability to be directly admitted into college programs in engineering, computer science, and other STEM fields of study. For more, see NCES ("Indicator 13") data on the topic, as well as DeRuy.
5. In addition to my own *Reframing the Subject* (2015), works by other rhetoric and writing studies scholars have argued this connection, as well as illustrated the value of class-based rhetorics in various communities. See, for example, Harvey Graff's *The Literacy Myth* (1979), Deborah Brandt's *Literacy in American Lives* (2001), Mary Soliday's *The Politics of Remediation* (2003), William DeGenaro's *Who Says* (2007), Steve Lamos's *Interests and Opportunities* (2011), and Rebecca Lorimer Leonard's *Writing On the Move* (2018), among many others.
6. See https://thielfellowship.org/faq.
7. *Harvard Alumni Bulletin*, vol. 40, no. 17, pp. 597. Conant's declaration was also highlighted in Jerome Karabel's important book, *The Chosen: The Hidden History of Admission and Exclusion at Harvard, Yale, and Princeton* (2006).
8. There are of course myriad ways that Gen Ed is organized on campuses. The general terms I use here correspond to those that Conant used in his time, covering broad areas of the cur-

riculum and without a specific interdisciplinary nomenclature. This was also before topics such as information literacy, digital literacy, and computing; and cultural studies, ethnic studies, and minority cultures; and during a time when English = literature, with a lack of subdivision between rhetoric and writing and literature. Thus, while I realize my terms here are a gross generalization, they represent a postwar expression of subject matter that Gen Ed should "cover," which continues to be shaped and reshaped on local levels today.

9. I say "first two years" here with the knowledge that many proponents of Gen Ed—particularly those at institutions where it is modeled on highly interdisciplinary study or designed to serve as a respite from a student's major program throughout all four years of study (e.g., engineering programs)—would take issue with this. The framing of Gen Ed as being completed within the first sixty credits lends itself to an equivalency with community college study, as well as to a focus within early college and other programs that do not contain what most institutions would call "advanced hours" toward the degree. However, the original concept of Gen Ed as articulated by the Harvard group is very clearly aligned with introductory study that often results in courses not requiring advanced knowledge nor being designed for working at higher levels of disciplinary expertise. Still, I acknowledge that the wide range of Gen Ed models in the US—which continue to evolve in response to various internal and external demands—are not completely represented by my emphasis here on first- and second-year studies.

10. For a longitudinal look at General Education before and after Harvard's Redbook, see Boning. For a more comprehensive study of General Education as an evolving curriculum across the US, see C. Wells, *Realizing General Education* (2016).

11. The details of these archives, and select conversations therein, is something I have also written about extensively elsewhere. See chapter 3 of Ritter, *To Know Her Own History*.

12. It's important to note that this is not problems *with* diversity—to think in terms of our current political climate—but problems *of* diversity of socioeconomic background and educational preparation, and how to address these through General Education. It is thus an examination of how to (insofar as is possible) *positively* ameliorate difference rather than punish those who highlight it. Admittedly, the Harvard plan did not serve as a panacea in this regard nor did it fully anticipate the longer-term ramifications on higher educational structures stemming from emerging fights over desegregation, as discussed later in this book.

13. James Bryant Conant was a strong proponent of "ability grouping," one outgrowth of which was ways to advance "gifted" students through what would eventually become the Advanced Placement Program. In Byron S. Hollingshead's words, such grouping allows education to be "differentiated only by ability in order that the bright might move faster than the dull" ("General Education" 78).

14. See the full VALUE rubrics at https://www.aacu.org/initiatives/value-initiative/value-rubrics.

15. See for example the Gen Ed outcomes at the University of Illinois Urbana-Champaign, at https://provost.illinois.edu/assessment/learning-outcomes-assessment/general-education-assessment/, or the University of Oklahoma, at https://www.ou.edu/assessment/general-education/learning-outcomes. For a broader interpretation of these areas, see the University of Utah outcomes at https://generaleducation.utah.edu/overlaps.php.

16. A short list of recent titles include Armstrong and Hamilton's *Paying for the Party: How College Maintains Inequality* (2015); McMillan Cottom's *Lower Ed: The Troubling Rise of For-Profit Colleges in the New Economy* (2017); Hamilton's *Parenting to a Degree: How Family Matters for College Women's Success* (2016); Abram Jack's *The Privileged Poor* (2020); Lee's *Class and Campus Life: Managing and Experiencing Inequality at an Elite College* (2016); Mettler's *Degrees of Inequality: How the Politics of Higher Education Sabotaged the American Dream* (2014); Mullen's *Degrees of Inequality: Culture, Class, and Gender in American Higher Education* (2010); and Stich's *Access to*

Inequality: Reconsidering Class, Knowledge, and Capital in Higher Education (2012). A journalistic take on this same subject matter is Tough's *The Years That Matter Most* (2019).

17. In terms of motivating factors, AP, early college, and dual credit are also means for saving significant tuition dollars. Thus we cannot talk about the demise of Gen Ed without talking about the lack of affordability of college for many in the United States. Even as forty-eight of the fifty states have tuition remission programs for low-income students (Georgia and New Hampshire being the exceptions), this alone is not enough to combat the rhetoric of General Education as an unnecessary expense.

18. In a broader sense, rhetoric and writing studies certainly has long had its eye on how the archives may reveal truths about present-day conditions that affect our labor and our ideology in writing programs. Examples include Gold's *Rhetoric at the Margins*, Stanley's *The Rhetoric of Remediation*, Wan's *Producing Good Citizens*, and Ostergaard and Rix Wood's *In the Archives of Composition*. The stories told in this book extend the dialogue with these and my other fellow field historians.

19. "Seamless transfer" is a term of art in the higher education business. It means that students may come from another college (typically an in-state community college with which a four-year campus has an articulation agreement) without any "seams" between their previous and future work. The courses all transfer with previously agreed-upon equivalencies, and the process for students is without additional effort or justification on their part. In evoking this term, I do not mean to denigrate seamless transfer, which has student advantages. Rather, I highlight how systems such as this tend to be expanded and even perverted to apply to any manner of pre-college experience that should, at the very least, have a few exposed curricular seams.

20. As I have written about elsewhere, basic writing was a zero-credit, ungraded course (English 098) when I arrived at my first institution (Southern Connecticut State University) in fall 2000. We fought to have that changed such that by the time I left in 2008, we had a renumbered sequence of English 110, 111, and 112, with basic writing being the first of these and bearing 3 credits plus a letter grade. See Ritter, "Extra-Institutional Authority."

Chapter 1: Educating the Great Community

1. See, for example, the discussion of a recent (2022) survey of 178 CAOs (chief administrative officers) at public, private, and nonprofit institutions in the US regarding Gen Ed at https://www.insidehighered.com/views/2022/05/26/addressing-disconnects-gen-ed-opinion.

2. As I discuss in chapter 4, the American Philosophical Association does a particularly good job of promoting the discipline to a variety of stakeholders. I do not know if this is why Philosophy remains popular at Penn (nor does the *Gazette* article offer ideas), but I do observe that Philosophy is a humanities unit that is engaging in forward thinking regarding Gen Ed and other curricular matters.

3. For more specifics about recent student demographics and academic qualifications at Penn, see https://admissions.upenn.edu/how-to-apply/resources-programs/incoming-class-profile.

4. In using the term "humanistic inquiry," I follow the principles set forth by several institutions promoting this approach today, including Emory University's Initiative for Arts and Humanistic Inquiry, whose guiding questions are the following: "What does it mean to live in a world undergoing radical environmental, climatic, social, economic, and political upheaval? How are understandings of the person, the social, and the human anchored in regional, cultural, and historical specificity? How is humanity adapting to rapid and radical technological change? How will individuals and societies find and articulate meaning in the future, and what new forms of community and creative expression will emerge?" (https://provost.emory.edu/arts-humanistic-inquiry/).

5. Such a system would follow the findings of Harvard faculty, who, according to Byron Hollingshead, understood that "a bright youngster from an obscure high school is a better academic risk for the University than a medium ability boy from the best preparatory school in the land" (79).
6. Penn State's overhaul of their General Education program is particularly notable. Virginia Tech's overhaul is designed around the interdisciplinary Pathways program (https://www.pathways.prov.vt.edu/), as is the Gen Ed curricula in humanities and social sciences at RPI (https://hass.rpi.edu/advising/hass-integrative-pathways). University of Nebraska–Omaha has a comprehensive website (https://www.unomaha.edu/general-education/faculty-and-staff-resources/gen-ed-reform-models.php) that espouses liberal education principles and provides numerous examples and resources for reform. Finally, the AAC&U offers a conference serving those looking for QEP (quality enhancement plan) or other Gen Ed projects (https://www.aacu.org/event/conference-on-general-education-pedagogy-and-assessment).
7. As an example, see Steven Mintz's October 25, 2023, *Inside Higher Ed* essay, "Reinventing the Humanities for Our Fragmented Time," which also nods to the paucity of humanistic principles at work in Gen Ed courses in this area of study.
8. See https://www.theheagroup.com/blog/college-majors-pay-most for an analysis of both top-earning and most popular four-year and two-year college majors, as of May 2023.
9. For example, a course in the biological sciences that meets a broad Gen Ed requirement in historical perspectives in the humanities by being on the "history of biology" but neither uses best practices in teaching history nor employs historical methods in its design or assignments. Students thus may learn interesting things about historical events in science but will not learn how to "do" history as a subject focused on humanistic inquiry and methods. For a particularly dark take on this, see Brennan and Magness, "The Gen Ed Hustle."
10. I have worked with many conscientious advisors (and faculty) who understand the original mission of Gen Ed and attempt to convey it to students. But they are limited in their efforts by institutional rhetorics that privilege a discourse that does not value education qua education. This efficiency mindset is demonstrated in the Education Commission of the States report from July 2022, which indicates that "48 states and the District of Columbia have state-level dual enrollment policies [and] 28 states have established multiple dual enrollment programs through state policy." Indeed, it is rare to find a state university system without a robust credit articulation program between its high schools and colleges, with first-year writing usually at the top of that list of articulated courses.
11. See, for example, https://edtrust.org/press-release/black-and-latino-students-shut-out-of-advanced-coursework-opportunities/ and from 2014, https://www.theatlantic.com/politics/archive/2014/12/the-race-gap-in-high-school-honors-classes/431751/, each of which outlines the paucity of advanced courses for Black and Latino students in high schools and the consequences on their subsequent enrollment in Gen Ed requirements in college. See also arguments that introductory STEM courses "weed out" minority students who would otherwise pursue these majors and careers (Hatfield et al.). While granting more access solves enrollment disparity and puts less pressure on minority and other marginalized students enrolled in Gen Ed college courses, I do not know that it solves the overall problem of the rhetorical framing of Gen Ed as remedial, nor the problem of efficiency models that discourage *all* students from taking college courses on college campuses.
12. By "remedial" I mean placement into standard college courses that are widely credit-bearing and universally agreed components of the core curriculum. This would include Calculus I, First-Year Writing, and other standard introductory courses. When the "average" student starts college with double-digit credit hours and sophomore (or junior) standing, students *without* such credits—who are also not white, or lower-income, or first-generation—are comparatively framed as "behind" in their studies.

13. Indeed, at present we Americans have gone over the edge of the "Enrollment Cliff" that resulted from a downturn in births during the 2008 recession; this has caused drops in the college-age population nationwide, with the Northeast and Midwest being the most affected (for an overview, including the projected "second wave," see https://www.chronicle.com/article/colleges-were-already-bracing-for-an-enrollment-cliff-now-there-might-be-a-second-one).
14. For more information on Victory Gardens, see the National Agricultural Library site at https://www.nal.usda.gov/exhibits/ipd/small/exhibits/show/victory-gardens/victory-garden-aids.
15. Dwight D. Eisenhower and A. A. Vandegrift, respectively, in Eisenhower et al., "Liberal Education in the Military Forces."
16. See https://www.archives.gov/milestone-documents/servicemens-readjustment-act for a concise summary of the GI Bill's creation and legacy, by the National Archives. Current policy related to the GI Bill and the post-9/11 Montgomery GI Bill can be found at the Veterans Affairs website: https://www.va.gov/education/about-gi-bill-benefits/. The bill's subsequent revisions and eligibility restrictions also made national news in June 2023: https://www.insidehighered.com/news/government/2023/06/28/lawsuit-arguing-va-shortchanges-vets-heading-supreme-court.
17. For a discussion of enrollment trends in the decades following the GI Bill's implementation, including detailed statistics by race and gender as well as overall numbers of two- and four-year postsecondary institutions in each decade, see Clotfelter, "Patterns of Enrollment and Completion" (https://www.nber.org/system/files/chapters/c6079/c6079.pdf).
18. See recent projections (May 2023) from the NCES (https://nces.ed.gov/programs/coe/indicator/cha/undergrad-enrollment) for a recent view of projected college enrollments.
19. See https://nces.ed.gov/programs/coe/indicator/cpb/college-enrollment-rate.
20. McGrath's views, and the principles of the General Education movement, echo those of the 1947 *Report of the President's Commission on Higher Education*, which included other equalizing efforts such as the expansion of American two-year colleges, as detailed in Sullivan.
21. Hancher's assertions are later reflected in McGrath's editorial, "Teachers of General Studies," published in *JGE* volume 1, number 2 (1947). McGrath argues that faculty are not prepared to teach introductory subjects, citing a study which found that "the vast majority of the holders of such degrees [mathematics] entered the field of teaching [with] no specific preparation for this occupation" (83) and thus part of General Education's mission should be to expand graduate education to include foundations in introductory subjects and the pedagogies required to teach them, with a concomitant reduction in time "devoted to research and the thesis" (84). John C. Gerber, soon to become president of NCTE, similarly argued in his 1949 *JGE* essay (vol. 3, no. 2) that "the training of college teachers in the field of communication should begin in the undergraduate years" and that a "general seminar for all graduate students regardless of their field" in teaching communication skills should be required (127). Such a call prefigures graduate pedagogy seminars for students teaching first-year writing today.
22. Such arguments, in the negative, today ironically make easier the segregation of "teaching" versus "research" faculty across disciplines at many elite institutions, including the proliferation of a teaching class of contingent faculty in first-year writing, who have on a national scale a widely variable institutional status and associated benefits. Cowley, of course, was not in favor of such bifurcation of labor, but such is one complicated labor-based inheritance of General Education as experienced in many disciplines, including rhetoric and writing studies.
23. For a more in-depth look at Charles Roberts and his work as Director of Freshman Rhetoric at the University of Illinois Urbana-Champaign, with a particular focus on his role in the 1955 Illinois Decision on the discontinuation of basic writing in the university, see Ritter, "With 'Increased Dignity and Importance.'"

24. The subsequent realignment of the purposes and scope of *CCC*, the governing organization of CCCC, and the history of the communication course are well documented in two articles addressing these topics: George and Trimbur, "Communication Battle"; Finnegan and Wallace, "Origin Stories."
25. In contrast to Gray's article, the liberal arts "problem" essay focuses on how to teach bright versus "dull" students in the same classroom, and the university "problem" essay navigates the difficulty of graduate teaching assistants in composition courses—a problem that Charles Roberts and his administrative team at the University of Illinois would address in later issues of *CCC*.
26. A partial echo of Gray's argument is present in Erwin R. Steinberg's October 1951 *CCC* essay, "Some Basic Assumptions for Courses in English Composition," where he contends "It is unwise . . . to attempt to set up an 'ideal' course and then pour the students into it. The students in a liberal arts college are different from those in an engineering school . . . those in a women's college different from those in an all-male school. The freshman class which entered in 1947 (mostly veterans) was different from the class which entered last September, and the class which enters five years from now may well be different still. . . . Berating the high schools for not doing their job and insisting on trying to make students do what they ought to be able to do does not solve the problem either for the instructor or the class. Yet that is exactly what is being done . . . under the guise of 'maintaining standards'" (12).
27. See the National Institute for Learning Outcomes Assessment 2019 brief, "A Historical Overview of Assessment: 1980s-2000s," for more on the start of the "assessment movement."

Chapter 2: "The Interests of the State"

1. For more, see https://ticas.org/wp-content/uploads/2023/11/Hillman-Geography-of-Opportunity-Brief-1_2023.pdf.
2. Such duplication regulations are sometimes applied unevenly within a state system, however; one example is a recent lawsuit filed by students against the State University System of Florida, charging that predominately white institutions (PWIs) were allowed to offer duplicate programs whereas HBCUs (historically Black colleges and universities) were not, effecting a two-tiered system (*Denton, Stevens, Dansby, Peterson, Harris, and Doe vs. The Board of Governors for the State University System of Florida*, September 22, 2022, https://storage.courtlistener.com/recap/gov.uscourts.flnd.445246/gov.uscourts.flnd.445246.1.0.pdf). For a discussion of longer histories of this problem at other institutions, see Pluviose.
3. Such out-of-state migration is explicitly addressed in the 1943–1944 Annual Report of the USG (University System of Georgia), which declares that "Far more young men and women of this state go out of the state for graduate work than take such work in Georgia. This is not from choice on their part, but from necessity. Looked at from any standpoint it represents a loss of valuable human material for Georgia because so many of our most promising men and women settle permanently outside of the state as a result of connections formed while taking graduate work away from here" ("Annual Report" 10).
4. See Board of Regents, "Semester Enrollment Report." Note that the overall diversity of demographics represented in the aggregate figures are possible in part due to the USG's inclusion of two HBCUs as well as other formerly two-year colleges, where women and minority students are historically high.
5. The census may be found here: https://www.census.gov/library/stories/state-by-state/georgia-population-change-between-census-decade.html.
6. Board of Regents Statement, January 1, 1932.
7. Texas has an elaborate set of regulations designed to create maximal efficiency in postsecondary education, including a statement on duplication of programs, outlined in a 2019

report at https://reportcenter.highered.texas.gov/training-materials/presentations/04-25-19-iv-a-ppt/.
8. Indeed, in a memo from Chancellor Sanford to the USG Committee on Education, dated April 17, 1943, Sanford argues that Fort Valley State College, whose mission was "the training of teachers primarily for rural schools and of vocational education," should "begin at once to lay the foundation for cooperation with the Atlanta University for advanced work in the arts and sciences. It should give advanced degrees as are not given by other institutions. In other words, avoid all duplication of effort on the higher levels." Steadman V. Sanford, Letter to the Committee on Education, Board of Regents, State of Georgia, April 17, 1943. Board of Regents, University System Files. RCB 35746, record group 033-01-03, Georgia Archives.
9. See the complete listings at https://www.usg.edu/academic_affairs_handbook/assets/academic_affairs_handbook/docs/TCSGUSGTransfer.pdf.
10. The USG Core still allows for one campus-specific requirement at each institution to be determined outside the core. This requirement falls under area B, "Institutional Options," and accounts for 3–7 hours of the 42 total Core required hours.
11. See UGA's Core curriculum requirements at https://bulletin.uga.edu/GenEdCoreBulletin. These may be compared with the USG core curriculum for its other institutions, found here: https://www.usg.edu/student_affairs/assets/student_affairs/documents/OverviewofUSGCoreCurriculum.pdf, which notably state, "This document provides general guidance only, and nothing in this document is binding on any University System of Georgia institution or on the University System as a whole."
12. As I have written about elsewhere, UNC–Chapel Hill, NC State, and The Woman's College (now UNCG) consolidated in 1931, one year before the USG system was created, but the larger statewide consolidation of the current sixteen campuses in the UNC system happened in 1972.
13. Additional campuses continue to engage in even more drastic consolidation measures for economic reasons. Two examples are in a 2020 *Chronicle of Higher Education* article that examined reasons for consolidation in Georgia, Pennsylvania, and Maine, including avoiding the demise of particular campuses, saving operational costs, and other finance-minded efficiencies (https://www.chronicle.com/article/more-states-are-looking-at-consolidating-their-public-colleges-does-it-work). A more extensive research report from 2021 focused on Georgia, Texas, and Wisconsin, and questioned whether consolidations result in better equity for student populations: "Without an explicit focus on racial, ethnic, and socioeconomic equity at the planning stage, it is far from certain that minoritized students and other stakeholders will benefit from the consolidation, and unlikely that institutional and system leaders, policymakers, or the public will even know how they fare" (Kurzweil et al. 3). As many readers know, such recent consolidations in Vermont, Wisconsin, and Pennsylvania have resulted in entire campus closures and many faculty and staff jobs lost.
14. See the chronology also at https://www.usg.edu/assets/usg/docs/USG75years.pdf.
15. For example, in fiscal year 2025, Georgia Tech received new state appropriations of $60.2 million, based on an increase of 4 percent in the incoming first-year class for fall 2024 versus fall 2023, following a 14 percent increase in undergraduate applications for fall 2024 over fall 2023. Georgia Tech's total FY24 budget was the highest in the state system, at just under $2 billion, with a tuition revenue of $490 million and sponsored (restricted use) funds of $510 million. The largest budget among regional universities was Kennesaw State, at $713 million (tuition revenue $215 million, sponsored funds $84 million), and the largest budget among state universities was University of North Georgia at $269 million (tuition revenue $73.2 million, sponsored funds $47 million). In contrast, Abraham Baldwin Agricultural College, an HBC that no longer functions in this capacity, had a budget of just over $57 million, with a tuition revenue of $9.6 million, and sponsored funds of $11 million (https://fiscalservices.kennesaw.edu/docs/FY24_Budget_Appendix_I_-_Exhibits_1-4.pdf).

Part of these disparities are long-standing funding differences between PWIs and HBCUs starting with the second Morrill Act in 1890. A 2024 report from the Century Foundation summarizes these issues as applicable in 2024 (D. Smith).

16. I am not a historian of racial segregation or integration, nor do I pretend to be. But many other scholars are, and in their important work is where the vast and troubling narratives of structural inequities in higher education for African Americans may be found. As I discuss later in this chapter, Annie Mendenhall's *Desegregation State* is one such work. Another useful gloss of the challenges of desegregation for African American students and teachers is R. Scott Baker's article "The Paradoxes of Desegregation: Race, Class, and Education, 1935–1975."

17. As of this writing, there are four R1 universities in the USG, four comprehensive universities, nine "state" universities, and nine "state" colleges, some of which were two-year colleges created before the USG absorbed these under a new designation. Three of these institutions—Albany State, Fort Valley State, and Savannah State—are also historically Black colleges and universities (https://www.usg.edu/institutions/). The USG system is separate from the Technical Colleges System of Georgia, or TCSG, which includes twenty-six two-year technical colleges and has its own standardized curriculum, and which also has participated in transfer agreements with the USG since 2012 (https://www.tcsg.edu/why-tcsg/).

18. See, for example, the 2005 publication by the Center for American Progress, "Fast Track to College: Increasing Postsecondary Success for All Students," which states, "Specifically, the development of three 'fast track to college' alternatives to the traditional high school senior year would enable students to get a head start toward the goal of education through grade 14: An Academic Head Start on College; An Accelerated Career/Technical College; and A Gap Year, or College in the Community." (https://cdn.americanprogress.org/wp-content/uploads/kf/FastTrack-FINAL%2012%2001.pdf).

19. See https://www.admissions.uga.edu/admissions/transfer/transfer-pathway-faq/.

20. See https://admission.gatech.edu/transfer/transfer-pathway-programs.

21. A growing subset of research in writing studies focuses on transfer student learning and success across institutional types. One excellent, recent example of this work is Christie Toth's *Transfer in an Urban Writing Ecology* (2023).

22. See https://ccrc.tc.columbia.edu/tracking-transfer-state-outcomes.html for the full reports from the Community College Research Center, which tracks national as well as state-specific rates.

23. See, for example, Emory University's two-year campus for first- and second-year studies, Oxford College. Located about an hour from the main campus, Oxford advertises itself as a smaller, residential campus and as "one of two entry points for Emory undergraduates. You'll find two different experiences for your first and second years of college available through one application process" (https://oxford.emory.edu/admission/index.html). At Northeastern University (MA), significant numbers of first-year students are part of the "Specialized Entry" program where students attend one of NU's international campuses for their first semester before returning to the Boston campus in January (https://nuin.northeastern.edu/). This program also allows NU to claim a more selective rate of admission, as these students are not counted in their statistics for first-time freshmen. See numerous Reddit threads critical of NEU's practices archived here: https://www.reddit.com/r/NEU/comments/m7fx0q/nu_in_program/.

24. To be very clear: I am not implying that Sanford believed in the Nazi regime. Further, I recognize that Hitler's actual influence was not visible to many Americans prior to 1939. Nonetheless, for a chancellor of a large university system to make these comparisons at this juncture in history seems to me to be ill-chosen, at best, unless he was explicitly hailing a system that would exclude students who were deemed less worthy of higher education, i.e.,

Black students (and also women, except for their value in normal schools as future teachers).
25. The report also explicitly mentions Earl McGrath, founding editor of *JGE*, and his focus on the importance of humanistic study within General Education.
26. For another excellent history of segregation in higher education that covers a wider range of institutions, see Joy Ann Williamson-Lott's *Jim Crow Campus: Higher Education and the Struggle for a New Southern Social Order* (2018), from which I quote above.
27. It is important to note that Georgia Tech also did not admit its first woman student until 1952; comparatively, UGA admitted its first woman student in 1918. Yet archival discussions of whether and how to allow women students on campuses in the USG are not completely straightforward, as witnessed in the response to the proposal to allow wives of returning servicemen studying in the USG under the GI Bill to also enroll in college courses alongside their husbands. As articulated in a letter on this topic from UGA President Harmon Caldwell to Marion Smith, Chairman of the Board of Regents, on February 7, 1946: "It is probably that most of the women would enter the freshman or sophomore class. All classes for students of these grades are filled to capacity. . . . [If] the wives of these [500 enrolled veterans] should enroll, twelve new teachers, costing approximately $30,000.00 per year, would have to be added to the budget. If this privilege were extended to women, it would encourage even larger numbers to come here to take advantage of the offer of a free college education." The letter thus proposes that wives be allowed to audit and that wives alternatively be admitted under a plan in which they pay 50 percent of the regular tuition, which would "discourage those who have no real interest in college work and who might plan to take courses just to pass the time away" (Caldwell memo to Smith, State of Georgia Archives, "Exhibit B," February 7, 1946, Files of Committee on Finance and Organization, RCB 35746, Record Group 033-01-035, Georgia Archives).

Meanwhile, just a little over one year later, a request was made by Guy H. Wells, president of the Georgia State College for Women, to the USG Committee on Education, to admit men students to the junior and senior classes, effective fall 1947. His request follows the inclusion of men at colleges in Florida and North Carolina at the junior and senior levels, also citing UNC–Chapel Hill's practice at the time of only admitting "girls" to the junior and senior classes. Wells states that "there is no doubt about the trend in this country toward co-education, but in spite of this, I would prefer to see this unit remain a womans college, provided the Regents would adopt the pattern of education set by states like North Carolina" (G. Wells). And in 1962, in the minutes of the Committee on Languages and Literatures of the University System Advisory Council, there is a comment that "a girl who entered Tech from the junior year of high school" with "an all A record with the exception of one B" was not allowed to major in Physics at Tech, per a Board of Regents rule. Committee chairman Wright noted that "Tech takes all students who made As in their first quarter of language instruction and gives them special instruction—their only reward, better education" ("Minutes of the Committee" 2–3).
28. For more details, see https://cspcs.sanford.duke.edu/cspcs-publication/general-education-board-1903-1960/.
29. I have chosen to keep this antiquated and offensive term in place in all archival references, to preserve the original context of the documents. I do not sanction this term, obviously, but in historical discussions of African Americans in Georgia and the South more broadly, it was the term widely used in both informal and formal correspondence, policies, and documents, and so I will keep its use intact here to fully represent the historical record.
30. Sanford's earlier letter to Mann in the correspondence file, dated August 16, 1943, details how the USG institutions are operating during war time, including "three [junior colleges] operating on a peace time basis," i.e., without active-duty military male students on campus, and three other junior colleges with such students enrolled. Sanford also previews his forthcoming letter to Mann by saying, "this letter will be followed by a second letter informing

you of the progress being made to give the Negroes substantially equal opportunities as the whites. We intend to support the fourteenth amendment to the Constitution of the United States as soon as it is possible. The problem has always been difficult, but more so until the war ends."
31. For the full document, see https://dlg.galileo.usg.edu/data/dlg/ggpd/pdfs/dlg_ggpd_s-ga-bu500-pr4-bm1-b2002-bh5.pdf.
32. Board of Regents minutes 05/30/41.
33. For more on the Cocking Affair, see a synopsis at https://www.georgiaencyclopedia.org/articles/government-politics/cocking-affair/. Press in the Black community was also critical of Talmadge, for example in the *Atlanta Daily World* article on November 20, 1941, "Says Governor Admires Hitler," which detailed how President Buell G. Gallagher of Talladega College in Alabama—a historically Black college—felt about Talmadge and his actions within the Board of Regents and more broadly (including book-banning legislation). Gallagher is quoted as saying, "There is a strange and appalling parallel between the racial doctrines and practices of men like Governor Talmadge and men like Adolf Hitler" (1).
34. "Funds Move to Crack Down on State Schools," *Atlanta Daily World*, July 30, 1941, 6.
35. "A Noble Beginning," *Atlanta Daily World*, January 6, 1939, 6.
36. Sanford letter to BOR, April 17, 1943. Board of Regents, University System Files. RCB 35746, Record Group 033-01-03, Georgia Archives. The Gaines reference here is to *Missouri ex. rel Gaines v. Canada*, 305 US 337 (1938) regarding the legality of separate schools for Black and white students in a state that practiced segregation through 1950. Lloyd L. Gaines's appeal regarding his denied admission to the University of Missouri School of Law on the basis of his race was upheld by the US Supreme Court in 1939, though he never enrolled at the university, and disappeared after the decision was publicized.
37. Among other recommendations stated in this 1943 report were that "the programs of the three colleges for Negroes should be materially strengthened with respect to staff, facilities, and diversity of programs offered in General Education at the undergraduate level. It is not believed desirable to attempt graduate work in any one of them at the moment. That should be left to the future" (83). It further noted that "provision should be made for scholarships in professional fields open to Negroes although the state may not provide instruction for whites in that subject. The opportunities for the Negro are so limited that every possible avenue should be opened to him" (84). This report also makes clear that General Education is the primary goal of the junior college, in both white and Black colleges, and that students transferring to Georgia Tech would have difficulty meeting standards based on their General Education coursework at the junior colleges (109, 111).
38. A (very) critical response to Strayer's 1948 report for Washington, DC, segregated schools, "The Cost of Segregated Public Schools in the District of Columbia," was published in *The Journal of Negro Education*, in which Paul Cooke, an instructor at Miner Teachers College in DC, rails against Strayer's recommendations, which would in his view result in the "ghettoing of Negro high school education" (95).
39. The 1950 "Allocation of Functions" report recommends that junior colleges be "disassociated" from the University system and administered by local boards of education. However, the system continued to include the junior colleges thereafter. Recommendation 8 in the 1965 report by the Georgia General Education Improvement Council characterizes (what are now termed) community colleges as "the primary means by which local area and community needs should be met for education beyond the high school" that should "be integral and fully coordinated parts of the University System of higher education" (General Education Improvement Council 30). It also notes in recommendation 7 that "admission standards for the University System as a whole should be such that every student who is capable of completing a college education be admitted and encouraged to graduate from some institution within the system" (30). These two recommendations in tandem solidify the place of

two-year colleges in the USG, both structurally and financially (given that enrollments in such colleges serve to be profitable avenues for the USG, who would educate, ideally, "every student" capable).
40. These actions were informed by a report from the Executive Secretary of the Georgia Commission on Education that analyzed the *Brown v. Board of Education* decision. That report noted, among other things, that "it is only State action through State law that is within the purview of the Oliver Brown case and the Fourteenth Amendment. Nothing emphasizes this so well as the Court's distorted holding . . . that children of the colored race cannot learn and study as well in their own schools as in mixed schools, and that when the State by State law, classifies the children into the two racial groups into which they were born, the State, by State law, thus creates an inequality of protection" (18).
41. As late as 1954, Georgia Tech's "Aims and Objectives" document encourages faculty to pursue more sabbatical leaves (at a time when such leaves were available; the State of Georgia no longer grants such leaves, as a system) (35).
42. The financial impetus for efficiency in Gen Ed options and their delivery is foretold in a memo from June 22, 1961, written by Arthur Gignilliat, Administrative Assistant to the Chancellor, to the chairmen and members of the academic committees of the USG. He notes that "The Education Committee of the Board of Regents is anxious to stretch the dollars spent in Georgia for higher education as far as possible. With the 'tidal wave' of students expected during the next five years, it is more cogent than ever that we consider ways and means of teaching students effectively in larger sections. . . . Your local administration will need your assistance in overhauling the traditional recitation section, and in eliminating very small classes."
43. A later memo (February 7, 1967) from J. Dixon Wright, Chairman of the Academic Committee on Languages and Literature at Georgia Tech, to committee members asked for a list of courses in area IV (courses appropriate to the major field of study) for the Core curriculum. In this memo, Wright offers that "In view of the current interest on the part of system officialdom in the feasibility of system-wide uniform course numbering, please present your information, insofar as possible, in terms of both course numbers and statement of general course content for all courses." This request pre-dates USG's implementation of CCN by thirty years and provides evidence that such conversations were in play long before 1997.
44. For state-by-state policies, Education Commission for the States.
45. See the USG database at https://www.usg.edu/academic_affairs_handbook/section2/C748.
46. For more information about Gen Ed goals in the USG, see https://www.usg.edu/academic_affairs_handbook/section2/C738/#p2.4.1_general_education_learning_goals.
47. Seamless transfer can also apply to what academic administrators call "downward" transfer—that which comes from credits earned at a four-year school taken into a two-year school for students to apply to an associate's degree. The more traditional "upward" pathway is of the most public concern to advocates for transfer students, however, for example those who administer the TOP (Transfer Opportunity Project) and ACT (Articulation of Credit Transfer) programs housed at CUNY (City University of New York): https://www.cuny.edu/about/administration/offices/oira/policy/a2b/about-2/.
48. See guidelines for the HOPE and Zell at https://www.gafutures.org/hope-state-aid-programs/hope-zell-miller-scholarships/.
49. One might observe not only distinct differences in institutional goals, but also differing levels of engagement with student type and overall purpose across the various USG institutional mission statements. For further discussion of rhetorical purposes of mission statements, see, for example, Taylor and Morphew (2010), "An Analysis of Baccalaureate College Mission Statements," and Trina Marie Marquez's dissertation, *Words Matter: A Content Analysis Study of Private and Public Higher Education Mission Statements in the Middle States Region* (2016).

50. Early examinations of CCN and General Education include Ratcliff and Jones's examination of the validity of a core curriculum in articulation of transfer student Gen Ed credit, findings which "did not support the efficacy of a statewide common course numbering system." In contrast, Arnold (2003), whose study as part of the Joint Boards Articulation Commission in the state of Oregon compares and summarizes the Gen Ed transfer programs across all fifty states, comes to the conclusion that Oregon should consider such a common course-transfer system statewide along the lines of "strong" systems in Arizona, Florida, Idaho, Illinois, and North Carolina (https://files.eric.ed.gov/fulltext/ED477586.pdf).
51. Ultimately, though, such aims are important to the bottom line: as of fall 2023, 12.3 percent of all students seeking a four-year college degree nationwide were transfer students who had attended one or more prior institutions, with this figure representing a 7.7 percent increase in "upward" transfers (National Student Clearinghouse Research Center, "College Transfer Enrollment").
52. For analysis of the purposes and effects of history textbooks in Texas, see https://www.texasmonthly.com/being-texan/state-history-textbook-erases-the-stories-black-hispanic-texans/ as well as Goldstein, "Two States."
53. See https://www.flgov.com/2023/05/15/governor-ron-desantis-signs-legislation-to-strengthen-floridas-position-as-national-leader-in-higher-education/ for the full details on the bill from Governor Ron DeSantis's office. And on January 30, 2025, Florida once again revised its statewide Gen Ed curriculum to focus on a "greatly reduced number of courses" that excluded any offerings addressing "identity politics," per the Trump Administration's executive order against the same in governmental operations. For more details, see the *Chronicle* article here: https://www.chronicle.com/article/floridas-universities-approve-a-new-gen-ed-curriculum-after-law-restricted-exploratory-content?sra=true.
54. The UT core's components are further outlined at https://catalog.utexas.edu/general-information/academic-policies-and-procedures/core-curriculum/#text.
55. In January 2023, Florida rejected the course based on it being "inexplicably contradictory to Florida Law" and also lacking in "educational value" (Mazzei and Hartecollis, "Florida Rejects A.P."). In February 2023, the College Board affirmed its commitment to the AP African American History course in the following statement: https://newsroom.collegeboard.org/our-commitment-ap-african-american-studies-scholars-and-field. In December 2023, Florida reversed its decision and announced that the course would be allowed to be offered in the 2024–2025 school year (Alfonseca, "AP African American Studies Course"). The State of Georgia filed a similar ruling regarding the funding of the AP African American Studies course, and also a reversal of that ruling, in July 2024.
56. See https://ufdc.ufl.edu/WL00001594/00001/images/0.
57. See https://www.flrules.org/Gateway/View_notice.asp?id=28489790.
58. For complete descriptions of all courses, see https://flscns.fldoe.org/Reports/CourseDescriptionReport.aspx?instituion=&dis=163&prefix=ENC&discontinued=0&Type=CourseDescriptions.
59. See the description of ENGL 1101 and all USG common course listings at https://www.usg.edu/academic_affairs_handbook/section2/C748.
60. See https://fyc.kennesaw.edu/students/english1101.php.
61. See https://sites.gatech.edu/bfhandbook/writing-and-communication-program-courses/english-1101-and-1102/.
62. See https://wcprogram.lmc.gatech.edu/courses/composition.
63. See https://web2.augusta.edu/pamplin/english-world-languages/college-composition.php. For the Frameworks document in full, see https://wpacouncil.org/aws/cwpa/pt/sd/news_article/242845/_parent/layout_details/false.
64. For a full list of press releases detailing each of these moves by the USG, see https://www.usg.edu/news/archive/category/campus_consolidations.

65. This same site includes a link to "Associate Degree [*sic*] You Deserve," which lets students know that earning an associate degree, among other benefits, "shows the world you can FINISH what you started" and "looks GREAT on your resume." It also notes that "You may have already earned your Associate Degree!" and not even know it. "If you are currently enrolled in one of the institutions below (that do not award associate degrees) and you left your associate degree institution without a degree, request a transcript from your current institution to be sent to your associate degree institution. Click on one of the links below to request a transcript from your current institution." Without labeling it as such, this is *backwards transfer* at work, further emphasizing the interchangeability of courses and requirements across USG institutions. (https://www.usg.edu/curriculum/associate_degree_you_deserve).

Chapter 3: To AP or Not to AP

1. CLEP offers freestanding examinations that are not tied to high school courses or any coordinated programming. As such, these exams are often (but not always) taken by returning students who seek credit for prior learning. The CLEP program offers exams in thirty-four areas, and many CLEP exams are framed as focused on what is "usually taught" in a college course, which of course highlights the problems with what is "usual" across the diversity of college requirements in the US today (https://clep.collegeboard.org/clep-exams). Scores range from 20 to 80, with the CLEP site noting that the ACE (American Council on Education) recommends 50 as a threshold score for college credit (https://clep.collegeboard.org/scores/understand-scores). Not all colleges and universities accept CLEP credit, but the slogan for CLEP on the College Board website promotes its value as thus: "The College-Level Examination Program® (CLEP) helps you receive college credit for what you already know, for a fraction of the cost of a college course" (https://clep.collegeboard.org/clep-benefits-for-everyone), thereby using similar rhetoric to what the AP program promotes, with emphasis on prior learning keyed more explicitly to returning adults and the rhetoric of adult learning programs that award college credit for life and work experiences. Two examples of such programs are DePaul University's School of Continuing and Professional Studies in Chicago, Illinois, which tells prospective students that "your experience has value" (https://scps.depaul.edu/Pages/default.aspx), and Charter Oak State College in Connecticut, which exhorts students to "get the credit [they] deserve" (https://www.charteroak.edu/cpl/).
2. IB offers an integrated curriculum in select high schools across the globe. Unlike AP, students in IB must take the full curriculum and thereafter take examinations on the subject matter, some of this starting in primary schools, in order to receive an IB diploma. At the time of this writing, there were 1,935 K–12 schools in the US who participated in IB, 944 of which offered the Diploma program at the high school level. The seven subject areas covered in the diploma examinations for IB are Studies in Language and Literature (which includes work in specific languages other than English), Language Acquisition, Individuals and Societies, Sciences, Mathematics, The Arts, and Interdisciplinary, with "extended essay" subject exams in ten other subareas.

    Unlike rising AP pass rates for individual exams, IB pass rates are falling; in 2021, 87.2 percent of IB students passed the diploma, compared with 72.4 percent in 2023. In the US, 4,726 students at 393 high schools received an IB diploma (https://www.ibo.org/globalassets/new-structure/about-the-ib/pdfs/dp-statistical-bulletin-november-2023_en.pdf). Passing rates are determined by a process outlined here: https://www.ibo.org/about-the-ib/what-it-means-to-be-an-ib-student/recognizing-student-achievement/about-assessment/dp-passing-criteria/. Individual colleges and universities assess IB for credit in areas that best correspond with the individual IB exams, with scores of 5, 6, and 7 being the usual thresholds for exemption of the related college course.

3. Tyler Branson's 2022 book *Policy Regimes* characterizes the public narratives of dual enrollment, strongly supported by state legislators, as "a *reasonable* way for college students and their parents to save money, to *get through* entry-level college composition courses, and to *enter the workforce* more quickly, which will, proponents suggest, spur growth in the economy" (101).
4. Such is actually a false equation, as (1) the exam does not guarantee exemption, (2) many students taking the exam do not pass it, and (3) low-income students often have institutional or Pell Grant funding that reduces or eliminates their college tuition, such that a Gen Ed course could be "free" versus the costs of the AP exam. I do not mean to claim that in all cases, college courses are "cheaper" than credit by examination. But particularly when the public discourse considers these experiences *educationally equal*, we need to parse out the actual costs in dollars, as well as the social costs of taking fewer college courses in order to gain a college degree.
5. For readers unfamiliar with QEPs, the link below offers some general information about how they work for reaccreditation under the regional organization that governs accreditation of Midwestern institutions, the Higher Learning Commission (HLC). Each of the other regional accrediting agencies in the US—Middle States Commission on Higher Education (MSCHE), the New England Association of Schools and Colleges (NEASC), the Southern Association of Schools and Colleges (SACS), and the Western States Association of Schools and Colleges (WASC) also use QEPs: https://www.hlcommission.org/Accreditation/quality-initiative.html.
6. See, for example, https://www.engineeringchallenges.org/challenges.aspx.
7. See http://undergrad-education.illinois.edu/initiatives/grand-challenge-learning-pilot/index.html for more information.
8. The amount of credit that students can bring in for a four-year college degree varies from campus to campus. At my first institution, students could bring in up to 90 credits. At UIUC, they were only allowed 60, i.e., the typical credits gained through a two-year college degree. AP (and IB and CLEP) credits figure into this total, as does dual enrollment / dual credit coursework. These act as course *exemptions* but in reality, are calculated as course *credits*. WPA readers are familiar with non-credit-bearing exemptions, for example, via portfolio review, placement mechanisms, and so on. AP, in contrast, is always credit-bearing.
9. Throughout this book, I frame Gen Ed courses as being "on" college campuses. I'm aware, of course, that many Gen Ed courses, as well as entire college degrees, are now offered online. For the purposes of my argument, I am still considering those "on" campuses, as they are offered by the college or institution and are part of a credit-bearing program of courses called General Education. Though I have opinions about the proliferation of online courses and degrees, I am subdividing that out as a separate argument from pre-college Gen Ed credit versus "on"-campus Gen Ed courses and programs.
10. While I am primarily arguing here about the rhetoric of exemption, such rhetoric also has economic underpinnings in public discourse. Thus, we also cannot forget that the College Board is a business, one that in 2023 received "at least" $90 million from the federal government, in part to underwrite fee waivers for low-income students taking AP exams, many of whom did not earn a passing score or college credit. As this brief article from *The New York Times* argues, increased revenue is critical for the College Board, as more colleges and universities stop requiring the SAT or ACT for admission purposes—the SAT being another College Board product, which thereby means lost revenue in that sector of their business: https://www.nytimes.com/2023/11/18/us/college-board-ap-examscourses.html. See also the recent article by Tanouye on the profits gained by College Board from the AP program, which in 2022 came to $500M.
11. My thanks to David for giving me permission to quote him in this chapter.
12. The issue of AP credit showing up as transfer credit on a student's transcript is one familiar to advisors. Dual credit / dual enrollment courses also generally appear as transfer

credit—and can also represent the start of the student's academic GPA on that campus. Thus, some advisors caution against taking a DE/DC course in which the student may perform poorly, as the low course grade will put them behind in their academic standing before they have even arrived on campus. AP, by contrast, is not graded, so there are no such consequences to the GPA.
13. See https://apcentral.collegeboard.org/about-ap/ap-a-glance.
14. See the fee table here: https://apstudents.collegeboard.org/exam-policies-guidelines/exam-fees.
15. High schools are rated and ranked based on how many students enroll in AP courses and how many of those students get a "3" on exams. As a result, teachers are also pressured to get as many students as possible to take the corresponding AP exam at year's end. For example, the widely used website GreatSchools.org has a "College Readiness Ranking" that includes three data points: high school graduation rate, college entrance exam results, and number of IB, AP, and dual credit / dual enrollment courses. Per the site, "The advanced courses component is based on the rate of student enrollment in at least one advanced course, including Advanced Placement (AP), International Baccalaureate (IB), or Dual Enrollment courses . . . and the rate of passing one or more AP exams. If a school does not offer advanced courses or the rates of participation are not provided, the rates of participation are assigned a zero (0)" (https://www.greatschools.org/gk/ratings-methodology/#methodology-college-readiness-rating.)

Similarly, *US News and World Report* weights "College Readiness" as 30 percent of their overall ranking of a high school, measuring "the proportions of 12th graders who took and earned a qualifying score on at least one AP or IB exam. Earning a qualifying score is worth three times more than just taking," and goes on to say that "Many schools without any AP or IB exam test-takers scored a zero on this ranking indicator. But adjustments were made so that schools without APs and IBs would not score significantly worse than schools with very few APs and IBs even after the scores were standardized. In summary, not having any AP or IB exams was not enough alone for a school to be at the bottom of the rankings" (Morse et al., "How US News"). Further, local (state) reports on high school quality and rankings also call out AP participation. For example, the State of Illinois's College and Career Readiness Guidance from April 2024 lists a "3" on English and Math Advanced Placement exams as one acceptable indicator of readiness (https://www.isbe.net/Documents/CCR-Guidance.pdf).
16. See https://reports.collegeboard.org/media/pdf/program-summary-report-2022.pdf.
17. Per the College Board regarding data collection of certain demographic groups, as stated in the "Data Notes" in the "Performance" report: "In June 2015, the categories used by College Board to collect student-reported race/ethnicity data were updated to align with changes to federal racial/ethnic definitions. Rather than being required to 'check one' identifier, students could 'check all.' Those students selecting 'Hispanic' in combination with any other identifier were, per the US Census, aggregated within the 'Hispanic' population, whereas students selecting any combinations of identifiers that did not include 'Hispanic' were aggregated within the 'Two or More Races' population. As a result of this 2015 change to self-reporting and aggregation, caution should be exercised when comparing 2015 and earlier years' racial/ethnic data with such data from 2016 and beyond. If fewer than ten exams earned a specific score point within a student group, no data disaggregating exams by score point is provided for that group. . . . Data describing Native American or Alaska Native exam participation and performance should be interpreted cautiously. Challenges to collection of student data made between 2019 and 2020 increased the rate of students' mistakenly selecting Native American or Alaska Native, impacting reported values for 2022 and 2023 in this report. A tribal affiliation field has been added to improve reportable data for future reports."

18. See https://www.usnews.com/news/best-states/slideshows/the-10-most-educated-states-in-the-us?slide=10 regarding Massachusetts; and Rahman, "Map Shows" regarding Mississippi. Note also the marked racial demographic differences between the two states.
19. Whole numbers are not available on the College Board site, but are accessible through third-party sites that request such data from the College Board. My numbers here come from "Total Registration," which has enrollment data by exam or subject, per year, and also includes comments from Trevor Packer, head of the Advanced Placement Program for the College Board on each AP exam: https://www.totalregistration.net/AP-Exam-Registration-Service/Compare-Score-Distributions.php?id=11&year=2024. Trevor Packer also famously tweets about AP at @AP_Trevor (https://x.com/ap_trevor?lang=en), which itself serves as another site of the rhetoric of AP.
20. See https://reports.collegeboard.org/ap-program-results/statewide-credit-policies.
21. Such policies are frequently framed as larger "college-ready" or "student success" policies that also encompass mandated cut scores for AP credit across the state's institutions. See, for example, the State of Illinois's "College and Career Success for All Students Act" (https://www.ilga.gov/legislation/ilcs/ilcs3.asp?ActID=2732&ChapterID=17). Others, such as the State of Oregon, are more simply designed for "transparency" to the public, including students seeking credits, as noted here: https://www.oregon.gov/highered/about/Documents/High-School-College/AP%20IB%20Statewide%20Course%20Credit%20Policy.pdf.
22. One may observe that the number of institutions accepting a 3 for credit is larger for AP Language and Composition than for AP Literature and Composition. This may be due to perceived differences in rigor between the exams, or more applicable content in the Language exam. The full searchable database is available publicly through drop-down menus on the AP website at https://apstudents.collegeboard.org/getting-credit-placement/search-policies/course/10 and https://apstudents.collegeboard.org/getting-credit-placement/search-policies/course/11.
23. The most recent enrollment data on the Atlanta Public Schools (or APS) from the National Center for Education Statistics shows over 50,000 students, with 25.2 percent of families at or below the poverty level, and 48 percent identifying as Black or African American and 5 percent as Hispanic or Latino (https://nces.ed.gov/ccd/districtsearch/district_detail.asp?Search=1&State=13&ID2=1300120).
24. See the details of this program at https://apcentral.collegeboard.org/exam-administration-ordering-scores/scores/awards/school-districts-awards.
25. A current list of institutions is at https://fairtest.org/test-optional-list/. Many, but not all of these institutions have dropped the requirement in order to increase diversity and equity in admissions, noting the long-standing observation that such tests are biased against minority students and others. For a critical take on this endeavor as specific to the SAT and college admissions, see David Leonhardt's January 2024 *New York Times* article, "The Misguided War on the SAT" (https://www.nytimes.com/2024/01/07/briefing/the-misguided-war-on-the-sat.html).
26. Each AP course has its own page that provides overview of the curricula as well as information about the structure of the correspondent exam. Note also that for AP English Language and Composition, recommended prerequisites for the course are "none": https://apstudents.collegeboard.org/courses/ap-english-language-and-composition.
27. Of course, in many other developed countries, students can attend postsecondary institutions for free. The more expensive college becomes, the more resentful the US populace grows over tuition costs. Individual states are making inroads toward such free programs, however; Michigan Governor Gretchen Whitmer announced on July 9, 2024, that the state would provide free community college for all high school graduates, a plan reminiscent of Obama's America's College Promise in 2015. See Michigan's plan at https://www.michigan.gov/whitmer/news/press-releases/2024/07/09/gov-whitmer-secures-tuition-free-community-college-for-michigan-high-school.

28. As of July 2025, the end of the US Department of Education was a looming reality, as *The New York Times* reported (VanSickle).
29. See Packard's *The Status Seekers* (1959).
30. For details on acceptance at Columbia, see https://bulletin.columbia.edu/general-studies/academic-policies/ap-credit/.
31. I want to add here—on the off chance that Melissa's parents or high school counselors will read this book—that I have no idea what major Melissa pursued, what her financial or academic circumstances were in high school or are now, whether or when she graduated from Columbia, or what choices led her to take the AP courses that she did.
32. See various student-led Reddit threads on the subject of AP Scholar awards and their value in college admissions processes, where the consensus opinion is the same as mine. For example: https://www.reddit.com/r/APStudents/comments/w0gyof/got_the_ap_scholar_award_what_do_i_get/.
33. Designed specifically for international AP test-takers, the APID is described as "a globally recognized certificate awarded to students who display exceptional achievement across a variety of disciplines. Available to international students attending secondary schools outside the U.S. and to U.S. high school students applying to universities outside the country, the APID certifies outstanding academic excellence with a global perspective."
34. Note that these are different from another set of awards that existed in the past, which included state and national honors designations and are outlined at https://apstudents.collegeboard.org/help-center/what-were-criteria-awards-ap-no-longer-offers.
35. See, for example studies, on AP student stress and high school achievement inside and outside the classroom by Foust, Hertberg-Davis, and Callahan (2009); Suldo, Shaunessy-Dedrick, Ferron, and Dedrick (2018); and Xiong (2024). AP stress and "burnout" from pre-college advanced curricula has also been the subject of many doctoral dissertations in the last decade, indicating a trend in the research, toward the affective, qualitative measures of AP.
36. In 2024, my high school, Iowa City West High, offered twenty-five AP courses, including AP Capstone and AP Research Seminar (https://www.iowacityschools.org/academics-programs/programs-of-study-high-school).
37. A (positively) contrasting view is held by Handell and Williams—both of whom were executives on the College Board—in their *Change* article, "Reimagining Remediation," which focuses on two-year colleges students: "We need to insist on challenging learning environments for our weakest students. We know that our best students respond well to challenging learning environments. We engage them in learning communities and present them with demanding curricula, such as Advanced Placement. . . . We often reward our less fortunate students, however, with the 'drill-and-kill' approach that characterizes a great many of our remedial interventions" (31). At the same time, they emphasize the need for "prevention over remediation," which unfortunately frames preparatory work in medical-esque terms not dissimilar from basic writing's mid-century label of "Hospital English."
38. Similar rhetoric is present on the site *Georgia Transfer*, operated by the University System of Georgia, which allows students to see where each AP exam will transfer by USG institution, with the tagline at the top left corner of the site: "Make Every College Credit Count" (https://www.gatransfer.org/tools/find-exam-score-transfer-credit).
39. See the latest statistics from November 2023 here: https://nscresearchcenter.org/completing-college/.
40. "SRO 1985 APP Participation Regional/State Volumes." Louise McBee Papers, UA97-074, Box 40, folder 30, Hargrett Rare Book and Manuscript Library, University Archives, The University of Georgia Libraries.
41. Delgado and Paul, "Georgia's Advanced Placement Program: Historical Trends and Descriptive Statistics." May 30, 2017 (https://gosa.georgia.gov/georgias-advanced-placement-program-historical-trends-and-descriptive-statistics-0).

42. See https://www.georgiacenter.uga.edu/courses/teaching-and-education/advanced-placement-summer-institutes.
43. Geoff Freer to Louise McBee letter, March 9, 1988, University of Georgia Archives.
44. See the currently available list of workshops at the College Board's institute registration page, at https://eventreg.collegeboard.org/c/calendar/54ae034d-96ef-4609-8458-c7c7a76ad3b9.
45. Current Pell guidelines, including how funding is calculated, are available at https://studentaid.gov/understand-aid/types/grants/pell/calculate-eligibility. For an example of other gap funding awarded to low income students, see the University of Illinois Urbana-Champaign's "Illinois Commitment" program, which provides full tuition and fees for eight semesters for students whose families reside in Illinois and earn less than $67,100 per year (as of the 2024–2025 academic year guidelines): https://osfa.illinois.edu/illinois-commitment/.
46. See more about this initiative at https://secure-media.collegeboard.org/digitalServices/pdf/membership/regional-2012/Reforming-Schools_EXCELerator-Handout.pdf.
47. See the full statement here: https://secure-media.collegeboard.org/digitalServices/pdf/excelerator/AP-Equity-and-Access_IB_June-2012_FINAL.pdf/.
48. Readers are allowed to work up to fifty hours weekly between the hours of 7:00 a.m. and midnight when scoring online from home. In-person readers work more hours.
49. In materials I received prior to the COVID-19 pandemic in 2018, as part of the packet given to the AP VIP tour group, "online distributed scoring opportunities" were available for AP Computer Science Principles, European History, French Language and Culture, Research, Seminar, Spanish Language and Culture, US History, and World History. However, online scoring of exams such as AP Language and AP Literature was still in person.
50. One might observe, however, Annie Abrams's description of how speed and coverage rule over scaffolded, humanistic learning in her analysis of AP US History (aka APUSH) as taught via the virtual "AP Classroom" platform. Abrams observes how the blistering speed and hyper-efficiency of the course stands in strong contrast to actual interactive teaching and learning in college: "At the college level, events, ideas, and people gain or lose historical significance through argumentation, but for AP teachers and students the calendar of topics is fixed. By dictating elements like breakneck speed through chronology . . . it aligns more closely with AP Classroom than with any theoretically cogent view of history" (112). Abrams further asserts that the College Board structures AP as an exam-based system that requires "submission to depersonalized, infallible authority" (119).
51. As a comparative, I recall my own AP Literature and Composition exam response in 1987 on Faulkner's *The Sound and the Fury*. I was awarded a score of 4, which exempted me from freshman rhetoric at the University of Iowa. I doubt the AP readers found my exam sophisticated or insightful, but instead, something just above competent. Or maybe I just got lucky, and my essay was scored during the middle of the week.
52. The platform for interaction with the table leader was Zoom, but the program used for scoring online was ONE—or "Online Network for Evaluation," which Julie commented crashed "several times" during the week's reading but which was deemed the most secure by the College Board among several other interface options available for scoring.
53. As profiled in a July 25, 2024, story in *Inside Higher Ed*, the number of "passing" scores for AP exams have increased over the past year, due to a new method of scoring called EBSS, or Evidence-Based Standard Setting, which has raised questions that the College Board is eager to answer in defense, and which is on display in the examples Dan and Julie discuss in their interviews (Knox, "Settling the Score").
54. See the most recent NCES data here: https://nces.ed.gov/pubs2018/2018434.pdf.
55. See https://www.insidehighered.com/news/quick-takes/2024/02/14/college-board-fined-selling-students-information regarding the 2024 class action lawsuit against AP regard-

ing the sale of student information; see Strauss, "Class-Action Lawsuit," regarding the 2020 class action lawsuit regarding missing test responses; and see https://highschool.latimes.com/fountain-valley-high-school/opinion-the-college-board-screwed-up-big-time-on-the-2020-ap-exams/ for criticism of the 2020 AP examination process overall, including its complications for students with disabilities.

Chapter 4: Liberatory Mythologies

1. See, as three recent examples, Chen and Simone; Miller and Martorell; and the "Illinois Report Card 2022–2023" (Illinois).
2. See https://wac.colostate.edu/repository/exhibits/dartmouth/introduction-what-was-the-dartmouth-seminar/. For other takes on the history of the discipline, see Nystrand et al.; Varnum; and Goggin.
3. See O'Neill et al.; Yood; Bazerman; and Everett and Hanganu-Bresch.
4. Of course, rhetoric as a discipline is a separate issue. Writing studies, in the formation I employ in this chapter and in this book, has a history associated with English *departments* and English curricula, given the history of the required first-year course. Thus, in this analysis, I am focusing on the (rhetorical) construction of writing studies as separate from rhetoric, even though I recognize—and well remember—the discipline's identity being framed in decades past as both rhetoric and composition, and composition and rhetoric. Rhetoric itself is still, to my mind, a key part of writing studies in theory and in practice. But it has been dropped from the discipline's nomenclature to a great degree over the last decade.
5. You can learn more about CIP codes at https://nces.ed.gov/ipeds/cipcode/Default.aspx?y=56.
6. Such was the result of a 2008 CCCC task force that included Linda Ferreira-Buckley, Kay Halasek, Gail Hawisher, Doug Hesse, Krista Ratcliffe, and David Russell. See a full announcement of this work on the Doctoral Consortium of Rhetoric and Composition Programs site at https://ccccdoctoralconsortium.org/announcements/.
7. In other such industry classifications, rhetoric and composition / writing studies also is considered part of English. See for example the National Endowment for the Humanities, where it is generally classified as a subdivision of English studies.
8. It would be hypocritical not to include myself in this category of instructors, as my PhD is in English with a specialization in Creative Writing.
9. A significant departure from this "orphan" model is the pedagogy of Writing About Writing, pioneered by Elizabeth Wardle and Doug Downs, which introduces students to the field of writing studies in the first-year writing class itself. See their 2007 *CCC* article for a good overview of this pedagogy (Downs and Wardle).
10. These authors, including Crowley, take issue with abolitionist arguments both contemporary and historical, as they argue that "what unites historical efforts to abolish the required first-year writing course across disparate periods is a fundamentally elitist view of the English department mission and its move toward disciplinarity" which they find "contrary to the purposes driving composition studies" (Roemer et al., "Reframing" 378).
11. Importantly, DE/DC courses are also frequently a site of what WPAs and admission officers sometimes call "credit wash." This is the practice of, for example, a student taking a DE first-year writing course that receives credit at a local community college, getting that credit on one's transcript, and then bringing it into a four-year institution where credit from the community college in any form is accepted. Such "washing" fulfills credit agreements between the participating high school and the community college, even if the four-year university does not participate in these agreements regarding DE/DC.
12. The state of Connecticut offered the first dual credit course in 1955, but most DE/DC programming has been in place since the mid-1980s.

13. An interesting operational wrinkle that comes up with DE/DC courses is the viability of FERPA (Family Educational Rights and Privacy Act of 1974). FERPA "gives parents certain rights with respect to their children's education records. These rights transfer to the student when he or she reaches the age of 18 or attends a school beyond the high school level" (https://www2.ed.gov/policy/gen/guid/fpco/ferpa/index.html). These rights include seeing a student's academic record and receiving direct communication about their academic progress, or lack thereof. College students over the age of eighteen are afforded freedom from parental interference in their academic records by virtue of their attendance, which for some may be very important if familial situations are unsafe or unstable. The notion of "attendance" is complex in DE/DC situations, however, since such students are typically considered non-degree-seeking. Further, for those whose DE/DC program requires travel to college campuses (including in early college programs, another formation of DE/DC that allows students to earn a community college degree while still in high school), students as young as fourteen or fifteen years old may be learning beside students older than eighteen, which provides quandaries for DE/DC instructors who have to plan for lessons that are appropriate to both age groups—a difficult task, especially in a first-year writing classroom where assignments may address personal or political issues that rely on mature points of view on the part of the students. For more on FERPA navigation and DE/DC, see Ison et al.
14. It is important to clarify that I am focusing here on DE/DC courses offered in the high school setting. These are distinct from DE/DC courses wherein high school students travel to college campuses to take the courses there. These have issues as well (including but not limited to minors as young as 15 being in college classrooms). But they do not relocate first-year writing in a high school, in the ways I am describing here.
15. Though much of my argument in this book is framed toward four-year college and university enrollments, structures, and politics, as these are the areas where efficiency-based rhetorics of exemption and transfer focus as a whole, it is important to remember that our colleagues teaching and conducting research at two-year colleges are a critical part of the field of writing studies and are a significant group of scholars dedicated to the first-year course and its students.
16. TYCA, or the Two-Year College Association, has its own position statement on concurrent enrollment, which can be found at https://ncte.org/wp-content/uploads/2020/10/Concurrent_Enrollment.pdf. Unfortunately, like the position papers and statements I profile later in this chapter from the Conference on College Composition and Communication (CCCC), this statement is more than a decade old, having been published in 2012, and the threat of DE/DC has become even more dire since then.
17. The full text of the 2024 manual may be found here: https://tea.texas.gov/texas-schools/accountability/academic-accountability/performance-reporting/2024-accountability-manual-full.pdf.
18. For further discussion, see, for example, Lamos, "Basic Writing"; Kynard; and Perryman-Clark.
19. In 2021, UT–Austin was in talks with the politically conservative Liberty Institute regarding a plan to create a civics course in OnRamps for UT–Austin students. Such was part of a larger plan to create a think tank on the UT-Austin campus that would be "dedicated to the study and teaching of individual liberty, limited government, private enterprise and free markets." As of the date of this writing, such a course is not in the OnRamps list of offerings, but this proposed partnership does illuminate how outsourcing college curricula in any form exposes it to external stakeholders whose values may or may not match those of students and faculty on college and university campuses (McGee).
20. See latest figures at https://www.utsystem.edu/about.
21. Both Brannon's and Calhoon-Dillahunt's assertions also follow in some measure on Chris Anson's 2013 CCCC Chair's Address, which is structured as a Socratic dialogue of sorts on

Notes : 227

current threats facing higher education, including facts about encroaching rhetorics of efficiency measures in higher education, the rising costs of college, myriad corporate interventions into course delivery models and competency-based education (including MOOCs), and the simultaneous reported decline of the liberal arts. The message of Anson's address is clear: More education across academia as well as the broader public is needed, followed by action, in order for writing studies to have any hopes of saving itself and other disciplines within General Education that are at imminent risk of erasure.

22. E.g., the "Tate-Lindemann Debate," conducted across two 1993 pieces authored by Erika Lindemann and Gary Tate, respective in *College English*. Central to this conversation was the place of literature in composition; it subsequently was widely referenced in relation to many aspects of writing studies' separation from English departments, representative as they were of the primacy of literary studies.

23. See for example Hesse, "Who Owns Writing?" (2005); Valentino, "Rethinking the Fourth C" (2010); Tinberg, "The Loss of the Public" (2014); Adler-Kassner, "Because Writing Is Never Just Writing" (2017); and Hassel (2022).

24. By comparison, in 2012 there were twenty-four policy statements listed, categorized under the headings of: "Digital Literacy and Assessment"; "Ethical Issues"; "Language Issues"; and "Professional Issues." CCCC policies and position statements have thus increased by more than 50 percent over a period of less than fifteen years. See http://web.archive.org/web/20180212023210/http://cccc.ncte.org/cccc/resources/positions.

25. I am focusing only on philosophy as a comparative field here, for multiple reasons: because it does excellent public-facing work, because I have some firsthand experience in a philosophy department, and because space limitations keep me from doing similar deep dives into other disciplines. Had I more space, the American Historical Association (or AHA) site, https://www.historians.org/, would certainly receive equal analysis, as it showcases a similar keen attention to promoting the value of the discipline of history to the public. AHA's tagline, "Everything Has a History," is quite enviable, and its page, "Why History Matters," which includes its own advocacy site, is worth a careful read as well. I would further note that the AHA's recent "History Gateways" project has especially strong benefits for General Education students, and is thus key to mention here (see https://www.historians.org/teaching-learning/undergraduate-education/reconsidering-the-introductory-history-course/).

26. The place where I was able to access the 2013 NCTE policy statement was on Professor Mary Jo Reiff's personal site, http://mjreiff.com/uploads/3/4/2/1/34215272/nctepolicybrief.pdf. Many thanks to Mary Jo for at some point preserving this document for reference and use by others.

27. Like the 2013 NCTE policy statement, the 2012 CCCC policy statement is no longer archived on the CCCC or NCTE websites but is available via the Internet Wayback Machine. See the statement's full text at http://web.archive.org/web/20180214103910/http://cccc.ncte.org/cccc/resources/positions/dualcredit.

28. The growth of enrollment in DE/DC programs has been significantly aided by state government investment in funding for students in these programs, covering materials such as books and supplies. See Knox ("Can High Schoolers") for a quick overview of some of these state efforts.

29. I cannot prove that the advocacy of the APA has led to Penn's own particular enrollment trends in Philosophy. They could instead be related to philosophy as a popular prelaw course, or to a very popular faculty member who is valued by generations of students. But of all the courses that a pundit might think is "useless" in today's career-focused paradigm, it's pretty interesting that philosophy remains strong at Penn, in the face of other humanities courses falling off students' collective radar.

30. Such dual ownership of key figures came up during a conversation I had with a faculty member in our philosophy department, in which I asked her whether Aristotle was a *rhetori-*

cian or a *philosopher*. She responded—without taking a beat—"he's a philosopher of course," and proceeded thereafter to persuasively explain to me why this was the case. She was, in turn, surprised to learn that I might have thought otherwise, especially since she was not familiar with writing studies, nor its kinship with rhetoric.

31. One of two widely read blogs in philosophy, *The Daily Nous*, keeps track of such closures at https://dailynous.com/category/cuts-and-threats-to-philosophy-programs/. Among recent philosophy program cuts (actual or seriously threatened) are those at SUNY Fredonia, SUNY Potsdam, Manhattanville College, UW–Milwaukee, and Warren Wilson College. *The Daily Nous*, which is maintained by Justin Weinberg at the University of South Carolina, is also an important site of internally facing advocacy for the field, as it is widely read by philosophers (according to the site, to the tune of 7.5 million viewers per year) and is virtually up to the minute on developments in higher education that affect the field.
32. While fundraising and philanthropy are not part of my focus here on writing studies' public engagement efforts, it is worth noting this, too, as a possible model for writing studies in the future.
33. Important to note here is the international foundations of philosophy as a field. Many strong philosophy programs are located outside the US, and since the field itself is not primarily of American invention, as writing studies arguably is, its reach and membership is global. So, while CCCC speaks almost entirely to a US audience (with membership in Canada, and some scholars also living in Australia and elsewhere globally), philosophy is speaking in its policies and statements to a far more global audience, one not as easily unified in identity and thus even more of a challenge to corral and conjoin ideologically in policy statements.

Conclusion: Will the Circle Be Unbroken

1. For the full proposal, see https://civicsalliance.org/general-education-act/. A similar initiative has been forwarded by the Hoover Institute, without hailing General Education specifically, at https://www.hoover.org/news/new-alliance-civics-academy-working-promote-university-civics-education-nationwide.
2. See Kelderman et al.
3. For details of Project 47 and its potential damage to US educational systems, see Owen Dahlkamp's July 5, 2024, article in *The Atlantic Monthly*. For Trump and Project 2025, see Shao, Yourish, and Kim's detailed analysis on February 14, 2025, in *The New York Times*.
4. See the memo distributed to UNC system faculty dated February 5, 2025, by Andrew Tripp, System Senior Vice President for Legal Affairs and General Counsel, which stated that "effective immediately, all General Education requirements and major-specific requirements mandating completion of course credits related to diversity, equity, and inclusion, or any other topic identified in Section VII of the Equality Policy are suspended. Inclusion of these and other synonymous General Education requirements may contradict the Jan. 21 EO directive to '[e]xcise references to DEI and DEIA principles, *under whatever name they may appear*.' (Jan. 21 EO, Sec. 3) [emphasis added] . . . DEI requirements of the same substance, but identified by a different name, could further jeopardize federal funding." This edict was in direct response to President Trump's national orders regarding the elimination of DEI programming at all state agencies.
5. See also a discussion of Henderson's concept in the March 2, 2024, article by Conor Friersdorf in *The Atlantic Monthly*.
6. For additional discussion of the broad social and policy changes in American higher education during this time that came into conflict with postwar ideals, see chapter 5 of John Drury's *Education and Social Change* (2016), "Education, Equity, and Social Policy: Postwar America to the 1970s."

7. See the American Psychological Association, "Fact Sheet: Education and Socioeconomic Status," for more details.
8. See the full NSSE tableau table for this module at https://tableau.bi.iu.edu/t/prd/views/CivicEngagementTopicalModule/Dashboard1?%3Aembed=y&%3AisGuestRedirectFrom Vizportal=y.
9. At the time of this writing, Penn State was also in the process of further consolidating commonwealth campus leadership, secondary to budget cuts that came, in part, from an almost 4 percent decline in total enrollments since 2019. See Spitalniak for more discussion of these changes.
10. For a vision that aligns with the work of Penn State, see Russell Stone on the value of making Gen Ed visible to public audiences, including through community partnerships.
11. Such a vision was prescient, as on May 3, 2024, the University of Wisconsin–Milwaukee proposed the elimination of its College of General Studies, which was a site for students coming from the Washington County and Waukesha campuses, which now would be closed as well (https://uwm.edu/generalstudies/about/waukesha-closure/program-discontinuance-proposal/). Such a closure would lay off thirty-five tenured faculty and lead to nonrenewals for sixty-four academic and professional staff in the college (Gunn, "UW–Milwaukee Faculty").

Works Cited

Abram Jack, Anthony. *The Privileged Poor: How Elite Colleges Are Failing Disadvantaged Students*. Harvard UP, 2020.

Abrams, Annie. *Shortchanged: How Advanced Placement Cheats Students*. Johns Hopkins UP, 2023.

Academic Senate for California Community Colleges. "Towards a Common Course Numbering System." November 1995. https://www.asccc.org/sites/default/files/publications/CCNF95_0.pdf.

Adler-Kassner, Linda. *The Activist WPA: Changing Stories About Writing and Writers*. Utah State UP, 2008.

Adler-Kassner, Linda. "Because Writing Is Never Just Writing." *College Composition and Communication*, vol. 69, no. 2, 2017, pp. 341–353. 2017 CCCC Chair's Address.

Adler-Kassner, Linda, and Susanmarie Harrington. "Responsibility and Composition's Future In the Twenty-First Century: Reframing 'Accountability.'" *College Composition and Communication*, vol. 62, no. 1, 2010, pp. 73–99.

"Aims and Objectives of the Georgia Institute of Technology." September 1954. Record Locator MFS-MF38, box 1, Georgia Institute of Technology Archives, Atlanta, GA.

Alfonseca, Kiara. "AP African American Studies Course Finalized for Next Year." *ABC News*, December 6, 2023. https://abcnews.go.com/US/ap-african-american-studies-course-finalized-next-school-year/story?id=105418166.

"Allocation of Functions." 1950. Standing Committees—Education, RCB 35746, record group 033-01-035, Georgia Archives.

American Association of Colleges and Universities (AAC&U). "Trending Topic: What Is Liberal Education?" 2025. https://www.aacu.org/trending-topics/what-is-liberal-education.

American Psychological Association. "Fact Sheet: Education and Socioeconomic Status." https://www.apa.org/pi/ses/resources/publications/factsheet-education.pdf.

"Annual Report for 1943–1944 from the Regents of the University System of Georgia to His Excellency Honorable Ellis Arnall." June 30, 1944. https://dlg.galileo.usg.edu/data/dlg/ggpd/pdfs/dlg_ggpd_y-ga-bu500-pr4-ba1-b1943-h44.pdf.

Anson, Chris. "Climate Change." *College Composition and Communication*, vol. 65, no. 2, 2013, pp. 324–344. 2013 CCCC Chair's Address.

Armstrong, Elizabeth A., and Laura T. Hamilton. *Paying for the Party: How College Maintains Inequality*. Harvard UP, 2015.

Arnold, Jim. "Statewide Transfer Policy: The Transferable General Education Core Curriculum." Joint Boards Articulation Commission, 2003. ERIC. https://files.eric.ed.gov/fulltext/ED477586.pdf.

"Articulating High School and College Work: The Report of Workshop No. 12." *College Composition and Communication*, vol. 1, no. 2, 1950, pp. 37–39.

Artze-Vega, Isis, et al. "Privileging Pedagogy: Composition, Rhetoric, and Faculty Development." *College Composition and Communication*, vol. 65, no. 1, 2013, pp. 162–184.

Baker, R. Scott. "The Paradoxes of Desegregation: Race, Class, and Education, 1935–1975." *American Journal of Education*, vol. 109, no. 3, 2001, pp. 320–343.

Bazerman, Charles. "Standpoints: The Disciplined Interdisciplinarity of Writing Studies." *Research in the Teaching of English*, vol. 46, no. 1, 2011, pp. 8–21.

Beasley, James. "*The Journal of General Education* and an Institutional Return to Rhetoric." *The Journal of General Education*, vol. 61, no. 2, 2012, pp. 126–140.

Berlin, James A. *Rhetoric and Reality: Writing Instruction in American Colleges, 1900–1985*. Southern Illinois UP, 1987.

Board of Regents, University System of Georgia. "A Brief History 1932–2002." Office of Media and Publications, 2002.

Board of Regents, University System of Georgia. "Semester Enrollment Report, Spring 2024." https://www.usg.edu/research/assets/research/documents/enrollment_reports/Spring_2024_SER_Final.pdf.

Bok, Derek. *Universities in the Marketplace: The Commercialization of Higher Education*. Princeton UP, 2003.

Boning, Kenneth. "Coherence in General Education: A Historical Look." *The Journal of General Education*, vol. 56, no. 1, 2007, pp. 1–16.

Brandt, Deborah. "Drafting U.S. Literacy." *College English*, vol. 66, no. 5, May 2004, pp. 485–502.

Brandt, Deborah. *Literacy in American Lives*. Cambridge UP, 2001.

Brannon, Lil. "Unintended Consequences: A Comment on the CCCC Position Statement 'Scholarship in Composition: Guidelines for Faculty, Deans, and Department Chairs.'" *College Composition and Communication*, vol. 66, no. 3, 2015, pp. 516–522.

Branson, Tyler. "College Composition at Midwest High: Field Notes from a Concurrent Enrollment Classroom." *The Dual Enrollment Kaleidoscope: Reconfiguring Perceptions of First-Year Writing and Composition Studies.* Christine Denecker and Casie Moreland, eds. Utah State UP, 2022, pp. 178–194.

Branson, Tyler. *Policy Regimes: College Writing and Public Education Policy in the United States.* Southern Illinois UP, 2022.

Brenan, Megan. "Americans' Confidence in Higher Education Down Sharply." *Gallup*, July 11, 2023. https://news.gallup.com/poll/508352/americans-confidence-higher-education-down-sharply.aspx.

Brennan, Jason, and Phillip Magness. "The Gen Ed Hustle." *Cracks in the Ivory Tower: The Moral Mess of Higher Education.* Oxford UP, 2019, pp. 157–185.

Bringsjord, Elizabeth L., Daniel J. Knox, David Lavallee, and Kenneth P. O'Brien. "SUNY Seamless Transfer Policy and Shared Governance." *Shared Governance in Higher Education: Demands, Transitions, Transformations*, vol. 1, edited by Sharon F. Cramer, SUNY P, 2017.

Burdick, Melanie, and Jane Greer. "Navigating the Landscape of Professional Development: Dual Enrollment Teachers Map College Composition into the High School Classroom." *The Dual Enrollment Kaleidoscope: Reconfiguring Perceptions of First-Year Writing and Composition Studies.* Christine Denecker and Casie Moreland, eds. Utah State UP, 2022. 89–108.

Caldwell, Harmon. Letter to Board of Regents, University System of Georgia. "Exhibit B." February 7, 1946. Files of Committee on Finance and Organization, RCB 35746, record group 033-01-035, Georgia Archives.

Caldwell, Harmon. Letter to Howard W. Rogerson, United States Commission on Civil Rights, December 18, 1963. Board of Regents, Chancellor Subject Files, RCB 30124, record group 033-01-051, Georgia Archives.

Calhoon-Dillahunt, Carolyn. "2018 CCCC Chair's Address." *College Composition and Communication*, vol. 70, no. 2, 2018, pp. 273–293.

Carnevale, Anthony P., and Stephen J. Rose. "Socioeconomic Status, Race/Ethnicity, and Selective College Admissions." In *America's Untapped Resource: Low Income Students in Higher Education.* Richard D. Kahlenberg, ed. Century Foundation Press, 2004.

Challenge Success Group, Stanford University Graduate School of Education. "The Advanced Placement Program: Living Up to Its Promise?" 2013. https://challengesuccess.org/wp-content/uploads/2021/04/ChallengeSuccess-AdvancedPlacement-WP.pdf.

Charters, W. W. "Patterns of Courses in General Education." *The Journal of General Education*, vol. 1, no. 1, 1946, pp. 58–63.

Chen, Xianglei, and Sean Simone. "Remedial Coursetaking at U.S. Public 2-Year and 4-Year Institutions: Scope, Experiences, and Outcomes." National Center for Educational Statistics, September 2016. https://nces.ed.gov/pubs2016/2016405.pdf.

Clotfelter, Charles T. "Patterns of Enrollment and Completion." In Charles T. Clotfelter et al., eds. *Economic Challenges in Higher Education.* U of Chicago P, 1991.

College Board. "A Brief History of the Advanced Placement Program." 2003. https://www.oakparkusd.org/cms/lib/CA01000794/Centricity/Domain/295/APUSH/AP_History_history.pdf.

College Board. "AP Participation." https://apcentral.collegeboard.org/media/xlsx/ap-participation-2013-2023.xlsx.

College Board. "AP Performance." https://apcentral.collegeboard.org/media/xlsx/ap-performance-2013-2023.xlsx.

College Board. "AP Reading Facts." 2018. Personal archive of author.

College Board. "AP Student Success at the College Level." 2018. Personal archive of author.

College Board. "Become an AP Reader." 2018. Personal archive of author.

College Board. "Tear the Paper Ceiling Partnership." September 21, 2022. https://bigfuture.collegeboard.org/explore-careers/tear-the-paper-ceiling-partnership.

Complete College America. "Momentum." https://completecollege.org/momentum/.

Complete College Georgia, University System of Georgia. "Completion by Performance." https://completega.org/content/completion-performance.

Conant, James Bryant. *The American High School Today: A First Report to Interested Citizens*. McGraw Hill, 1959.

Conant, James Bryant. *Education and Liberty: The Role of the Schools in a Modern Democracy*. Harvard UP, 1953.

Conant, James Bryant. *Education in a Divided World*. Harvard UP, 1948.

Conference on College Composition and Communication (CCCC). "Joint Position Statement on Dual Enrollment in Composition." November 2019. https://cccc.ncte.org/cccc/resources/positions/dualenrollment.

Conference on College Composition and Communication (CCCC). "Principles for the Postsecondary Teaching of Writing." November 2023. https://cccc.ncte.org/cccc/resources/positions/postsecondarywriting.

Conference on College Composition and Communication (CCCC). "Statement on Dual Credit / Concurrent Enrollment Composition: Policy and Best Practices." November 2012. http://web.archive.org/web/20180214103910/http:/cccc.ncte.org/cccc/resources/positions/dualcredit.

Connors. Robert. *Composition-Rhetoric: Background, Theories, and Pedagogy*. U of Pittsburgh P, 1997.

Cook, James. "Cocking Affair." *New Georgia Encyclopedia*, November 8, 2013. https://www.georgiaencyclopedia.org/articles/government-politics/cocking-affair/.

Cooke, Paul. "The Cost of Segregated Public Schools in the District of Columbia." *The Journal of Negro Education*, vol. 18, no. 2, spring 1949, pp. 95–103.

Council of Writing Program Administrators. *Framework for Success in Postsecondary Writing*. 2011. https://wpacouncil.org/aws/CWPA/asset_manager/get_file/350201?ver=7548.

Cowley, W. H. "Education for the Great Community." *The Journal of General Education*, vol. 1, no. 1, 1946, pp. 22–33.

Crowley, Sharon. *Composition in the University: Historical and Polemic Essays*. University of Pittsburgh P, 1998.

Current Population Reports: Population Characteristics. Department of Commerce, Bureau of the Census, Washington, DC, September 5, 1947.

Dahlkamp, Owen. "Donald Trump's Secret Weapon to Dismantle American Education." *The Atlantic Monthly,* July 5, 2024. https://www.thenation.com/article/politics/donald-trump-second-term-education-accreditation/.

"Dan" [AP Reader]. Personal interview with the author, July 10, 2024.

Davidson, Cathy. *The New Education: How to Revolutionize the University to Prepare Students for a World in Flux.* Basic Books, 2017.

Davison, Fred C. Annual Report, the University of Georgia, 1975–1976. University System Board of Regents Institution Annual Reports, RCB 993, record group 033-04-039, Georgia Archives.

DeGenaro, William. *Who Says? Working-Class Rhetoric, Consciousness, and Community.* U of Pittsburgh P, 2007.

Delgado, Brian, and Prateek Paul, "Georgia's Advanced Placement Program: Historical Trends and Descriptive Statistics." May 30, 2017. https://gosa.georgia.gov/georgias-advanced-placement-program-historical-trends-and-descriptive-statistics-0.

Denecker, Christine, and Casie Moreland, eds. *The Dual Enrollment Kaleidoscope: Reconfiguring Perceptions of First-Year Writing and Composition Studies.* Utah State UP, 2022.

Denecker, Christine, and Casie Moreland, eds. "Introduction: The Dual Enrollment Kaleidoscope." *The Dual Enrollment Kaleidoscope: Reconfiguring Perceptions of First-Year Writing and Composition Studies.* Utah State UP, 2022, pp. 11–25.

DeRuy, Emily. "When Calculus Isn't an Option." *The Atlantic Monthly,* June 7, 2016. https://www.theatlantic.com/education/archive/2016/06/where-calculus-class-isnt-an-option/485987/.

Downs, Douglas, and Elizabeth Wardle. "Teaching About Writing, Righting Misconceptions: (Re)Envisioning 'First-Year Composition' as 'Introduction to Writing Studies.'" *College Composition and Communication,* vol. 58, no. 4, June 2007, pp. 552–584.

Drury, John. *Education and Social Change: Contours in the History of American Schooling.* 5th ed., Routledge, 2016.

Education Commission of the States. "50-State Comparison." *Transfer and Articulation* 2022. https://reports.ecs.org/comparisons/transfer-and-articulation-2022-03.

Eisenhower, Dwight D., Chester W. Nimitz, and A. A. Vandegrift. "Liberal Education in the Military Forces: A Symposium." *The Journal of General Education,* vol. 1, no. 1, 1946, pp. 34–38.

Emory University Oxford College. "Admission and Aid." 2024. https://oxford.emory.edu/admission/index.html.

Everett, Justin, and Cristina Hanganu-Bresch, eds. *A Minefield of Dreams: Triumphs and Travails of Independent Writing Programs.* Utah State UP, 2017.

Fazlul, Ishtiaque, Todd Jones, and Jonathan Smith. "College Credit on the Table? Advanced Placement Course and Exam Taking." IZA Institute of Labor Economics, Discussion Paper Series, August 2021. https://papers.ssrn.com/sol3/papers.cfm?abstract_id=3908867.

Federal Student Aid, Office of the US Department of Education. "Calculating Pell Grant Lifetime Eligibility Used." https://studentaid.gov/understand-aid/types/grants/pell/calculate-eligibility.

Fincher, Cameron. "Planning for a Statewide System of Public Higher Education: Fifty Years of Trial, Error, and Eventual Success in Georgia." Paper presented at the University of Georgia College of Education's Meet the Scholar Series, February 24, 1984. ERIC 245 638.

Finn, Chester E., and Andrew E. Scanlan. *Learning in the Fast Lane: The Past, Present, and Future of Advanced Placement*. Princeton UP, 2019.

Finnegan, Cara A., and Marissa Wallace. "Origin Stories and Dreams of Collaboration: Rethinking Histories of the Communication Course and the Relationships Between English and Speech." *Rhetoric Society Quarterly*, vol. 44, no. 5, 2014, pp. 401–426.

Fisher, Walter T. "The Lopsided Harvard Report." *The Journal of General Education*, vol. 1, no. 3, 1947, pp. 195–199.

Florida Department of Education. "Florida Department of Education Statewide Course Numbering System: Institution Course Descriptions." July 28, 2024. https://flscns.fldoe.org/Reports/CourseDescriptionReport.aspx?instituion=&dis=163&prefix=ENC&discontinued=0&Type=CourseDescriptions.

Fore, Preston. "2 Trillion in Student Loan Debt Is in Limbo Under Trump." *Fortune*, January 30, 2025. https://fortune.com/article/student-loan-forgiveness-trump-adminstration-uncertainty/.

Foust, R. C., H. Hertberg-Davis, and C. M. Callahan. "Students' Perceptions of the Non-Academic Advantages and Disadvantages of Participation in Advanced Placement Courses and International Baccalaureate Programs." *Adolescence* 4, no. 174, 2009, pp. 289–312.

Freer, George. Letter to Louise McBee, March 30, 1988. Louise McBee Papers, UA97–074, box 40, folder 30, Hargrett Rare Book and Manuscript Library, University Archives, The University of Georgia Libraries.

Friersdorf, Conor. "What 'Luxury Beliefs' Reveal About the Working Class." *The Atlantic Monthly*, March 2, 2024. https://www.theatlantic.com/ideas/archive/2024/03/rob-henderson-memoir-yale-troubled/677620/.

Fry, Richard, Dana Bragg, and Kim Parker. "Public Views on the Value of a College Degree." Pew Research Center, May 23, 2024. https://www.pewresearch.org/social-trends/2024/05/23/public-views-on-the-value-of-a-college-degree/.

"The Function of the Communication Course in General Education: The Report of Workshop No. 2." *College Composition and Communication*, vol. 1, no. 2, May 1950, pp. 7–8.

"The Function of the Composition Course in General Education: The Report of Workshop No. 1." *College Composition and Communication*, vol. 1, no. 2, May 1950, pp. 5–6.

"Funds Move to Crack Down on State Schools." *Atlanta Daily World*, January 6, 1939, pp. 6–7.

Gallagher, Chris W. *College Made Whole: Integrative Learning for a Divided World*. Johns Hopkins UP, 2019.

Gardner, Lee. "More States Are Looking at Consolidating Their Colleges: Does It Work?" *The Chronicle of Higher Education*, July 30, 2020. https://www.chronicle.com/article/more-states-are-looking-at-consolidating-their-public-colleges-does-it-work.

Gates Foundation, Edge Research, and HCM Strategists. "Student Perceptions of American Higher Education." March 11, 2024. https://www.pewresearch.org/social-trends/2024/05/23/public-views-on-the-value-of-a-college-degree/.

"Gee Speaks on the Budget Deficit, Academic Transformation, and Huggins." *Daily Athenaeum*, August 25, 2023. https://www.thedaonline.com/news/university/gee-speaks-on-the-budget-deficit-academic-transformation-and-huggins/article_5600875c-4059-11ee-81d2-dffc69b12c86.html.

General Education Improvement Council, Atlanta, Georgia. "Status Report on Recommendations of the Governor's Commission to Improve Education." July 1, 1965. Board of Regents, Chancellor Subject Files. RCB 30124, record group 033-01-051, Georgia Archives.

George, Diana, and John Trimbur. "The Communication Battle, or Whatever Happened to the 4th C?" *College Composition and Communication*, vol. 50, no. 4, 1999, pp. 682–698.

Georgia Advisory Committee to the United States Commission on Civil Rights. *Desegregation of Public School Districts in Georgia: 35 Public School Districts Have Unitary Status, 74 Districts Remain Under Court Jurisdiction*. December 2007. https://www.usccr.gov/files/pubs/docs/GADESG-FULL.pdf.

Georgia Commission on Education. "GEA Release." September 28, 1954. Board of Regents Chancellor Subject Files. RCB 30124, record group 033-01-051, Georgia Archives.

"Georgia Legislature 1929 Session Report." Commission and Board Reports 1915–1971, F-7257, record group 001-05-007, Georgia Archives.

Gerber, John C. "The Conference on College Composition and Communication." *College Composition and Communication*, vol. 1, no. 1, 1950, p. 12.

Gerber, John C. "Problems of Communication in College Teaching." *The Journal of General Education*, vol. 3, no. 2, 1949, pp. 121–127.

Giani, Matt, Rebecca Lyle, and Tara O'Neill. "OnRamps to College Attainment: Examining the Impact of OnRamps Participation on College Persistence and Attainment." Education Research Center, the University of Texas at Austin, August 2023. https://repositories.lib.utexas.edu/items/f0b9b187-d4dc-4958-9d6b-6d048a532101.

Giani, Matt, Julie Schell, Emily Wade, and Harrison Keller. "Policy Brief: OnRamps to College: Examining the Impact of OnRamps Participation on College Enrollment." Education Research Center, the University of Texas at Austin, July 2018. https://repositories.lib.utexas.edu/items/f0b9b187-d4dc-4958-9d6b-6d048a532101.

Gignilliat, Arthur M. Memo to Chairmen and Members of Academic Committees, University System of Georgia, June 22, 1961. University System Advisory Council Files, RCB 33626, record group 033-01-092, Georgia Archives.

Goggin, Maureen. *Authoring a Discipline: Scholarly Journals and the Post–World War II Emergence of Rhetoric and Composition*. Routledge, 2000.

Goglia, M. J. Memo to Academic Committee Chairmen and Secretaries, re: Report of the Committee on Transfer of Credit, University System of Georgia. Board of Regents Minutes, RCB 33626, record group 033-01-092, Georgia Archives.

Gold, David. *Rhetoric at the Margins. Revising the History of Writing Instruction in American Colleges, 1873–1947*. Southern Illinois UP, 2008.

Goldstein, Dana. "Two States. Eight Textbooks. Two American Stories." *The New York Times*, January 12, 2020. https://www.nytimes.com/interactive/2020/01/12/us/texas-vs-california-history-textbooks.html.

Goldstein, Dana. "Why Is the College Board Pushing to Expand Advanced Placement?" *The New York Times*, November 18, 2023. https://www.nytimes.com/2023/11/18/us/college-board-ap-exams-courses.html.

Graff, Harvey. *The Literacy Myth: Literacy and Social Structure in the Nineteenth Century City*. Academic Press, 1979.

Gray, C. Harold. "The Problem of Freshman English in the Professional School." *College Composition and Communication* 2, no. 1, 1951, pp. 3–6.

Griffin, Marvin. *Education in Georgia: Nineteen Fifty-Five thru Nineteen Fifty-Eight*. Education, Negro Education Division, Negro Education Material 1924–1964. RCB 10924, record group 012-06-075, Georgia Archives.

Gunn, Erik. "UW–Milwaukee Faculty to Vote on a Plan That Could Lead to Layoffs for Tenured Profs." *Wisconsin Examiner*, August 6, 2024. https://wisconsinexaminer.com/2024/08/06/uw-milwaukee-faculty-to-vote-on-a-plan-that-could-lead-to-layoffs-for-tenured-profs/.

Haines, Julia. "The Ten Most Educated States in America." *US News and World Report*, May 7, 2024. https://www.usnews.com/news/best-states/slideshows/the-10-most-educated-states-in-the-us?slide=10 (accessed January 2025).

Hamilton, Grace, and Cameron Spurr. "Columbia Admits 2,319 Students to Class of 2028, Acceptance Rate Drops Slightly to 3.85 Percent." *Columbia Spectator*, March 28, 2024. https://www.columbiaspectator.com/news/2024/03/28/columbia-admits-2319-students-to-class-of-2028-acceptance-rate-drops-slightly-to-385-percent/.

Hamilton, Laura T. *Parenting to a Degree: How Family Matters for College Women's Success*. U of Chicago P, 2016.

Hammond, Miriam, LaToya Owens, and Brian Gulko. *HBCUs Transforming Generations: Social Mobility Outcomes for HBCU Alumni*. United Negro College Fund, 2021. https://hbcufirst.com/Portals/20/Research/2021-Social-Mobility-Report-UNCF.pdf.

Hancher, Virgil. M. "The Components of General Education." *The Journal of General Education*, vol. 1, no. 1, 1946, pp. 9–16.

Handell, Stephen J., and Ronald A. Williams. "Reimagining Remediation." *Change: The Magazine of Higher Learning*, vol. 43, no. 2, 2011, pp. 28–33.

Hansen, Kristine, and Christine Farris. *College Credit for Writing in High School: The "Taking Care of" Business*. National Council of Teachers of English, 2010.

Hansen, Kristine, et al. "Are Advanced Placement and First-Year College Composition Equivalent? A Comparison of Outcomes in the Writing of Three Groups of

Sophomore College Students." *Research in the Teaching of English*, vol. 40, no. 4, 2006, pp. 461–501.

Harvard Committee. *General Education in a Free Society: Report of the Harvard Committee.* Harvard UP, 1945.

Hassel, Holly. 2022 CCCC Chair's Address. *College Composition and Communication*, vol. 74, no. 2, 2022, pp. 391–404.

Hassel, Holly, and Joanne Baird Giordano. "Occupy Writing Studies: Rethinking College Composition for the Needs of The Teaching Majority." *College Composition and Communication* 65, no. 1, 2013, pp. 117–139.

Hatfield, Neil, Nathanial Brown, and Chad M. Topaz. "Do Introductory Courses Disproportionately Drive Minoritized Students out of STEM Pathways?" *SocArXiv*, no. 15, February 2022. https://doi.org/10.1093/pnasnexus/pgac167.

Haveman, Robert, and Kathryn Wilson. "Access, Matriculation, and Graduation." *Economic Inequality and Higher Education: Access, Persistence, and Success*, edited by Stacy Dickert-Conlin and Ross Rubenstein, Russell Sage Foundation, 2007, pp. 17–43.

Havighurst, Robert J. "Emotional Outcomes of General Education." *The Journal of General Education*, vol. 1, no. 1, 1946, pp. 39–44.

Henderson, Rob, Lindsay Crouse, and Kevin Oliver. "When Progressive Ideals Become a Luxury." *The New York Times*, July 10, 2024. https://www.nytimes.com/2024/07/10/opinion/campus-protests-progressive-henderson.html.

Hesse, Doug. "Who Owns Writing?" *College Composition and Communication*, vol. 57, no. 2, 2005, pp. 335–357. 2005 CCCC Chair's Address.

Higher Learning Commission (HLC). *Defining Student Success Data Recommendations: A Compendium of Paper from HLC's Defining Student Success Data Initiative.* 2019.

Hoang, Kayla. "Opinion: The College Board Screwed Up Big Time on the 2020 AP Exams." *The Los Angeles Times*, May 27, 2020. https://highschool.latimes.com/fountain-valley-high-school/opinion-the-college-board-screwed-up-big-time-on-the-2020-ap-exams/.

Hodges, Lacy, and Georgia Institute of Technology, Office of Undergraduate Education. "Georgia Tech's Four-Year Graduation Rate Reaches All-Time High." December 19, 2023. https://oue.gatech.edu/node/2813.

Hollingshead, Byron S. "General Education at Harvard." *The Journal of General Education*, vol. 1, no. 1, 1946, pp. 76–80.

Illinois, State of. "Illinois Report Card 2022–2023: Postsecondary Remediation." https://www.illinoisreportcard.com/state.aspx?source=trends&source2=postsecondaryremediation&Stateid=IL.

Ison, Matthew, et al. "FERPA and Dual Enrollment: Institutional Practice and Policy Considerations." *Journal of Applied Research in the Community College*, vol. 30, no. 2, 2023, pp. 131–140.

Johnson, Kristine. "Beyond Standards: Disciplinary Perspectives on Habits of Mind." *College Composition and Communication*, vol. 64, no. 3, 2013, pp. 517–541.

Jones, Joseph. "Location, Delivery, and the Historical Divide Between School and College English." *The Dual Enrollment Kaleidoscope: Reconfiguring Perceptions of First-Year*

Writing and Composition Studies, edited by Christine Denecker and Casie Moreland, Utah State UP, 2022, pp. 52–67.

Jordan, W. K. "The Future of the Social Studies." *The Journal of General Education*, vol. 1, no. 1, 1946, pp. 72–75.

"Julie" (AP Reader). Personal interview with the author, July 10, 2024.

Karabel, Jerome. *The Chosen: The Hidden History of Admission at Yale, Harvard, and Princeton*. Harper, 2006.

Kast, Brett. "New Michigan State Budget Includes Free Community College Tuition for High School Grads." *WXYZ Detroit News*, July 9, 2024. https://www.michigan.gov/whitmer/news/press-releases/2024/07/09/gov-whitmer-secures-tuition-free-community-college-for-michigan-high-school.

Kelderman, Eric, Jacqueline Elias, and Brian O'Leary. "What the Public Really Thinks About Higher Education." *The Chronicle of Higher Education*, September 5, 2023. https://www.chronicle.com/article/what-the-public-really-thinks-about-higher-education.

Kiester, Edwin J. "The Education of Earl McGrath." *Change*, vol. 9, no. 4, 1977, pp. 23–29.

Kinsley, Peter, and Sara Goldrick-Rab. "Making the Grade: The Academic Side of College Life Among Financial Aid Recipients." *The Working Classes and Higher Education: Inequality of Access, Opportunity, and Outcome*, edited by Amy Stich and Carrie Freie, Routledge, 2016, pp. 87–109.

Knox, Liam. "Can High Schoolers Save the Community College?" *Inside Higher Ed*, November 21, 2022. https://www.insidehighered.com/news/2022/11/22/community-colleges-struggle-dual-enrollment-grows.

Knox, Liam. "College Board Fined for Selling Student Data." *Inside Higher Ed*, February 14, 2024. https://www.insidehighered.com/news/quick-takes/2024/02/14/college-board-fined-selling-students-information.

Knox, Liam. "Settling the Score." *Inside Higher Ed*, July 25, 2024. https://www.insidehighered.com/news/admissions/traditional-age/2024/07/25/college-board-defends-changes-ap-scoring-methodology.

Kolluri, Suneal, Stephanie Owen, and Jack Schneider. "Rethinking the Goals of High School Rigor: Three Experts Weigh in on the AP Program and College Board." Brookings Institute, April 11, 2023. https://www.brookings.edu/articles/rethinking-the-goals-of-high-school-rigor-three-experts-weigh-in-on-the-ap-program-and-college-board/.

Kretchmar, Jen, and Steve Farmer. "How Much Is Enough? Rethinking the Role of High School Courses in College Admission." *Journal of College Admission*, summer 2013, pp. 29–33.

Kurzweil, Martin, et al. *Public College and University Consolidations and the Implications for Equity*. ITHAKA-SR, August 30, 2021.

Kynard, Carmen. "Writing While Black: The Colour Line, Black Discourses, and Assessment in the Institutionalization of Writing Instruction." *English Teaching: Practice and Critique*, vol. 7, no. 2, 2008, pp. 4–34.

Labaree, David F. *Someone Has to Fail: The Zero-Sum Game of Public Schooling.* Harvard UP, 2010.

Lamos, Steve. "Basic Writing: CUNY and 'Mainstreaming': (De)Racialization Considered." *Journal of Basic Writing,* vol. 19, no. 2, 2000, pp. 22–43.

Lamos, Steve. *Interests and Opportunities: Race, Racism, and University Writing Instruction in the Post-Civil Rights Era.* U of Pittsburgh P, 2011.

Lebduska, Lisa. "Composing in the Wake of War: The G.I. Bill and the Teaching of English." *Open Words,* 2014, pp. 65–79.

Lee, Elizabeth M. *Class and Campus Life: Managing and Experiencing Inequality at an Elite College.* ILR Press, 2016.

Lindemann, Erika. "Freshman Composition: No Place for Literature." *College English,* vol. 55, no. 3, 1993, pp. 311–316.

Lorimer Leonard, Rebecca. *Writing On the Move: Migrant Women and the Value of Literacy.* U of Pittsburgh P, 2018.

Lueck, Amy. *A Shared History: Writing in the High School, College, and University, 1856–1886.* Southern Illinois UP, 2019.

Mackenzie, Gordon N., and Hubert Evans. "The Challenge of General Education for the Secondary Schools." *The Journal of General Education,* vol. 1, no. 1, 1946, pp. 64–71.

Marquez, Trina Marie. *Words Matter: A Content Analysis Study of Private and Public Higher Education Mission Statements in the Middle States Region.* 2016. St. John Fisher University, PhD dissertation. https://fisherpub.sjf.edu/education_etd/286/.

Mays, Arthur B. "The Relationship Between General and Vocational Education." *The Journal of General Education,* vol. 2, no. 2, 1948, pp. 156–160.

Mazzei, Patricia, and Anemona Hartecollis. "Florida Rejects A.P. African American Studies Class." *The New York Times,* January 19, 2023. https://www.nytimes.com/2023/01/19/us/desantis-florida-ap-african-american-studies.html.

McCullar, Emily. "How One State History Textbook Erases the Stories of Black and Hispanic Texans." *Texas Monthly,* October 22, 2020. https://www.texasmonthly.com/being-texan/state-history-textbook-erases-the-stories-black-hispanic-texans/.

McGee, Katie. "UT Austin Working with Lt. Gov. Dan Patrick, Conservative Donors to Create 'Limited Government' Think Tank." *The Texas Tribune,* August 26, 2021. https://www.texastribune.org/2021/08/26/ut-austin-liberty-institute/.

McGrath, Earl James. "General Education: A Review." *The Journal of General Education,* vol. 2, no. 4, 1948, pp. 267–277.

McGrath, Earl James. "The General Education Movement: An Editorial." *The Journal of General Education,* vol. 1, no. 1, 1946, pp. 3–8.

McGrath, Earl James. "Teachers of General Studies: An Editorial." *The Journal of General Education,* vol. 1, no. 2, 1947, pp. 83–85.

McKay, Heather A., Renée Edwards, and Daniel Douglas. "Smoothing the Path for Transfer: Implementing Interstate Passport at Community Colleges." *New Directions for Community Colleges,* no. 197, 2022, pp. 71–80.

McMillan Cottom, Tressie. *Lower Ed: The Troubling Rise of For-Profit Colleges in the New Economy.* New Press, 2017.

Mendenhall, Annie. *Desegregation State: College Writing Programs After the Civil Rights Movement*. Utah State UP, 2022.

Mettler, Suzanne. *Degrees of Inequality: How the Politics of Higher Education Sabotaged the American Dream*. Basic Books, 2014.

Michaels, Gene. Letter to Virginia Trotter, July 30, 1985. Louise McBee Papers, UA97–074, Box 1, folder 22, Hargrett Rare Book and Manuscript Library, University Archives, The University of Georgia Libraries.

Miller, Trey, and Paco Martorell. "Using Corequisite Remediation to Help Students Progress to College-Level Courses." Manpower Demonstration Research Corporation, July 2022. https://www.mdrc.org/work/publications/using-corequisite-remediation-help-students-progress-college-level-courses.

Mintz, Steven. "Reinventing the Humanities for Our Fragmented Time." *Inside Higher Ed*, October 25, 2023. https://www.insidehighered.com/opinion/blogs/higher-ed-gamma/2023/10/25/reinventing-teaching-humanities-our-fragmented-time.

"Minutes of the Committee on Languages and Literatures of the University System Advisory Council." April 20, 1962. University System Advisory Council Files, RCB 33626, record group 033-01-092, Georgia Archives.

"Minutes of the Meeting of the Administrative Committee on Transfer of Credit, University System Advisory Council." May 6, 1971. University System Advisory Council, RCB 33627, record group 033-01-092, Georgia Archives.

Moner, William, Phillip Motley, and Rebecca Pope-Ruark, eds. *Redesigning Liberal Education: Innovative Design for a Twenty-First Century Undergraduate Education*. Johns Hopkins UP, 2020.

Morse, Robert, Eric Brooks, and Owen Turnbull. "How US News Calculated the 2024 Best High Schools Rankings." *US News and World Report*, April 22, 2024. https://www.usnews.com/education/best-high-schools/articles/how-us-news-calculated-the-rankings.

Morton, Jennifer A. *Moving Up Without Losing Your Way: The Ethical Costs of Upward Mobility*. Princeton UP, 2021.

Mullen, Ann L. *Degrees of Inequality: Culture, Class, and Gender in American Higher Education*. Johns Hopkins UP, 2010.

Mullen, Ann L. "You Don't Have to Be a College Graduate to be Intelligent: First-Generation Students' Perspectives of Intelligence and Education." *The Working Classes and Higher Education: Inequality of Access, Opportunity, and Outcome*, edited by Amy Stich and Carrie Freie, Routledge, 2016, pp. 140–156.

National Center for Education Statistics (NCES). "Indicator 13: High School Coursetaking." August 2016. https://nces.ed.gov/programs/raceindicators/indicator_rcd.asp.

National Center for Education Statistics (NCES). *120 Years of American Education: A Statistical Portrait*. US Department of Education, 1993.

National Council of Teachers of English (NCTE). "First-Year Writing: What Good Does It Do?" (policy research brief). 2019. http://mjreiff.com/uploads/3/4/2/1/34215272/nctepolicybrief.pdf.

National Institute for Learning Outcomes Assessment. "Assessment Brief: A Historical Overview of Assessment: 1980s–2000s." January 2019. https://www.learningout comesassessment.org/wp-content/uploads/2019/08/Assessment-Briefs-History.pdf.

National Student Clearinghouse Research Center. "College Transfer Enrollment Grew by 5.3% in the Fall of 2023." February, 28, 2024. https://www.studentclearing house.org/news/college-transfer-enrollment-grew-by-5-3-in-the-fall-of-2023/.

Needham, Arnold E. "The Need for the 'Permissive' in Basic Communications." *College Composition and Communication*, vol. 1, no. 3, 1950, pp. 12–18.

Newfield, Christopher. *Unmaking the Public University: The Forty-Year Assault on the Middle Class*. Harvard UP, 2008.

"A Noble Beginning." *Atlanta Daily World*, January 6, 1939, p. 6.

North, Stephen. *The Making of Knowledge in Composition Studies: Portrait of an Emerging Field*. Heinemann, 1987.

Nystrand, Martin, Stuart Greene, and Jeffery Wiemelt. "Where Did Composition Studies Come From? An Intellectual History." *Written Communication*, vol. 10, no. 3, 1993, pp. 267–333.

Office of General Education, Pennsylvania State University. "General Education at Penn State." https://gened.psu.edu/.

Office of General Education, Pennsylvania State University. "General Education Learning Objectives and Foundation and Domain Criteria." https://gened.psu.edu/faculty-staff/about-general-education/learning-objectives-and-foundation-and-domain-criteria.

Ohmann, Richard. "English and the Cold War." *The Cold War and the University: Toward an Intellectual History of the Postwar Years*, Noam Chomsky, et al., New Press, 1997, pp. 73–106.

Oladipo, Gloria. "Trump's Plans to Axe US Education Department Puts Marginalized Students Most at Risk, Experts Warn." *The Guardian*, January 21, 2025. https://www.theguardian.com/us-news/2025/jan/21/trump-education-department.

Oliver, Kenneth. "The One-Legged, Wingless Bird of Freshman English." *College Composition and Communication* vol. 1, no. 1, 1950, pp. 3–6.

O'Neill, Peggy, Angela Crow, and Larry W. Burton, eds. *A Field of Dreams: Independent Writing Programs and the Future of Composition Studies*. Utah State UP, 2002.

Opportunity@Work. "The Paper Ceiling." https://www.tearthepaperceiling.org/the-paper-ceiling.

Ostergaard, Lori, and Henrietta Rix Wood. *In the Archives of Composition: Writing and Rhetoric in High Schools and Normal Schools*. U of Pittsburgh P, 2015.

Packard, Vance. *The Status Seekers: An Exploration of Class Behavior in America and the Hidden Barriers That Affect You, Your Community, and Your Future*. McKay, 1959.

Pandey, Erica. "America's Diploma Divide: States with Fewer Grads Went for Trump." *Axios*, November 7, 2024. https://www.axios.com/2024/11/07/college-degree-voters-split-harris-trump.

"Pedagogy." *OnRamps*, University of Texas at Austin, 2024. https://onramps.utexas.edu/what-we-offer/distance-ed/teachers/pedagogy/.

Perryman-Clark, Staci. "African-American Language, Rhetoric, and Students' Writing: New Directions for STROL." *College Composition and Communication*, vol. 64, no. 3, 2013, 469–495.

Pinckney, R. P. "The Negro State Colleges." *Atlanta Daily World*, May 18, 1939, p. 5.

Pluviose, David. "Civil Rights Panel: Historically White Program Duplication Threatens HBCUS." *Diverse Education*, May 7, 2006. https://www.diverseeducation.com/institutions/hbcus/article/15082017/civil-rights-panel-historically-white-program-duplication-threatens-hbcus.

Popp, Trey. "Course Corrections." *The Pennsylvania Gazette*, January/February 2025, pp. 24–35.

"The Proposed Plan of Reorganization as Set Forth in the Committee Substitute to House Bill 397 (Session of 1929)." Section 59. Commission and Board Reports 1915–1971, F-7257, record group 001-05-007, Georgia Archives.

Propst, H. Dean. "Statement by the Chancellor." Virginia Trotter Papers, Box 13, Folder 29, University of Georgia Archives, Athens, GA.

Rahman, Khaleda. "Map Shows Least Educated States in America." *Newsweek*, February 16, 2024. https://www.newsweek.com/map-shows-most-least-educated-states-1869928.

Ratcliff, James L., and Elizabeth A. Jones. "Are Common Course Numbering and a Core Curriculum Valid Indicators in the Articulation of General Education Credits Among Transfer Students?" Center for the Study of Higher Education, Pennsylvania State University. Paper Presented at American Educational Research Associaion, Chicago, Illinois, April 1991. https://files.eric.ed.gov/fulltext/ED338140.pdf.

Rhodes, Terrel. *Assessing Outcomes and Improving Achievement*. Association of American Colleges, 2010.

Richards, I. A. "The 'Future' of the Humanities in General Education." *The Journal of General Education*, vol. 1, no. 3, 1947, pp. 232–237.

Richardson, Jeanita W., and J. John Harris III. "Brown and Historically Black Colleges and Universities (HBCUs): A Paradox of Desegregation Policy." *The Journal of Negro Education*, vol. 73, no. 3, summer 2004, pp. 365–378.

Ritter, Kelly, "Extra-Institutional Authority and the Public Value of the WPA." *WPA: Writing Program Administration*, vol. 29, no. 3, 2006, pp. 45–64.

Ritter, Kelly. "The Importance of Disciplinary Dexterity in Humanities Leadership." *Profession*, February 29, 2024. https://profession.mla.org/the-importance-of-disciplinary-dexterity-in-humanities-leadership/.

Ritter, Kelly. *To Know Her Own History: Writing at the Woman's College, 1943–1963*. U of Pittsburgh P, 2012.

Ritter, Kelly. *Reframing the Subject: Postwar Instructional Film and Class-Conscious Literacies*. U of Pittsburgh P, 2015.

Ritter, Kelly. "With 'Increased Dignity and Importance': Re-Historicizing Charles Roberts and the Illinois Decision of 1955." *College Composition and Communication*, vol. 69, no. 3, 2018, pp. 458–493.

Roach, Paul F. "The Social Function of General Education." *The Journal of General Education*, vol. 2, no. 3, 1948, pp. 246–250.

Roberts, Charles. "Editorial Comment." *College Composition and Communication*, vol. 1, no. 1, 1950, pp. 13.

Roberts, Charles. "Editorial Comment." *College Composition and Communication*, vol. 1, no. 4, 1950, pp. 16.

Roemer, Marjorie, Lucille Schultz, and Russell Durst. "Reframing the Great Debate on First-Year Writing." *College Composition and Communication*, vol. 50, no. 3, 1999, pp. 377–392.

Rosenbaum, James. *Beyond College for All: Career Paths for the Forgotten Half*. Russell Sage Foundation, 2004.

Roth, Michael S. *Beyond the University: Why Liberal Education Matters*. Yale UP, 2015.

Sams, Henry W. "Composition and Logic." *The Journal of General Education*, vol. 6, no. 4, 1952, pp. 268–279.

Sanford, Steadman V. "Ladies and Gentlemen . . ." (untitled speech). 1935 Chancellor's Speeches, RCB 14614, record group 033-01-030, Georgia Archives.

Sanford, Steadman V. "Dangers." 1938. Chancellor Speeches, RCB 14614, record group 033-01-030, Georgia Archives.

Sanford, Steadman V. "Ladies and Gentlemen . . ." (untitled speech). Letter to the Committee on Education, Board of Regents, State of Georgia. April 17, 1943. Board of Regents, University System Files. RCB 35746, record group 033-01-03, Georgia Archives.

Sanford, Steadman V. "Ladies and Gentlemen . . ." (untitled speech). Letter to A. R. Mann, General Education Board, August 16, 1943. Board of Regents Chancellor Subject Files, RCB 30124, record group 033-01-051, Georgia Archives.

Sanford, Steadman V. "Ladies and Gentlemen . . ." (untitled speech). Letter to A. R. Mann, General Education Board, August 23, 1943. Board of Regents Chancellor Subject Files, RCB 30124, record group 033-01-051, Georgia Archives.

Schilb, John. *Rhetorical Refusals: Defying Audiences' Expectations*. Southern Illinois UP, 2007.

Schneider, Barbara. "And Yet the Gap Persists." *The Dual Enrollment Kaleidoscope: Reconfiguring Perceptions of First-Year Writing and Composition Studies*, edited by Christine Denecker and Casie Moreland, Utah State UP, 2022, pp. 27–44.

Schneider, Jack. "Privilege, Equity, and the Advanced Placement Program: Tug of War." *Journal of Curriculum Studies*, vol. 41, no. 6, 2009, pp. 813–831.

Schudde, Lauren, Huriya Jabbar, and Catherine Hartman. "How Political and Ecological Contexts Shape Community College Transfer." *Sociology of Education* 94, no. 1, 2020, pp. 65–83.

Shao, Elena, Karen Yourish, and June Kim. "How Trump's Directives Echo Project 2025." *The New York Times*, February 14, 2025. https://www.nytimes.com/interactive/2025/02/14/us/politics/project-2025-trump-actions.html.

Sharp-Hoskins, Kellie. *Rhetoric in Debt*. Penn State UP, 2023.

Smith, Denise. *Nourishing the Nation While Starving: The Underfunding of Black Land-Grant Colleges and Universities*. Century Foundation, July 24, 2023. https://tcf.org/content/report/nourishing-the-nation-while-starving-the-underfunding-of-black-land-grant-colleges-and-universities/.

Smith, Wilson, and Thomas Bender, eds. *American Higher Education Transformed, 1940–2005: Documenting the National Discourse.* Johns Hopkins UP, 2008.

Soliday, Mary. *The Politics of Remediation: Institutional and Student Needs in Higher Education.* U of Pittsburgh P, 2003.

Spitalniak, Laura. "Dive Brief: Penn State to Pare Down Commonwealth Leadership After Buyout Offers." *Higher Ed Dive*, June 12, 2024. https://www.highereddive.com/news/penn-state-commonwealth-leadership-restructure-buyouts/718753/.

"SRO 1985 APP Participation Regional/State Volumes." Louise McBee Papers, UA97-074, box 40, folder 30, Hargrett Rare Book and Manuscript Library, University Archives, The University of Georgia Libraries.

Stabley, Rhodes. "After Communications, You Can't Go Home Again." *College Composition and Communication* 1, no. 3, 1950, pp. 7–11.

Stanley, Jane. *The Rhetoric of Remediation: Negotiating Entitlement and Access to Higher Education.* U of Pittsburgh P, 2010.

Steinberg, Erwin R. "Some Basic Assumptions for Courses in English Composition." *College Composition and Communication*, vol. 2, no. 3, 1951, pp. 11–16.

Stich, Amy. *Access to Inequality: Reconsidering Class, Knowledge, and Capital in Higher Education.* Lexington Books, 2012.

Stich, Amy, and Carrie Freie, eds. *The Working Classes and Higher Education: Inequality of Access, Opportunity, and Outcome.* Routledge, 2016.

Stone, Russell. "Promoting the Public Impact of General Education." *The Journal of General Education*, vol. 69, nos. 3–4, 2020, pp. 142–153.

Strauss, Valerie. "Class-Action Lawsuit Filed Against College Board About Botched AP Tests." *The Washington Post*, May 20, 2020. https://www.washingtonpost.com/education/2020/05/20/class-action-lawsuit-filed-against-college-board-about-botched-ap-tests/.

Strayer, George. *A Report of the Survey of the University System of Georgia.* December 15, 1949. dig.galileo.usg.edu/data/dig/ggpd/pdfs/dig_ggpd_s-ga-bu500-b-pm1-b1949-bs9.pdf.

Suldo, S. M., E. Shaunessy-Dedrick, J. Ferron, and R. F. Dedrick. "Predictors of Success Among High School Students in Advanced Placement and International Baccalaureate Programs." *Gifted Child Quarterly* 62, no. 4, 2018, pp. 350–373.

Sullivan, Patrick. "Democracy's Unfinished Business: Rethinking How We Prepare Teachers of English." *Pedagogy*, vol. 21, no. 1, 2021, pp. 55–81.

Synnott, Marcia. "A Contentious History of Admissions Policies at American Colleges and Universities: Issues and Prospects." *Higher Education: Theory and Research*, edited by L. W. Perna, Springer, 2021, pp. 1–49.

Talmadge, Herman E. Letter to Eugene Cook, September 14, 1954. Board of Regents Chancellor Subject Files, RCB 30124, record group 033-01-051, Georgia Archives.

Tanouye, Dylan. "The College Board Has Become Indistinguishable from a Hedge Fund." *Tufts Daily*, January 17, 2024. https://www.tuftsdaily.com/article/2024/01/the-college-board-has-become-indistinguishable-from-a-hedge-fund.

Tate, Gary. "A Place for Literature in Freshman Composition." *College English*, vol. 55, no. 3, 1993, pp. 317–321.

Taylor and Morphew, "An Analysis of Baccalaureate College Mission Statements." *Research In Higher Education*, no. 51, 2010, pp. 483–503.

Thelin, John. *A History of American Higher Education*. Johns Hopkins UP, 2004.

Thompson, Clarissa A., Michelle Eodice, and Phuoc Tran. "Student Perceptions of General Education at a Large University: No Surprises?" *The Journal of General Education*, vol. 64, no. 4, 2015, 278–293.

Tinberg, Howard. "The Loss of the Public." *College Composition and Communication*, vol. 66, no. 2, 2014, pp. 327–341. 2014 CCCC Chair's Address.

Tinberg, Howard, and Patrick Sullivan, eds. *What Is College-Level Writing?* National Council of Teachers of English, 2006.

Tinberg, Howard, and Patrick Sullivan, eds. *What Is College-Level Writing? Assignments, Reading, and Student Writing Samples*. Vol. 2, National Council of Teachers of English, 2010.

Tough, Paul. *The Years That Matter Most: How College Makes or Breaks Us*. Mariner Books, 2019.

Tripp, Andrew. "Memorandum Regarding Federal Contracting Compliance." University of North Carolina System. February 5, 2025. https://www.unc.edu/wp-content/uploads/2025/02/February-5-Memorandum-Regarding-Federal-Contracting-Compliance.pdf.

University of Illinois Urbana-Champaign. "Campus Conversation on Undergraduate Education, Grand Challenge Learning Initiative." http://undergrad-education.illinois.edu/initiatives/grand-challenge-learning-pilot/index.html.

University of North Carolina System. "Understanding the Advanced Placement Credit Policy." https://www.northcarolina.edu/understanding-the-advanced-placement-credit-policy/.

University System of Georgia. "2.4: General Education CORE Curriculum: the IMPACTS Core." *Academic and Student Affairs Handbook*. July 19, 2024. https://www.usg.edu/academic_affairs_handbook/section2/C738/#p2.4.1_general_education_learning_goals.

"The University System of Georgia." 1939. House Committee on Economy and Energy files, F-7260, record group 001-05-007, Georgia Archives.

"University System of Georgia Equivalent Full-Time Enrollments." All Institutions General File, 1956–1964. RCB 30124, record group 033-01-051, Georgia Archives.

US News and World Report. "Centennial High School." 2024. https://www.usnews.com/education/best-high-schools/illinois/districts/champaign-community-unified-school-district-4/centennial-high-school-6542.

Valentino, Marilyn. "Rethinking the Fourth C." *College Composition and Communication*, vol. 62, no. 2, 2010, pp. 393–399. 2010 CCCC Chair's Address.

Vander Schee, Brian A. "Changing General Education Perceptions Through 'Perspectives' and the Interdisciplinary First-Year Seminar." *International Journal of Teaching and Learning in Higher Education*, vol. 23, no. 3, 2011, pp. 382–387.

VanSickle, Abbie. "Supreme Court Clears the Way for Trump's Cuts to the Education Department." *The New York Times*, July 14, 2025. https://nytimes.com/2025/07/14/us/politics/supreme-court-education-department.html.

Varnum, Robin. "The History of Composition: Reclaiming Our Lost Generations." *Journal of Advanced Composition*, vol. 12, no. 1, 1992, pp. 39–55.

Vee, Annette. "Introduction: What Was the Dartmouth Seminar?" *Dartmouth '66 Seminar* (exhibit), WAC Clearinghouse, December 2020. https://wac.colostate.edu/repository/exhibits/dartmouth/introduction-what-was-the-dartmouth-seminar/.

Waggaman, John S. "Indicators and Costing of Florida's Education Goals." US Department of Health, Education, and Welfare, National Institute of Education, August 24, 1975. ERIC 114 953.

Wan, Amy. *Producing Good Citizens: Literacy Training in Anxious Times*. U of Pittsburgh P, 2014.

Wapman, K. Hunter, et al. "Quantifying Hierarchy and Dynamics in US Faculty Hiring and Retention." *Nature*, vol. 610, October 2022, pp. 120–127.

Wells, Cynthia. *Realizing General Education: Reconsidering Conceptions and Renewing Practice* [ASHE Higher Education Report]. Wiley, 2016.

Wells, Guy H. Letter to Chancellor R. R. Paty, June 4, 1947. Standing Committee on Education Files, RCB 35746, record group 033-01-035, Georgia Archives.

Westfall, Jonathan J. "Memo to Members of the University of Georgia AAUP." July 13, 1945. Eugene P. Odum Papers, ms 3257, Series 1, Box 151, Folder 34. University Archives, The University of Georgia Libraries.

Williamson-Lott, Joy Ann. *Jim Crow Campus: Higher Education and the Struggle for a New Southern Social Order*. Teachers College Press, 2018.

Works, George A. "Report to the Regents of the University System of Georgia." 1943. https://dlg.galileo.usg.edu/data/dlg/ggpd/pdfs/dlg_ggpd_s-ga-bu500-b-pm1-b1943-br4.pdf.

Wright, J. Dixon. Memo to the Academic Committee on Languages and Literature, Georgia Institute of Technology, February 7, 1967. Board of Regents Minutes, RCB 33626, record group 033-01-092, Georgia Archives.

Wynn, Colleen, and Elizabeth Ziff. "General Education Classes Strengthen Democracy." *The Progressive*, September 7, 2023. https://progressive.org/op-eds/general-education-classes-strengthen-democracy-wynn-ziff-230907/.

Xiong, Ruiwen. "An Analysis of AP Classes Growth and the Effects on Student Stress." *International Journal of High School Research* 6, no. 1, 2024, pp. 136–144.

Yood, Jessica. "Writing the Discipline: A Generic History of English Studies." *College English*, vol. 65, no. 5, 2003, pp. 526–540.

Zimmerman, Jonathan. *The Amateur Hour: A History of College Teaching in America*. Johns Hopkins UP, 2020.

Zimpher, Nancy L., Laura A. Dunek, and Jessica Fisher Neidl. "The Evolving Social Contract for Higher Education in the Twenty-First Century: Serving the Public Good While Incentivizing Economic Growth." *Challenges in Higher Education Leadership*. Routledge, 2017, pp. 129–39.

Index

AAC&U. *See* American Association of Colleges and Universities (AAC&U)
AAPT. *See* American Association of Philosophy Professors (AAPT)
AAUP. *See* American Association of University Professors (AAUP)
AAVE, 157
ability grouping, 208n13
Abraham Baldwin Agricultural College, 88–89
Abrams, Annie, 125–26, 132, 224n50
Academic Senate for California Community Colleges, 96
Accountability Manual (State of Texas Education Agency), 164
accreditation, 220n5
ACT. *See* Articulation of Credit Transfer (ACT)
ACT (test), 6, 112, 118, 121, 156, 165, 218n50
The Activist WPA (Adler-Kassner), 21, 173
Adler-Kassner, Linda, 21, 170, 173
"An Administrative Code for the University System of Georgia," 82
Administrative Committee on the Transfer of Credit, at USG, 91
Advanced Placement (AP), 6, 7, 22, 23–24, 220n8; for African American History course in Florida, 95, 97, 218n55; African American History course in, 218n55; Asians in, 116–17, 119; Blacks in, 24, 116–17; *Brown v. Board of Education* and, 125; Capstone in, 122, 149, 223n36; class action lawsuit against, 224n55; Columbia University and, 128; as competitive advantage, 124–30; Conant on, 10, 49; cost savings from, 209n17; curricula overview for, 222n26; "Daily Practice Sessions" for, 127; DEI and, 130–39; for democracy, 110; EBSS for, 224n52; economies of scale of, 147–51; efficiency in, 132; in elementary school, 139; for English, 58; exams for, 115–22, 125, 126, 129, 132–33, 139–47; first-generation students and, 128; in Florida, 136; FYC and, 156; in Georgia, 119, 136; Harvard University and, 120, 126, 129; high school rating and ranking on, 120, 221n15; Hispanics in, 116–17; for history, 23, 115, 129, 132, 224n50; humanities and, 114; IB and, 108–9; K–12 schools and, 139; Language and Composition in, 110, 113–14, 115, 140–51, 222n22; liberal education and, 132; Literature and Composition in, 110, 113–14, 115, 119–20, 133, 222n22, 224n51; in middle school, 139; in Minnesota, 134–35; Native Americans in, 116–17; no age limit for, 115;

OnRamps and, 165, 167; for philosophy, 187; in PLA, 138; price of, 109; required credits for, 119; Research in, 122, 223n36; restrictions on, 133; retesting of, 118; rhetoric for, 27–28; rhetoric of competition for, 108, 121–30; rhetoric of efficiency for, 108, 139–47; rhetoric of exemption for, 107–51; rhetoric of remediation for, 108, 130–39; social sciences and, 114; Stanford University and, 124–25; stress and burnout from, 223n35; student choice and, 110–13; student loans and, 122–23; Studio Art in, 122; subsidizing of, 115; temporal span for, 115; as transfer credit, 220n12; at UGA, 135, 136; at UNC, 133, 192–93; University of Iowa and, 224n51; for University of Pennsylvania, 35; at University of Wisconsin, 134, 136; VIP in, 147–49; for World History, 115; WPA and, 119; writing programs/courses and, 110, 113–14, 115, 118–19, 133, 140–51, 222n22

African American History course, 95, 97, 218n55

African Americans. *See* Blacks

"After Communications, You Can't Go Home Again" (Stabley), 56

Agenda47, 192

Agricultural and Mechanical Arts, in USG, 69

Agricultural and Mechanical Schools, in USG, 69

Agricultural College, in USG, 69

AHA. *See* American Historical Association (AHA)

AI, 157

"Aims and Objectives," at Georgia Tech, 74, 217n41

Alabama, 216n33

Albany State College, 80, 81, 84, 102, 214n17

A-Level (GCE Advanced level), 134

Allocation of Functions, at USG, 81, 216n39

The Amateur Hour (Zimmerman), 194

American Association of Colleges and Universities (AAC&U), 17–18, 37, 94, 202, 210n6

American Association of Philosophy Professors (AAPT), 183

American Association of University Professors (AAUP), 73, 188–89

American Higher Education Transformed 1940–2005 (Smith, W., and Bender), 11

The American High School Today (Conant), 41, 49

American Historical Association (AHA), 186, 227n25

American Philosophical Association (APA), 181–84, 209n2, 227n29

"Americans' Confidence in Higher Education Down Sharply" (Brenan), 192

America's College Promise, 222n27

Anson, Chris, 226n21

AP. *See* Advanced Placement (AP)

APA. *See* American Philosophical Association (APA)

APID, 223n33

AP Participation, 116–17

AP Performance, 116–17

APS. *See* Atlanta Public Schools (APS)

AP Scholar Awards, 129–30

AP US History (APUSH), 23, 132, 224n50

Aristotle, 227n30

Arizona State University, 137

Armstrong State College, 75–76, 79

Arnold, Jim, 218n50

articulation agreements, 63, 137

Articulation of Credit Transfer (ACT), 217n47

Asians/Asian Americans, 116–17, 119, 157

Associate Degree, 219n65

Atlanta Daily World, 80

Atlanta Public Schools (APS), 222n23

Atlanta University, 213n8

Augusta University, 101

Austin State, 95

Baby Boom, 39

backwards transfer, 219n65

Baker, R. Scott, 214n16

Beasley, James, 51, 52

Bender, Thomas, 11

"Benefits of Taking the AP Exam" (College Board), 126–28

Berlin, James, 15, 51, 168–69

BigFuture, 197–99

biological sciences, 210n9

birth classes, 50

Bishop, Elizabeth, 22

Blacks (African Americans), 215n29; in AP, 24, 116–17; in APS, 222n23; college value for, 7; FYC for, 157; Gen Ed for, 19; at Georgia Tech, 76, 102; in high school, 207n4, 210n11; in OnRamps, 164, 167; in rhetoric courses, 157; with STARs, 196; in STEM, 207n4, 210n11; at UGA, 76, 78–79; at USG, 27, 65, 69, 72, 75, 80–81, 83, 84, 86–87, 215n30. *See also* historically Black colleges and universities; segregation

Bok, Derek, 9

branch campuses, at USG, 70–72, 91–92, 95

Brandt, Deborah, 16, 37–38

Brannon, Lil, 169–70, 226n21

Branson, Tyler, 21, 108, 153, 171, 220n3
Brenan, Megan, 192
Bringsjord, Elizabeth L., 93
Brookings Institute, 125
Broward College, 100
Brown, Oliver, 217n40
Brown v. Board of Education, 87–89, 125; Georgia and, 63, 69, 72, 74, 76, 77, 85, 217n40
Buck, Paul H., 11
Burdick, Melanie, 153
Burke, Kenneth, 109

calculus, 140, 210n12
Caldwell, Harmon, 79, 87, 215n27
Calhoon-Dillahunt, Carolyn, 168–70, 226n21
California, 96–97
California State Colleges, 68
Cambridge Pre-U, 134
capitalism, 9, 38
Capstone, in AP, 122, 149, 223n36
Carnegie Mellon, 120
Carnevale, Anthony P., 195
CCA. *See* Complete College America (CCA)
CCC. *See College Composition and Communication* (CCC)
CCCC. *See* Conference on College Composition and Communication (CCCC)
CCG. *See* Complete College Georgia (CCG)
CCN. *See* Common Course Numbering (CCN)
"The Challenge of General Education for Secondary Schools" (Mackenzie and Evans), 48–49
Challenge Success, 124–25
Charters, W. W., 48
The Chronicle of Higher Education (CHE), 190–93
CIP. *See* Classification of Instructional Program (CIP)
City University of New York (CUNY), 217n47
Civil Rights Act of 1964, 79
Civil Rights Movement, 194
Classification of Instructional Program (CIP), 159
CLEP. *See* College-Level Examination Program (CLEP)
Cocking, Walter D., 79–80
Cocking Affair, 80, 81, 216n33
cognitive learning, 43
Coldwell, Harmon, 79–80
College Board, 7, 10, 21, 112, 113, 126, 127–28, 220n10, 221n17; BigFuture of, 197–99; Opportunity@Work and, 197–98; Tear the Paper Ceiling and, 198–99. *See also* Advanced Placement (AP); College-Level Examination Program (CLEP)
college/college degrees: CCA for, 19–20; corporations and, 9; for employment, 6–7; free programs for, 222n27; Gen Ed courses for, 33–36; hands-on learning for, 18; intergenerational wealth and, 194–95; public views on, 6–7, 190–96; time-to-degree metric for, 138–39; transfer credits for, 220n8; by transfer students, 217n51. *See also specific topics*
College Composition and Communication (CCC), 26, 30–60, 212n24; English studies and, 52; on Gen Ed as liberation, 51–58; writing programs/courses in, 53–54
College Credit for Writing in High School (Hansen and Farris), 21, 172
College English, 52
College-Level Examination Program (CLEP), 6, 7, 108, 134, 138, 198, 219n1, 220n8
College Made Whole (Gallagher, C.), 203
College of General Studies, at University of Wisconsin, 229n11
college-ready, 137, 139, 222n21
Colleges for Negroes, 83
Columbia University, 9, 127, 128
Columbus Junior College, 79
Committee on Transfer of Credit, at USG, 90
Common Course Numbering (CCN): efficiency of, 92, 99; in Florida, 97–102; in Illinois, 96; seamless transfer and, 92–94; in Texas, 94–97; at USG, 62–63, 67–68, 74–77, 83, 91–94, 100–102; for writing programs/courses, 100–102
community relations, 156
Complete College America (CCA), 19–20, 137
Complete College Georgia (CCG), 137–38
"Components of General Education" (Hancher), 45
"Composing in the Wake of War" (Lebduska), 53
Composition in the University (Crowley), 154–55, 157
computational sciences, at USG, 67
Conant, James Bryant, 10, 11, 14–15, 23, 25, 31, 48, 207n8; on ability grouping, 208n13; *The American High School Today* by, 41, 49; on AP, 49; *Education in a Divided World* by, 41, 58–59; *General Education in School and College* by, 41
concurrent enrollment, 171–72, 226n16
Conference on College Composition and Communication (CCCC), 53–54, 58; APA and, 184, 185; on DE/DC, 168, 172, 174–77; on FYC, 160, 168–75, 178–79; realignment

of, 212n24; Strategic Governance Mission Statement of, 171–72; task force of, 225n6; "Workshop Reports" from, 54–56
Connecticut, 225n12
Connors, Robert, 160
Cook, Eugene, 84–85
core curriculum: ACT and, 218n50; Gen Ed as, 17, 27; at Georgia Tech, 90, 217n43; philosophy courses and, 185–86; at USG, 62–63, 66–68, 75, 76–77, 83, 87–91, 102–6, 213n10, 213n11, 217n43
Core IMPACTS. *See* IMPACTS
Council of Writing Program Administrators (CWPA), 101, 171, 173, 174
COVID-19 pandemic, 7, 140, 192, 200
Cowley, W. H., 46–47, 211n22
credit-by-exemption programs, 16
credit wash, 225n11
Crowley, Sharon, 154–55, 157, 160, 225n10
cultural understanding courses, 37
CUNY. *See* City University of New York (CUNY)
CWPA. *See* Council of Writing Program Administrators (CWPA)
"Daily Practice Sessions," for AP, 127
"Dangers" (Sanford), 77
Dartmouth Conference, 157
Darton State College, 102
Davidson, Cathy, 18
DE/DC. *See* dual enrollment/dual credit (DE/DC)
Defining Student Success Data Recommendations (HLC), 138
DEI. *See* diversity, equity, and inclusion (DEI)
democracy: AP for, 110; Gen Ed for, 12–13, 14, 36–39, 59, 187; in late-stage capitalism, 9; liberal education for, 9, 17; NSSE and, 200, 201; Truman Commission Report on, 39; writing programs/courses for, 52
Democratic Party, 6, 192
Demos, Raphael, 11
Denecker, Christine, 108, 170
"Department Advocacy Toolkit" (APA), 182–84
Department of Education, 7, 123, 192
Department of Health, Education, and Welfare (HEW), 79
DeSantis, Ron, 218n53
Desegregation State (Mendenhall), 75–76, 214n16
Dewey, John, 51
diversity, equity, and inclusion (DEI), 37; in APA, 181; AP and, 130–39; first-generation students and, 157–60; in Florida, 95; in Gen Ed, 74, 189, 208n12; in OnRamps, 165; in Texas, 95; at UNC, 192–93, 228n4; at USG, 74, 92
Douglas, Daniel, 94
Downs, Doug, 225n9
downward transfer, 217n47
dual enrollment/dual credit (DE/DC), 28, 47–48, 49, 220n8, 226n14; CCCC on, 168, 172, 174–77; competitive advantage of, 124; in Connecticut, 225n12; cost savings from, 209n17; as credit wash, 225n11; efficiency of, 108, 210n10; employment and, 220n3; FERPA and, 226n13; for FYC, 108, 152–87; high school rating and ranking on, 221n15; K–12 schools and, 153; OnRamps, at UT, 28, 160–68, 226n19; for philosophy, 187; state government funding for, 227n28; for University of Pennsylvania, 35; at USG, 162. *See also* Advanced Placement (AP)
The Dual Enrollment Kaleidoscope (Denecker and Moreland), 108
Durst, Russell, 152

Early, Mary Frances, 76
early college, 49; cost savings from, 209n17
EBSS. *See* Evidence-Based Standard Setting (EBSS)
Educational Policies Commission, 46
Educational Testing Service (ETS), 10
Education and Liberty (Conant), 14
education-as-uplift principles, 51
Education for All American Youth (Educational Policies Commission), 46
"Education for the Great Community" (Cowley), 46
Education Goals, of Florida, 98
Education in a Divided World (Conant), 41, 58–59
Education in Georgia (Griffin), 85–87
Edwards, Renée, 94
efficiency: in AP, 132; of CCN, 92, 99; in core curriculum, 63; of DE/DC, 108, 210n10; in Gen Ed, 217n42; rhetoric of, for AP, 108, 139–47; social, 195; in Texas, 212n7; at USG, 64–74, 106, 217n42
Eisenhower, Dwight D., 39, 43
elementary school, AP in, 139
ELL. *See* English language learners (ELL)
Emory University, 214n23
"Emotional Outcomes of General Education" (Hollingshead and Havighurst), 49–50
employment: college degrees for, 6–7; DE/DC and, 220n3; Gen Ed for, 28–29; junior colleges for, 82; paper ceiling and, 28–29,

188–205; in philosophy, 181; STEM for, 8; University of Pennsylvania and, 34; in USG IMPACTS, 104, 105; vocational education for, 31, 41
English Journal, 52
English language learners (ELL), 137
English programs/courses: for AP, 58; *CCC* and, 52; at Georgia Tech, 93; rhetoric courses in, 225n7; writing programs/courses in, 225n4, 225n7, 227n22
enrollment cliff, 211n13
"Essential Learning Outcomes," of AAC&U, 17–18
Ethics and Public Policy Center, 189
ETS. *See* Educational Testing Service (ETS)
Evans, Hubert, 48–49
Evidence-Based Standard Setting (EBSS), 224n52
"Faculty Scholars," at PSU, 202, 203
Family Educational Rights and Privacy Act of 1974 (FERPA), 226n13
Farmer, Steve, 124
Farris, Christine, 21, 170, 172
fast track to college, 214n17
Fazlul, Ishtiaque, 120
FERPA. *See* Family Educational Rights and Privacy Act of 1974 (FERPA)
Ferreira-Buckley, Linda, 225n6
"Fields of Research in Rhetoric" (Sams), 51
50 mile rule, in Texas, 66
fine arts, at USG, 67
Finley, John H., Jr., 11
Finn, Chester E., 130–31, 133
first-generation students, 19, 28, 47; AP and, 128; DEI and, 157–60; in OnRamps, 164; STEM education for, 8; at University of Pennsylvania, 35
first-time freshmen (FTF), 162
first-year composition (FYC), 51; abolishment of, 225n10; advocacy models for, 179–87; centrality of, 57; DE/DC for, 108, 152–87; faculty for, 211n22; with history courses, 186; with philosophy courses, 179–87; public perception of, 154–57; as remedial, 210n12; rhetoric courses in, 168–79
Fisher, Walter T., 45
Florida: African American History course in, 95, 97, 218n55; AP in, 136; CCN in, 97–102; DEI in, 95; Education Goals of, 98; identity politics in, 218n53; K–12 schools in, 99; K–20 system in, 98, 99–100; State University System of Florida, 212n2; University of Florida, 27; writing programs/courses in, 100

Florida Academy for Nursing and Health Occupations, 100
Florida International University, 100
Florida State University, 98
Fort Valley State College, 80, 84, 213n8, 214n17
Fourteenth Amendment, 217n40
Framework for Success in Postsecondary Writing, of CWPA, 171, 173
FTF. *See* first-time freshmen (FTF)
"The Function of the Composition Course in General Education," 55
FYC. *See* first-year composition (FYC)

Gaines, Lloyd L., 81, 218n36
Gallagher, Buell G., 216n33
Gallagher, Chris, 18, 37, 203
Gates Foundation, 7
gateway courses, 20
GC. *See* Grand Challenge (GC)
GCE Advanced level (A-Level), 134
GEA Release, in Georgia, 84–85
General Education (Gen Ed), 25, 50, 208n9, 211n21; academics' perception of, 3–4, 16–17; Conant on, 207n8; core values of, 18; cost-saving and, 24; courses and choices in, 33–36; curricular sameness in, 61–106; for democracy, 12–13, 14, 36–39, 59, 187; in educational marketplace, 15–20; efficiency in, 217n42; for employment, 28–29; as equalizer, 7; experimental courses for, 14; financial profits from, 21–22, 38; fundamentals of, 5–10; in high school, 4, 13–14, 48–49; history of, 26–27; hopes for, 204–5; intellectual training from, 60; as liberation, 51–58; in Long Fifties, 30, 39–41; online courses in, 220n9; paper ceiling and, 28–29, 188–205; philosophies and student choice of, 30–60; in postwar era, 36–41; problems with term of, 16; public perception of, 4, 190–96; in public university systems, 61–106; restaurant metaphor for, 31–32; state policies and politics with, 27; values of, 41–51. *See also specific topics*
"General Education Act," 189
General Education in a Free Society. See the Redbook
General Education in School and College, 41
"The General Education Movement" (McGrath), 30
"The General Education of Teachers and of All Others" (Peik), 73
"General Education Planning Tool," at University of Pennsylvania, 201–2

George Works Report, 82
Georgia: AP in, 119, 136; *Brown v. Board of Education* and, 63, 69, 72, 74, 76, 77, 85, 217n40; GEA Release in, 84–85; K–12 schools in, 74, 75, 82, 84–85; K–16 schools in, 80, 85; School Segregation Amendment in, 84; segregation in, 73, 74, 75, 80, 84–85. *See also* University System of Georgia (USG)
Georgia Coastal Plains Experiment Station, 69
Georgia Experiment Station, 69
Georgia Institute of Technology. *See* Georgia Tech
Georgia Normal and Agricultural College, 80
Georgia Normal College, 69
Georgia Perimeter College, 102
Georgia Southern University, 102
Georgia State College, 80
Georgia State College for Women, 69, 215n27
Georgia State University, 102
Georgia Tech (Georgia Institute of Technology): Aims and Objectives at, 74, 217n41; Blacks at, 76, 102; budget for, 213n15; core curriculum at, 90, 217n43; English program at, 93; enrollment at, 88; Gen Ed at, 216n37; segregation at, 78, 79; student composition at, 65; women at, 215n27; writing programs/courses at, 101–2
Georgia Transfer, 223n38
Gerber, John C., 53–54, 211n21
German model, 42, 87
GI Bill (Servicemen's Readjustment Act), 13, 39, 40, 50, 53, 211n16, 211n17, 215n27
gifted students, 31, 208n13
Gignilliat, Arthur, 217n42
Giordano, Joanne Baird, 169
globalization courses, 37
GMAT. *See* Graduate Management Admission Test (GMAT)
Goggin, Maureen, 160
Goglia, M. J., 90
Graduate Management Admission Test (GMAT), 141
graduate teaching assistants, 158, 194, 212n25
Grand Challenge (GC), at University of Illinois, 110–12
Gray, C. Harold, 57–58
GreatSchools.org, 221n15
Greer, Jane, 153
Griffin, Marvin, 85–87

Halasek, Kay, 225n6
Hancher, Virgil, 39–40, 45–46
Handell, Stephen J., 223n37

Hansen, Kristine, 21, 170
Harrington, Susanmarie, 170
Harris, J. John, III, 88–89
Hartman, Catherine, 97
Harvard University, 9–15; AP and, 120, 126, 129. *See also* University Committee on the Objectives of General Education in a Free Society
Hassel, Holly, 169
Haveman, Robert, 195
Havighurst, Robert J., 49–50
HBCUs. *See* historically Black colleges and universities (HBCUs)
Henderson, Rob, 193–95
Hesse, Doug, 225n6
HEW. *See* Department of Health, Education, and Welfare (HEW)
Higher Learning Commission (HLC), 138, 220n5
high-impact practices, 17
high school: Blacks in, 207n4, 210n11; college degree views from, 7; college-level work in, 48; DE/DC in, 226n14; Gen Ed in, 4, 6, 13–14, 48–49; of Harvard Committee members, 11; Latinos in, 210n11; rating and ranking of, 221n15; textbooks, in Texas, 95. *See also specific topics*
Hispanics (Latinx): in AP, 24, 116–17; in APS, 222n23; college value for, 7; FYC for, 157; Gen Ed for, 19; in high school, 210n11; in OnRamps, 164; in rhetoric courses, 157; with STARs, 196; in STEM, 210n11; at USG, 65
historically Black colleges and universities (HBCUs), 63, 212n2; in Alabama, 216n33; average earning power from, 89; *Brown v. Board of Education* and, 88–89; budgets for, 213n15; Gen Ed at, 216n37; segregation and, 218n36; transfer from, 89; in USG, 65, 70, 76, 88–89, 212n3, 212n4, 213n15, 214n17
history: AP for, 23, 115, 129, 132, 224n50; FYC with, 186; in USG IMPACTS, 103, 105
History Gateways project, of AHA, 227n25
Hitler, Adolf, 73, 214n24, 216n33
HLC. *See* Higher Learning Commission (HLC)
Hoadley, Leigh, 11
Hollingshead, Byron S., 11, 49–51, 208n13
Holmes, Hamilton, 76
Hoover Institution, 189
HOPE Scholarship, 92–93
humanistic inquiry, 36, 49, 51, 59, 60, 209n4
humanities, 35, 37; AP and, 114; biological sciences and, 210n9; first-generation faculty

in, 5; knowing in, 49–50; loving in, 49–50; at USG, 67; in USG IMPACTS, 103, 104
Hunter, Charlayne, 76

IB. *See* International Baccalaureate (IB)
The Idea and Practice of General Education, 10
Illinois, 96. *See also* University of Illinois
Illinois English Bulletin, 52
IMPACTS, at USG, 102–6
Indiana University, 172
information literacy courses, 37
Inside Higher Ed, 224n53
International Baccalaureate (IB), 6, 35, 108–9, 124, 134, 220n8; high school rating and ranking on, 221n15; pass rates for, 219n2; in PLA, 138
Interstate Passport (IP), 94
Iowa. *See* University of Iowa

Jabbar, Huriya, 97
James G. Martin Center for Academic Renewal, 189
JGE. *See The Journal of General Education* (JGE)
Johnson, Kristine, 171
"Joint Position on Dual Enrollment in Composition," 174
Jolliffe, David, 113–14, 129
Jordan, Wilbur K., 11, 40
The Journal of General Education (JGE), 26; first issue of, 39–40; on Gen Ed values, 41–51; the Redbook and, 30–60; University of Chicago and, 51. *See also specific articles*
"*The Journal of General Education* and an Institutional Return to Rhetoric" (Beasley), 51
junior colleges, in USG, 81–84, 89–90, 216n39

K–12 schools, 59, 99, 137; AP and, 139; DE/DC and, 153; in Georgia, 74, 75, 82, 84–85; with IB, 219n2; TEKS for, 167; writing programs/courses in, 171
K–16 schools, 14, 69–70, 80, 85, 171
K–20 system, 98, 99–100
Kennesaw State University, 93, 102
Kenyon Report, 126
Kolluri, Suneal, 125
Kretchmar, Jen, 124

Labaree, David F., 195
labor model for teaching, 22–23
Language and Composition, in AP, 110, 113–14, 115, 140–51, 222n22
language arts teachers, 178
Latinx. *See* Hispanics

LDGE. *See* lower-division General Education (LDGE)
LEAP, 94
Lebduska, Lisa, 53
legacy families, 41
liberal education, 3, 13; AAC&U on, 17; AP and, 132; decline of, 35; for democracy, 9, 17; GI Bill and, 53; problems with term of, 16–17; re-examination of, 14; at USG, 77, 83
Liberty Institute, 226n19
Lindemann, Erika, 227n22
literacy competency test, at USG, 76
Literature and Composition, in AP, 110, 113–14, 115, 118–20, 133, 222n22, 224n51
Long Fifties, 30, 39–41
"Looking for an Argument" (Weaver), 51
"Lopsided Harvard Report" (Fisher), 45
loving, in humanities, 49–50
lower-division General Education (LDGE), 94
luxury beliefs, 193, 194

Mackenzie, Gordon N., 48–49
Maine, 213n13
Mann, A. R., 77–78, 215n30
Massachusetts, 117
mass classes, 194
mathematics, 8, 37, 43, 67, 96–97, 103
Mays, Arthur B., 42
McGrath, Earl James, 24–25, 30, 42–45, 52, 59–60; on humanism courses, 215n25; *Report of the President's Commission on Higher Education* and, 211n20
McKay, Heather A., 94
Medical College, in USG, 69
Mendenhall, Annie, 75–76, 214n16
Mettler, Suzanne, 53
Michaels, Gene, 135
Michigan, 222n27
middle school, AP in, 139
Middle States Commission on Higher Education (MSCHE), 220n5
Minnesota, 134–35. *See also* University of Minnesota
"The Mission of American Universities" (Conant), 10
Mississippi, 117
Moner, William, 18
Monga, Ashwani, 104–5
MOOCs, 226n21
Morehouse, 88
Moreland, Casie, 108, 170
Morrill Act, 78
Morrison, Theodore, 11

Morton, Jennifer M., 71, 128
MSCHE. *See* Middle States Commission on Higher Education (MSCHE)

National Alliance of Concurrent Enrollment Partnerships (NACEP), 162, 174–75
National Association of Scholars, 189, 192
National Center for Education Statistics (NCES), 40, 159
National Council of Teachers in English (NCTE), 52, 168, 170–78, 227n26, 227n26
National Survey of Student Engagement (NSSE), 199–203
Native Americans, 116, 157
natural sciences, 8, 67
Nazis, 214n24
NCES. *See* National Center for Education Statistics (NCES)
NCTE. *See* National Council of Teachers in English (NCTE)
NEASC. *See* New England Association of Schools and Colleges (NEASC)
"'The Need for the Permissive' in Basic Communications" (Needham), 57
Needham, Arnold E., 57
The New Education (Davidson), 18
New England Association of Schools and Colleges (NEASC), 220n5
Newfield, Christopher, 202–3
Nimitz, Chester W., 39
North, Stephen, 157
North Carolina. *See* University of North Carolina (UNC)
Northeastern University, 214n23
NSSE. *See* National Survey of Student Engagement (NSSE)

Obama, Barack, 222n27
"Objectives and Organization of the Composition Course," 55–56
"Occupy Writing Studies" (Hassel and Giordano), 169
Oglethorpe University, 135
Ohmann, Richard, 38
Oliver, Kenneth, 56
ONE. *See* Online Network for Evaluation (ONE)
"The One-Legged, Wingless Bird of Freshman English" (Oliver), 56
Online Network for Evaluation (ONE), 224n52
OnRamps, at UT, 28, 160–68, 226n19
Opportunity@Work, 196–98
Oregon, 218n50
Owen, Stephanie, 125

Packard, Vance, 128
paper ceiling, 28–29, 188–205; credentialing and, 196–99; NSSE and, 199–203
"The Paradoxes of Desegregation" (Baker), 214n16
PASSHE. *See* Pennsylvania State System of Higher Education (PASSHE)
"Patterns of Courses in General Education" (Charters), 48
Payne Fund Studies, 48
Peik, W. E., 73
Pell Grants, 34–35, 93, 139, 220n4, 224n45
Penn Career Services, 34–35
Pennsylvania, 213n13. *See also* University of Pennsylvania
The Pennsylvania Gazette, 33–35
Pennsylvania State System of Higher Education (PASSHE), 68
Pennsylvania State University (PSU), 202, 203, 210n6
Pew Research Center, 6
Phelps, Louise Wetherbee, 159
Philosophy and Rhetoric, 187
philosophy programs/courses, 227n25, 227n30; AP for, 187; core curriculum and, 185–86; DE/DC for, 187; FYC with, 179–87; global audience for, 228n33; at SUNY, 228n31; at University of Iowa, 180–81; at University of Pennsylvania, 187, 209n2, 227n29
physical sciences, 8, 25
physics, AP for, 129
PLA. *See* Prior Learning Assessment (PLA)
Policy Regimes (Branson), 21, 220n3
political science, 103, 105
"Postsecondary Teaching of Writing" (CCCC), 177
predominately white institutions (PWIs), 76, 89, 212n2, 213n15, 218n36
Princeton University, 120, 128
Prior Learning Assessment (PLA), 138
program duplication, 66, 212n2, 213n7, 213n8
Project 2025, 192
Propst, H. Dean, 66–67
PSU. *See* Pennsylvania State University (PSU)
"Public Philosophy Committee," of APA, 181–82
PWIs. *See* predominately white institutions (PWIs)

quality enhancement plan (QEP), 110–12, 210n6, 220n5

R1 universities, 71, 76–77, 87–88, 164, 214n17. *See also specific universities*

Radcliffe College, 13, 40
Ratcliffe, Krista, 225n6
the Redbook (*General Education in a Free Society*), 10, 11, 12; AP and, 126; CCC and, 30–60; CCN and, 94, 99; *JGE* and, 26–27, 30–60
Redesigning Liberal Education (Moner), 18
"Reframing the Great Debate on First-Year Writing" (Roemer, Schultz, and Durst), 152
Reframing the Subject (Ritter), 207n5
"Reimagining Remediation" (Handell and Williams), 223n37
Rensselaer Polytechnic Institute, 58
Reorganization Act, for USG, 65–66, 70
Report of the President's Commission on Higher Education, 211n20
A Report of the Survey of the University System of Georgia. See Strayer Report
Republican Party, 6, 192
Research, in AP, 122, 223n36
restaurant metaphor for, 31–32
Rhetoric and Reality (Berlin), 168–69
Rhetoric in Debt (Sharp-Hoskins), 122–23
rhetoric of competition, for AP, 108, 121–30
rhetoric of efficiency, for AP, 108, 139–47
rhetoric of exemption, for AP, 107–51
rhetoric of remediation, for AP, 108, 130–39
rhetoric programs/courses: for AP, 27–28; in English department, 225n7; in FYC, 168–79; in Gen Ed, 8–9, 15–26; in OnRamps, 167–68; for truths of present-day conditions, 209n18
Rhodes, Terrel L., 18
Richards, Ivor A., 11
Richardson, Jeanita W., 88–89
Roach, Paul F., 47
Roberts, Charles, 52, 53–54, 212n25
Rockefeller Foundation, 77
Roemer, Marjorie, 152, 160
Rogerson, Howard W., 79
Roosevelt, Franklin D., 39
Rose, Stephen J., 195
Roth, Michael, 32
Rulon, Phillip J., 11
Russell, David, 225n6

SACS. *See* Southern Association of Schools and Colleges (SACS)
Sams, Henry W., 51
Sanford, Steadman V., 61, 72–73, 213n8, 214n24; on Blacks, 80–81; "Dangers" by, 77; Mann and, 77–78, 215n30
SAT (test), 6, 22, 220n10; credits from, 112; dropping as admission requirement, 121;

FYC and, 156; OnRamps and, 165; retesting of, 118; for University of Pennsylvania, 35
Savannah State College, 75–76, 79, 81, 84, 214n17
Scanlan, Andrew E., 130–31, 133
Schlesinger, Arthur M., 11
Schneider, Jack, 132–33
School Segregation Amendment, in Georgia, 84
Schudde, Lauren, 97
Schultz, Lucille, 152
sciences: in Gen Ed, 37; in USG IMPACTS, 103. *See also specific types*
seamless transfer, 209n19, 217n47; CCN and, 92–94; at SUNY, 93; at USG, 16, 63
segregation, 214n16, 218n36; in Georgia, 73, 74, 75, 80, 84–85; at Georgia Tech, 78, 79; in K–12 schools, 59; in K–16 schools, 80; at USG, 63, 77–78, 81–84, 86–87, 89–90, 216n39
Senate Bill 266, in Texas, 95
Senate Bill 450, in Texas, 96
Servicemen's Readjustment Act. *See* GI Bill
"75 Years of Transforming Lives," at USG, 81–82
Sharp-Hoskins, Kellie, 122–23
Shortchanged (Abrams), 125–26
skilled through alternative routes (STARs), 196–97
Smith, Marion, 215n27
Smith, Wilson, 11
social efficiency, 195
"The Social Function of General Education" (Roach), 47
social mobility, 195
social sciences, 37, 43, 67, 103, 114
social solidarity, 50
"Some Basic Assumptions for Courses in English Composition" (Steinberg), 212n26
Someone Has to Fail (Labaree), 195
"Soul and Self," 46–47
Southern Association of Schools and Colleges (SACS), 80, 220n5
Southern Polytechnic State College, 102
South Georgia College, 83
South Georgia Junior College, 69
special education, 12
Special Studies, at USG, 76
SRTOL. *See* students' right to their own language (SRTOL)
Stabley, Rhodes R., 56, 57
Stanford University, 124–25
STARs. *See* skilled through alternative routes
"Statement on the Role of Philosophy Departments in Higher Education" (APA), 182, 184
State Normal School, in USG, 69

258 : INDEX

State of Texas Education Agency, 164
State University of New York (SUNY), 68, 93, 228n31
State University System of Florida, 212n2
"Status Report on Recommendations of the Governor's Commission to Improve Education," 89–90
Steinberg, Erwin R., 212n26
STEM, 8, 207n4, 210n11
Stephens College, 48
Strategic Governance Mission Statement, of CCCC, 171–72
Strayer, George, 81
Strayer Report (*A Report of the Survey of the University System of Georgia*), 81–84, 89–90, 98, 216n38
Struck, Peter, 35–36, 41
student loans, 122–23; forgiveness of, 7
students of color, 19, 28; CCA on, 20; at University of Pennsylvania, 35. *See also* Asians/Asian Americans; Blacks; Hispanics; Native Americans
students' right to their own language (SRTOL), 76, 157
student success, 63, 110, 138, 146, 222n21
Studio Art, in AP, 122
Sullivan, Patrick, 21
SUNY. *See* State University of New York (SUNY)
Syracuse University, 159

Talladega College, 216n33
Talmadge, Eugene, 79–80, 84
Talmadge, Herman E., 216n33
TAMU. *See* Texas A&M (TAMU)
Tate, Gary, 227n22
TCCNS. *See* Texas Common Course Numbering System (TCCNS)
TCSG. *See* Technical Colleges System of Georgia (TCSG)
"Teachers of General Studies" (McGrath), 211n21
Tear the Paper Ceiling, 196, 198–99
Technical Colleges System of Georgia (TCSG), 67, 214n17
TEKS. *See* Texas English Knowledge Skills (TEKS)
terministic screen, 109
Test of Written English (TWE), 141
Texas, 213n7, 213n13; CCN in, 94–97; DEI in, 95; efficiency in, 212n7; 50 mile rule in, 66; Senate Bill 266 in, 95; Senate Bill 450 in, 96. *See also* University of Texas (UT)

Texas A&M (TAMU), 95
Texas Association of Collegiate Registrars and Admissions Officers, 95
Texas Common Course Numbering System (TCCNS), 95–97
Texas Community College, 97
Texas English Knowledge Skills (TEKS), 167
Texas State (TSUS), 95
Texas Tech System, 95
Thiel, Peter, 9
Thiel Foundation, 9
Thomas B. Fordham Institute, 130
Tinberg, Howard, 21
"Too Many Courses" (Griffin), 87
Transfer Opportunity Project (TOP), 217n47
Transfer Pathways, at USG, 71–72
Trotter, Virginia, 135
Truman, Harry S, 43
Truman Commission Report, 39
Trump, Donald, 189, 192, 207n3, 218n53
TSUS. *See* Texas State (TSUS)
TWE. *See* Test of Written English (TWE)
Two-Year College Association (TYCA), 169, 174, 226n16

UGA. *See* University of Georgia (UGA)
Ulrich, Robert, 11
unbundling movement, 37
UNC. *See* University of North Carolina (UNC)
University Committee on the Objectives of General Education in a Free Society, 39; "The Function of the Composition Course in General Education" and, 55; on Gen Ed in high school, 48; at Harvard University, 11–12; restaurant metaphor for, 31–32. *See also* the Redbook
University of Arkansas, 113–14
University of Chicago, 9, 10, 51, 120
University of Georgia (UGA), 68, 69, 73; AP at, 135, 136; Blacks at, 76, 78–79; *Brown v. Board of Education* and, 87–88; enrollment at, 87; women at, 76, 215n27
University of Houston, 95
University of Illinois, 42, 110–12, 180, 212n25, 224n45
University of Iowa, 9, 24–25, 39–40; AP and, 224n51; philosophy courses at, 180–81. *See also* Hancher, Virgil; McGrath, Earl James
University of Minnesota, 10, 50, 73–74
University of Missouri, 218n36
University of North Carolina (UNC), 68, 213n12; AP at, 133, 192–93; DEI at, 192–93, 228n4; women at, 215n27

University of North Georgia, 213*n*15
University of North Texas System, 95
University of Pennsylvania, 33–36, 127; philosophy courses at, 187, 209*n*2, 227*n*29
University of South Carolina, 228*n*31
University of Texas (UT), 27; CCN at, 95, 97; OnRamps at, 28, 160–68, 226*n*19
University of Wisconsin, 68, 228*n*31; AP at, 134, 136; College of General Studies at, 229*n*11
University System of Georgia (USG), 61; Administrative Committee on the Transfer of Credit at, 91; Allocation of Functions at, 81, 216*n*39; "An Administrative Code for the University System of Georgia," 82; articulation agreements at, 63; Blacks at, 27, 65, 69, 72, 75, 80–81, 83, 84, 86–87, 215*n*30; branch campuses at, 70–72, 91–92, 95; CCN at, 62–63, 67–68, 74–77, 83, 91–94, 100–102; Committee on Transfer of Credit at, 90; consolidation of, 68–69, 213*n*13; core curriculum at, 62–63, 66–68, 75–77, 83, 87–91, 102–6, 213*n*10, 213*n*11, 217*n*43; DE/DC at, 162; DEI at, 74, 92; doctoral degrees at, 87; efficiency at, 64–74, 106, 217*n*42; enrollment in, 87–88; *Georgia Transfer of*, 223*n*38; HBCUs in, 65, 70, 76, 88–89, 212*n*3, 212*n*4, 213*n*15, 214*n*17; IMPACTS at, 102–6; junior colleges in, 81–84, 89–90, 216*n*39; K–16 schools at, 69–70; Latinos at, 65; liberal education at, 77, 83; literacy competency test at, 76; mission statement at, 93, 217*n*49; out-of-state migration from, 212*n*3; program duplication at, 66, 212*n*2, 213*n*8; PWIs in, 76, 213*n*15; R1 universities in, 71, 76–77, 87–88, 214*n*17; Reorganization Act for, 65–66, 70; seamless transfer at, 16; segregation at, 63, 77–78, 81–84, 86–87, 89–90, 216*n*39; "75 Years of Transforming Lives" at, 81–82; Special Studies at, 76; student composition at, 65; teacher training in, 213*n*8; Transfer Pathways at, 71–72; transfers in, 90–91; writing programs/courses at, 100–101. *See also* specific colleges and universities
Unmaking the Public University (Newfield), 202–3
USG. *See* University System of Georgia (USG)
US News and World Report (USNWR), 23–24, 34, 128, 221*n*15
UT. *See* University of Texas (UT)

Valdosta State College, 79
VALUE initiative, of AAC&U, 17, 202
Vandegrift, A. A., 39

Vermont, 213*n*13
veterans. *See* GI Bill
Victory Gardens, 39
Vietnam War, 194
VIP, in AP, 147–49
Virginia Tech University, 210*n*6
vocational education, 31, 41

WAC, 168
Waggaman, John S., 98
Wald, George, 11
Walmart, 197
Wapman, K. Hunter, 195
Wardle, Elizabeth, 225*n*9
Warren Wilson College, 228*n*31
WASC. *See* Western States Association of Schools and Colleges (WASC)
Weaver, Richard, 51
Weinberg, Justin, 228*n*31
Wells, Guy H., 215*n*27
Western Interstate Commission for Higher Education (WICHE), 94
Western States Association of Schools and Colleges (WASC), 220*n*5
Westfall, Jonathan J., 73
West Georgia College, 79, 83
Wharton School of Business, 34
What Is College-Level Writing? (Tinberg and Sullivan), 21
Whites: college value for, 7; Gen Ed for, 6; in pre–World War II colleges, 40. *See also* predominately white institutions (PWIs); segregation
Whitmer, Gretchen, 222*n*27
WICHE. *See* Western Interstate Commission for Higher Education (WICHE)
Williams, Ronald A., 223*n*37
Williamson, Joy Ann, 75
Williamson, Kent, 173
"Will the Circle Be Unbroken," 204–5
Wilson, Kathryn, 195
Wisconsin, 213*n*13. *See also* University of Wisconsin
women: admissions challenges of, 59; in philosophy courses, 181; at UGA, 76, 215*n*27; at UNC, 215*n*27
Works, George, 82
"Workshop Reports," from CCCC, 54–56
World History, AP for, 115
WPA. *See* writing program administrator (WPA)
Wright, Benjamin F., 11
Wright, Dixon, 217*n*43

Writing About Writing, 225*n*9
writing program administrator (WPA), 22, 101, 112, 119, 220*n*8, 225*n*11
writing programs/courses: AP and, 110, 113–14, 115, 118–19, 133, 140–51, 222*n*22; in *CCC*, 53–54; CCN for, 96–97, 100–102; for democracy, 52; in English departments, 225*n*4, 225*n*7, 227*n*22; in Florida, 100; fundraising and philanthropy for, 228*n*32; in Gen Ed, 8–9, 20–26; at Georgia Tech, 101–2; graduate teaching assistants in, 212*n*25; in K–12 schools, 171; in K–16 schools, 171; public conceptions of, 9; for truths of present-day conditions, 209*n*18; at USG, 67, 100–101; in USG IMPACTS, 103. *See also* first-year composition (FYC)
Wynn, Colleen, 188–89

Yale University, 120

Zell, 92–93
"Zero English," 52, 209*n*29
Ziff, Elizabeth, 188–89
Zimmerman, Jonathan, 194
Zimpher, Nancy L., 93
Zoom, 144, 224*n*52

About the Author

KELLY RITTER is chair of the School of Literature, Media, and Communication and professor of writing and communication at the Georgia Institute of Technology in Atlanta, Georgia. She is the author of four books and editor or coeditor of four collections, including *Beyond Fitting In: Rethinking First-Generation Writing and Literacy Education*. Her work has appeared in *CCC, College English, Rhetoric Review, Pedagogy, Profession, WPA: Writing Program Administration, Composition Studies, JAC, Slate, The Conversation,* and *The Chronicle of Higher Education* and in numerous edited collections.

www.ingramcontent.com/pod-product-compliance
Lightning Source LLC
Chambersburg PA
CBHW060555080526
44585CB00013B/567